Confessions of a Crabgrass Cowboy

Confessions of a Crabgrass Cowboy

From Lincoln Logs to Lava Lamps: Coming of Age in an Early American Suburb

William Schwarz

iUniverse, Inc.

New York Lincoln Shanghai

Confessions of a Crabgrass Cowboy

From Lincoln Logs to Lava Lamps: Coming of Age in an Early American Suburb

Copyright © 2007 by William Schwarz

iUniverse books may be ordered through booksellers or by contacting:

iUniverse
2021 Pine Lake Road, Suite 100
Lincoln, NE 68512
www.iuniverse.com
1-800-Authors (1-800-288-4677)

Because of the dynamic nature of the Internet, any Web addresses or links contained in this book may have changed since publication and may no longer be valid.

The views expressed in this work are solely those of the author and do not necessarily reflect the views of the publisher, and the publisher hereby disclaims any responsibility for them.

ISBN: 978-0-595-45169-2 (pbk)
ISBN: 978-0-595-89479-6 (ebk)

Printed in the United States of America

For Lisa, Kate, Alex, and Jake the Wonder Dog
But mostly for Lisa

CONTENTS

ACKNOWLEDGMENTS

One of the many lessons I learned in the three years it took to complete *Confessions of a Crabgrass Cowboy* is that no book, whether fiction or non-fiction, is never really the work of the author alone. Although my personal memories and imaginings are reflected throughout this account, the book would not have been possible without assistance from countless sources to fill in many of the blank spots and details that were necessary to make the entire effort sing as a whole. Therefore, I would like to acknowledge the following sources for helping me tell this story.

Elissa Stein, *Cheerleaders* (Chronicle Books, 2004), *Stewardess: Come Fly With Me* (Chronicle Books, 2006), and *Here She Comes: Beauty Queen* (Chronicle Books, 2006); Garrison Keillor, *Lake Wobegon Summer 1956* (Viking, 2001); Bob Greene, *Be True to Your School,* Antheneum, 1987; Steven Guarnaccia and Bob Sloan, *Hi Fi's & Hi Balls: The Golden Age of the American Bachelor* (Chronicle Books, 1997) and *A Stiff Drink and a Close Shave: The Lost Arts of Manliness* (Chronicle Books, 1995); Rod Kennedy, Jr., and Ken Waltzer, *Monopoly: The Story Behind the World's Best Selling Game* (MJF Books, 2004); Timothy Samuelson, *But Wait! There's More!* (Rizzoli Books, 2002); Stuart A. Kallen, *The 1950's: A Cultural History of the United States Through the Decades* (Lucent Books, 1999); Jim Heimann, ed., *The Golden Age of Advertising: The 60's* (Barnes

& Noble), *All American Ads: 60's*, and *All American Ads : 50's* (Taschen, 2003); Scott C. Zemen and Michael A Amundson, eds., *Atomic Culture: How We Learned to Step Worrying and Love the Bomb* (University Press of Colorado, 2004); Dian Hansen, *The History of Girly Magazine s*(Taschen, 2006); Kirven Blount, *What's Your Poison: Addictive Advertising of the 40's–60's* (Collector's Press, 2005); Gideon Bosker and Bianca Lencek Bosker, *Bowled Over: A Roll Down Memory Lane* (Chronicle Books, 2002); Brad and Debra Schepp, *TV Wonderland: The Enchantment of Early Television* (Collector's Press, 2005); Michael Gitter, Sylvie Anapol, and Erica Glaser, *"Do You Remember Technology: Geeks, Gadgets & Gizmos* (Chronicle Books, 2000) and *"Do You Remember TV* (Chronicle Books, 1999); Michael Gitter and Sylvie Anapol, *Do You Remember: The Book that Takes You Back* (Chronicle Books, 1996); Gina Cascone, *Pagan Babies and Other Catholic Memories* (Washington Square Press, 1982); Mark Falanga, The Suburban You: Reports from the Home Front (Broadway Books, 2004); Rachel C. Weingarten, *Hello Gorgeous: Beauty Products in America 40's–60's* (Collector's Press, 2006); William H. Young with Nancy K. Young, *The 1950's: American Popular Culture Through History* (Greenwood Press, 2004); Jel Foreman, ed., *The Other Fifties* (University of Illinois Press, 1997); Susan Douglas, *Where the Girls Are: Growing Up Female With the Mass Media* (Three Rivers Press, 1995); Michael Scheibach, *Atomic Narratives and American Youth: Coming of Age with the Atom, 1945–1955* (McFarland & Company, 2003): Edith Pavese and Judith Henry, *TV Mania: A Timelineof Television* (Harry N. Abrams, 1998); Whitney Matheson, *Atomic Home: A Guided Tour of the American Dream* (Collector's Press, 2004); Michael Karl Witzel, *Drive In DeLux* (Motorbooks International, 1997) and *The American Drive In: History and Folklore of the Drive In Restaurant in American Car Culture* (Motorbooks International, 1994); Don and Susan Sanders, *The American Drive In Movie Theater* (Motorbooks International, 1997) and *Drive In Movie Memories: Popcorn and Romance Under the Stars* (Carriage House Publishing, 2000); Hal Lifson, *1966: A Personal View of the Coolest Year in Pop Culture History* (Bonus Books, 2002); Bill Yenne, *Going Home to the Fifties* (Last Gap Pub., 2002); Alan Betrock, *I Was a Teenage Juvenile Delinquent Rock N*

Roll Horror Beach Party Movie Book: A Complete Guide to the Teen Exploi-tation Film (St. Martin's Press, 1986); Steven Guarnaccia, *School Days*, (Abbeville Press, 1992); David Halberstam (RIP), *The Fifties* (Villard, 1993); Adam Parfrey, et. al., *It's a Man's World: Men's Adventure Maga-zines, the Postwar Pulps* (Feral House, 2003); Richard Horn, *Fifties Style* (Beach Tree Books, 1985); Dan Ponzol, *A Century of Lionel Timeless Toy Trains* (Friedman Fairfax/Zicarddi, 2000); Beth Bailey, David Farber con-sultants, *The Fifties Chronicle* (Legacy Publishing, 2006); David Farber, consultant, *The Sixties Chronicle* (Legacy Publishing, 2004); Michael Bar-son, *Better Red Than Dead* (Hyperion, 1992); Andrew F. Wood, *Road Trip America* (Collector's Press, 2003); Susan Jonas and Marilyn Nissen-son, *Going, Going, Gone: Vanishing Americana* (Chronicle Books, 1994); Johanna Omelia and Michael Waldock, *Come Fly With Us* (Collector's Press, 2003); the Berkeley Pop Culture Project, *The Whole Pop Catalog* (Avon Books, 1991); Michael Barson and Steven Heller, *Red Scared: The Commie Menace in Propaganda and Popular Culture* (Chronicle Books, 2001); Max Collins, George Hagenauer, and Steven Heller, *Men's Adven-ture Magazines* (Taschen, 2004); Robin Langley Somner, *I Had One of Those Toys* (Crescent Books, 1992); Brittany A. Daley, et. al., Sin A Rama: Sleaze Paperbacks of the Sixties (Feral House, 2005); Steve Roden and Dan Goodsell, *Krazy Kids' Food* (Barnes & Noble, 2006); Evan Morris, *From Altoids to Zina: The Surprising Stories Behind Famous Name Brands* Simon & Schuster, 2004); Robert Rodriguez, *The 50's Most Wanted: The Top 10 Book of Rock & Roll Rebels, Cold War Crises, and All American Odd-ities* (Potomac Books, 2006); Stuart Shea, *The 60's Most Wanted: The Top 10 Book of Hip Happenings, Swinging Sounds, and Out of Sight Oddities* (Potomac Books, 2006); Carolyn Wyman, *Better Than Homemade: Amaz-ing Foods That Changed the Way we Eat* (Quirk Books, 2004); Paul Feig, *Superstu*d (Three Rivers Press, 2005); Cheery Berry, *Hoorah for the Bra: A Perky Peek at the Brassiere* (Stuart, Tabori & Chang, 2006; Nick Greeth, *Made in America: From Levis to Barbie to Google* (MBI Publishing, 2005); Mark Newgarten and Picturebox, Inc.., *Cheap Laffs: The Art of the Novelty Item* (Harry N. Abrams, 2004); Ruth Ann Hobdat, ed., Rose Colored 50's (Barnes & Noble, 2004); Charles Phoenix, *Americana the Beautiful: Mid*

Century Culture in Kodahchrome (Angel City Press, 2006); James Lileks, *Mommy Knows Worst: Highlights From the Golden Age of Bad Parenting* (Three Rivers Press, 2005); Danny Gregory, *Change Your Underwear Twice a Week: Lessons from the Golden Age of Filmstrips* (Workman Publishing, Inc.., 2004); Kristin Tillotson, *"Retro Housewife: A Salute to the Suburban Superwoman* (Collector's Press, 2004); The Editors of Time Life Books, *The American Dream: The 1950's* (Time Life Books, 1970); Tim Walsh, *Timeless Toys: Classic Toys and the Playmakers Who Created Them* (Andrews McMeel, 2005); Michael Barson and Steven Heller, Teenage Confidential: *An Illustrated History of the American Teen* (Barnes & Noble, 1998); Thomas Hine, *Populux* (Alfred Knopf, 1987); Jennifer McKnight Trontz, *Yes You Can: Timeless Advice from Self Help Experts* (Chronicle Books, 2000); Eric Neilson and Leif Nesheim, *Saucer Attack: Pop Culture in the Golden Age of Flying Saucers* (Kitchen Sink Press, 1997); Steve Kosareff, *Window to the Future: The Golden Age of Television Marketing and Advertisement* (Chronicle Books, 2005); Paul Sann, *Fads, Follies, and Delusions of the American People* (Crown Publishers, 1967); Les Daniels, *Superman: The Complete History* (Chronicle Books, 1998) and *Wonder Woman: The Complete History* (Chronicle Books, 2000); Ken Smith, *Mental Hygiene: Classroom Films 1945–1970* (Blast Books, 1999); Michael Barson, *Better Red Than Dead: A Nostalgic Look at the Golden Years of Russiaphobia, Red Baiting, and Other Commie Madness* (Hyperion, 1992); Robert Heide and John Gilman, *Dime Store Dream Parade: Popular Culture 1925–1955* (EP Dutton, 1979); Carole Kismaric and Marvin Heiferman, *The Mysterious Case of Nancy Drew and the Hardy Boys* (Simon & Schuster, 1998) and *Growing Up With Dick and Jane* (Collins Publishers, 1996); John and Gordon Javna, *60's: A Catalog of Memories and Artifacts* (St. Martin's Press, 1988); Joel Makower, *Boom: Talkin' About our Generation* (Tilden Press, 1985); Susan Waggoner, *It's a Wonderful Christmas: The Best of the Holidays 1940–1965* (Stewart, Tabori & Chang, 2004); Rita Lang Kleinfelder, *When We Were Young: A Baby Boomer Yearbook* (Prentice Hall, 1993); David Mansour, *From Abba to Zoom: A Pop Culture Encyclopedia of the Late 20th Century* (Andrews McMeel, 2005); Ron Goulart, *Comic Book Culture* (Collector's Press, 2007); and Dan Brownell, ed., *101 Greatest baby Boomer Toys* (KP Books, 2005).

In addition, technology has made an entire universe of information and ideas available that also deserve acknowledgment:

http://Yesterdayland,elsewhere.org; http://web.org;
http://www,fiftiesweb.com; http://www.geocities.com
http://www.cnn.com; http://www.tvacres.com;
http://www.home.howstuffworks.com http://www.straightdope.com;
http://www.badfads.com; http://www.roadsideamerica.com
http://www/giantlavalamp.com; http://www.obits.com;
http://www.javasbachelorpad.com
http://www.genmarket.com; http://www/tvhistory.com;;
http://www.daveschultz.com.dickandjane
http://www.findarticles.com; http://www.aaamoviesearch.com;
http://www.etcomtact.net
http://thesaurus.reference.com; http://www.rareexception.com;
http://www.amsueyourself.com
http://www.christmaspast.com; http://www.aslyahoo.com;
http://www.fiftiesweb.com
http://www.toontracker.com; http://www.mattelgames.com;
http://www.slate.msn.com http://conelrad.com;
http://www.noveltynet.com; http://www.filmnight.org.;
http://www.inventorsabout.com;
http://iamthebeatles.com/article1044.html;
http://www.urganlegends.com
http://tvtome.com; http://www.popcultmag.com;
http://www.anthoneysworld.com
http://itseemslkeysterday.com; http://a,ericanheritage.com;
http://media server.amazon.com
http://www.wtvzone.com; http://www.strangemag.com;
http://www.us.imdb.com; http://www.claus.com
http://www.zyra.net; http://www.theindependent.com;

http://www.noframes.com
http://www.octanecreative.com;
http://www.brownalumnimagazine.com http://www.mala.bc.ca/incline/
sex.html;
http://www.classicbands.com; http://www.centex.com
http://www.newday.com; http://www.eisenhower.archives.com;
http://www.driveintheater.com
http://www.lalaland.cl.msu; http://www.info.detroitnews.com
http://www.porkpiedemon.co.uk/slightly.htm;
http://www.jumptheshark.com; http://www.joebates.com
http://www.smithsonsianmag.com; http://www.tsimon.com/louie.htm
http://www.kyrene.k12.az.us/schools/brias/sunda/decade/1960.htm;
http://www.home.att.net
http://www.foodreference.com; http://www.stationwagon.com;
http://www.theautochannel.com
http://www.carofthecentury.com; http://www.Mrtraffic.com;
http://www.wikipedia.org
http://www.local.aaca.org; http://www.members.aol.com;
http://www.litb.com
http://www.leaveittobeaver.com; http://www.nostalgiacentral.com

FOREWORD

A few weeks ago here in the Champlain Valley of Vermont, I was plowing through the Farmer's Breakfast at our local family restaurant, Rosie's, accompanied by the manuscript of this book, which, once I'd begun, I didn't want to get too far away from me. I got to a certain section late in the book—I guarantee you'll know when you reach it—and I found myself laughing out loud, roaring, really, prompting about forty citizens to turn my way.

After they had gone back to their coffee and muffins and eggs, and I had wiped the tears from my eyes, my mind swept across the chain of childhood and adolescent stories of the Crabgrass Cowboy, the intrepid Patio Pioneer, and I wished I could instantly share it all with that panoply of humanity. People roughly my age—that of author William Schwarz—would go through all the Proustian associations awakened in me by the mere mention of certain brand names, or toys, or television shows, or Mouseketeers, for heaven's sake. And their children and grandchildren would not only be amused by the revelations of "ancient" history come alive, but they would recognize the universal truths of being young, regardless of the generation or the era with which one identified.

This memoir is a *hoot*, a riot of memories and revelations. And I should know: I was there, too. Bill Schwarz has been telling me stories for slightly more than four decades. We grew up in adjoining suburban towns, and when I affirm that his younger days mirror my own, you'd better believe it. We became buddies at 16—among many common enthusiasms, we loved music, and singing, and theatre—and met during one of those week-end high school music invitational festivals, crowded into gymnasium bleachers with a bunch of mutual friends from several towns.

A year of jokes, rambles, pranks, and exploits later (I'm grateful he left them out of this book), we were both looking forward to appearing in a local church youth group production of "Guys and Dolls." Alas, our math grades had recently headed dramatically south. Our parents reacted identically: we were struck from the show. On opening night, we showed up to cheer all our friends and classmates—*even the ones who'd stepped into the parts we felt had been written for us!*—and afterward, in the crowd outside the basement dressing room, with everyone being congratulated, Bill came up to me with a brave grin on his face: "David, I really loved your performance best of all!" "No, Bill," I insisted, "*you* were by far the better!" And forty years has not shaken us from that certainty.

As I said, it was with some relief that I found no mention of certain adventures we shared back when we were patio pioneers. But I recognized a good number of our friends and classmates, although it seems as if identities and events have been blurred to protect innocent and guilty alike. And Chuck, Gary, Billy, Lizzy, Barbara, Peter, Meredith, Steve, Carol, Maggie, Heidi, and John, I swear the secret is safe with me, too. I have a feeling there are more memoirs in Bill's future, and I know they'll be just as entertaining as this, just as I'm confident that he won't blast the foundations of all us solid citizens. He'd better not—remember, Bill, I let you marry my little sister! I wouldn't revoke my approval—there are some young ones, after all—but as a fellow writer, I could produce my own reminiscences about Bill. This is the doctrine of mutually-assured destruction, which we learned, I guess, while ducking and covering in elementary school hallways, or while Vice President Tricky Dick debated Soviet Premier Krushchev among the washing machines.

Bill's *Confessions of a Crabgrass Cowboy* speaks for an entire generation, just as the inimitable Russell Baker did for our parents, with a similar

warmth of heart and ironic wit. It deserves a place on every nightstand—
so, switch on your lava lamp, don your mouse ears, ponder the second
verse of "Louie, Louie," and, most certainly, Happy Trails to You!
DAVID HAWARD BAIN
David Haward Bain is the author of a number of nonfiction books including Empire Express: Building the First Transcontinental Railroad and The
Old Iron Road: An Epic of Rails, Roads, and the Urge to Go West. He
teaches creative writing at Middlebury

PROLOGUE

The Legend of Christa Speck

For the uninitiated, Christa Speck was a fresh-faced German lass and former bank secretary on whom God did bestow a most bountiful bosom. Once these two cantilevered marvels made their inaugural appearance in the September 1961 pages of *Playboy Magazine,* they went on to play an indispensable role in many a young man's erotic musings, including my own, musings that evolved from the simple puerile imaginings of preadolescence to the saucy and delightfully tumescent fantasies of my testosterone-addled puberty.

The fortunes of Miss Speck and I became inexorably intertwined in late 1961, barely one year into the term of an energetic new president named John Fitzgerald Kennedy and one year before The Beatles recorded their first smash hit, "Love Me Do." One Saturday, with the air already heady with the promise of change, a friend invited me to join him in rummaging about his dad's closet in search of forbidden fruit. The intent of this innocent, rainy-day expedition was to unearth the whereabouts of a World War II German bayonet rumored to be tucked away somewhere inside. Family lore held that his father, once a young, clear-eyed warrior, had carried it home along with several other artifacts from Europe in 1945. With all the stealth a pair of excitable eleven-year-olds could muster, bent as we were on unearthing an instrument designed solely for the purpose of eviscerating other human beings, we began our adventure.

Although never banned outright, to children a father's closet and sock drawer were in those days generally acknowledged to be off-limits. Exactly why was never fully explained to us; however, everyone of my acquaintance over the age of six understood intuitively that this was so. Lamentably, only later in life did I learn that no reciprocal arrangement existed for teenagers.

Trouble greeted us almost immediately when my host, intent on gaining access to the uppermost closet shelf, carelessly allowed his concentration to wander and dislodged an unseen stack of magazines. We froze as they spilled to the floor in a disagreeable heap. Hearts pounding, we listened for the slightest sound suggesting the approach of a curious adult, and only when it became clear that our efforts had gone unnoticed did we simultaneously leap into action. So intent were we on removing all evidence of our crime that neither one of us had the presence of mind to fully examine, much less appreciate, the nature of our discovery. But once it became clear that we remained undetected, the frenzied pace of our cleanup effort slowed enough for us to examine our find more closely.

As aficionados of the surly, ham-fisted Sergeant Slaughter, both of us immediately recognized the classic illustration of a leering, spectacled Japanese soldier on one of many magazine covers now piled at our feet. One magazine cover in particular stood out from the rest. It was entitled, *Tales of Adventure for the Rugged Man,* and portrayed a Son of Hirohito and several of his Samurai cohorts engaged in an enterprise that was patently un-soldierly: torturing a helpless civilian, and a comely, scantily clad female civilian at that!

The state of the poor woman's outfit was clearly not of her own choosing. To the contrary, she struggled ferociously in an effort, one might presume, to more properly cover a pair of silky thighs and two handsomely protruding breasts. What few pieces of clothing remained had been shredded and tattered, one supposed, by the repeated lashings applied so liberally at the hands of her tormentors. Oh, what strange stirrings this discovery produced!

Not content to dwell on our initial accomplishments, we pawed deeper into the pile only to be greeted by similarly titled publications like *True Adventures, For Men Only,* and *Men's Adventure Stories.* Most adhered to the same basic theme, and except for some variations in ethnicity, the antagonists were all portrayed as sneering, brutish louts who were impervious to the plight of their captives, while the captives themselves, although understandably distressed by the unusual circumstances in which they found themselves, all appeared to be in robust good health.

Further excavation revealed even more remarkable finds, leaving me both incredulous and exasperated at the degree to which my childhood had thus far been sheltered.

Our next discovery included several periodicals devoted entirely to female undergarments, including black nylon hosiery, garter belts, panties, brassieres, and an unusual assortment of other items I didn't recall ever having seen among the apparel in my mother's wardrobe. I was taken aback at the stark difference between these images and the droll, two-dimensional figures found in more mainstream publications like the Sears and Roebuck catalog. These were more provocative than anything I'd seen before, even though the ladies were engaged only in activities like bending to straighten a stocking seam, fasten a garter, or adjust the strap of a brassiere. Magazine after magazine, with names like *Silky Sirens, Nylon Jungle,* and *French Frills,* presented us with a plentitude of breathtaking compositions. Would I ever be able to look at my mother's underwear the same way again?

My breathing became slightly labored as we approached the bottom of the pile, but I knew intuitively this had nothing to do with our physical exertions. Fortunately, what was left seemed devoted to Hollywood film stars like Betty Grable, Heddy Lamar, and Rita Hayworth and the occasional humor digest masquerading as titillation. But as our task neared completion, lightning struck! There at the bottom of the pile was an object that had launched both countless hours of schoolyard discourse and a thousand boyhood fantasies — a copy of *Playboy Magazine.*

Like the first moon landing, the assassination of JFK or the loss of his virginity, a man can recall the events surrounding his first boyhood encounter with *Playboy* in exquisite detail. Many of my peers and I knew a great deal about this icon of popular culture long before I'd even seen my first issue. Rumors of its contents flourished in the playgrounds and school bathrooms of our youth, so the first time a boy found himself confronted with the real thing, the moment was electrifying.

Dumbstruck, we shook off our momentary reverie and simultaneously dove for the magazine in a tangled mass of arms and legs. For one brief, exhilarating moment I thought the prize was mine until my wily chum invoked a time-honored dispute resolution tactic called dibs.

In those days, dibs allowed that the possession of a disputed item automatically went to the first party who claimed it by saying the word *dibs*. In this particular situation, the honor went to my friend, and though I could scarcely argue the legitimacy of his claim, I found his actions inhospitable. Clearly, I had been outmaneuvered by a clever adversary, leaving me no choice but to acquiesce.

To his immeasurable credit, as well as my own considerable relief, my companion then suggested we share the fruits of our labor by repairing to his bedroom, where we could engage in a more deliberate investigation of our find. His enlightened thinking delighted me.

We quickened our efforts to restore order to the closet and soon we were both satisfied that no evidence of our duplicity remained save for the purloined magazine itself, which my cohort concealed down the front of his pants. The studied nonchalance of our demeanor was in stark contrast to our highly charged sense of anticipation. The last fifteen or twenty feet to his bedroom turned into a mad dash as we burst though the door and locked it behind us. Without so much as a pause to catch our breath, we then jumped on his bed, spread the centerfold out before us, and began to consume our visual feast like starved animals.

As kids, we sometimes used the term *boob* in reference to something other than a person of dubious mental acuity. *Bumpers* and *headlights* were often more than just auto accessories, *cans* and *jugs* more than containers for transporting liquids, and *maracas* not always just a Latin musical instrument. None of these words were inherently off-color, but let an unwary adult employ one of these double entendres in daily conversation and it was a guaranteed source of mirth for any boy within earshot.

My friends and I had each adopted our own idiomatic preferences for the female upper torso. *Tits* was the favored appellation, although *bazooms, knockers,* and *gazongas* were also perfectly acceptable depending on the level of panache and sophistication one wished to convey.

From my very first glance, I knew that the yardstick against which I would measure female beauty had changed forever. Gone were the lingerie models, the half-naked female captives, and even Susan Gabrielli, the prematurely developed darling of our sixth-grade class. In their place was the beautiful, sloe-eyed Christa Speck. Unlike her bra size, Miss Speck's curriculum vitae was quite modest. Nineteen years old, she found Jack Benny a turn-on, loved swimming and jazz, and disliked indecisive men. She aspired to be an actress (what Playmate didn't?), and, although not listed as such, her most notable accomplishment to date was a figure that measured 38-22-36.

I was transfixed, temporarily disengaged from the here and now by her transcendent beauty. But it wasn't just her tantalizing figure, or the graceful slope of her breasts that the sheerest of negligees only succeeded in making more pronounced, or those sleek, silky legs folded so demurely beneath her that mesmerized me. There was something else. Perhaps it was the way her eyes locked onto mine with a knowing gaze of recognition. She could've lived next door, and her appeal was based as much on this sense of familiarity as it was on her physical beauty. It was a pleasant albeit unnerving sensation.

My friend and I quickly picked our way through the rest of the magazine but soon returned it downstairs with the rest rather than risk discovery. Personally, I had no interest in any of the articles or other features, although years later I would vociferously claim otherwise. Indeed, the issue of editorial copy would over time become one of the biggest gripes we had about *Playboy,* and were it not for the infamous centerfold surrounded by its Playmate of the Month pictorial, it might well have become the girlie magazine equivalent of an artichoke, in that it simply was too much work to get to the good part. The publisher, whom we would come to know almost collegially as "Hef," even went so far as to try to articulate the magazine's philosophy, for goodness sake, as if testosterone-riddled boys needed any philosophical validation for their attraction to bare breasts.

It was getting on toward dinnertime and I had to think about going home. I was invited to stay for dinner, followed perhaps by an hour or so of color TV, one of the first on our street, but I declined. It was time to take stock of the day's revelations, and the walk home would give me that chance.

The sky was nearly dark by the time I left. The earlier showers had become a steady drizzle, and the eerie bluish light of a dozen TV sets illuminated the street in front of me like an airport runway. I zipped up my coat against the chill, tucked my chin down into my collar, and started home, accompanied only by the slap of my Keds on the wet pavement.

In the universe of eleven-year-old boys, females, unlike candy Lifesavers, did not come in a wild assortment of flavors. The two basic types were girls and grown-ups, the latter known also as ladies, as in "Hey, lady, you dropped something!" Although slight variations did exist between the two—grown-ups included mothers and teachers, while girls could be either sisters or female classmates—the categories were pretty clear. As a youngster, I had sometimes seen my mother undressed, but this produced in me only a mild sense of curiosity. Occasionally, I would burst into the bathroom, interrupting my older sister mid-shower, and catch a brief glimpse of her approaching maturity before she'd shriek, *"Get out of here this instant, you little pervert."* These encounters aroused in me nothing beyond the urge to tease her mercilessly by observing how nicely her bee stings seemed to be healing, and doing so preferably just as she was about to leave on a date.

Was Miss Speck a girl or a grown-up? Strangely, I sensed she was both, a hybrid that somehow straddled two worlds. She had the physique of a grown-up, but the impish, almost playful demeanor of someone much younger. I felt like an anthropologist who'd just discovered the missing link.

Continuing down the street, I was struck by a second realization. At some point over the past couple of hours, I had crossed a divide in my relationships with these curious creatures, and there was no turning back. From now on it was going to be almost impossible to objectively consider any female, girl or grown-up, without some subliminal acknowledgment that she was something else as well. This puzzled me because it suggested that all females—mothers, teachers, sisters, and schoolmates—were at some fundamental level all the same thing, a premise I was not quite ready to accept. It would be years before I understood that the missing word was ... *woman.*

But the third epiphany of the day unnerved me the most. From the moment I set eyes on Miss Speck I felt strangely overpowered and slightly out of control. Don't ask me how, I just did, and this insight put me permanently at a disadvantage with females. Next week at school, for example, if Allison Van Gundy and I were paired as lab partners in science class, it was now a distinct possibility I would devote far more time admiring the evidence of her advancing metamorphosis than on creating a solution for growing sugar crystals.

I didn't ask for this!

As my own front yard drew near and the lights inside the house promised things warm and familiar, I suspected something far more significant had taken place that day besides getting my first glimpse of an über-breasted female in a *Playboy Magazine.* I didn't know for sure what it was, but I knew that nothing would ever be quite the same again.

CHAPTER I

Welcome to the Crabgrass Frontier

In 1945 Dad put down his rifle, Mom put down her welding torch, and they—along with millions more like them—became so fruitful and did multiply so prodigiously, it produced a mammoth population bubble, a population bubble we still refer to today as the baby boom. As the number of new families began to increase, so too did the need for space in which they might grow, both physically and culturally. Thus began a great migration from the urban neighborhoods, small towns, and farms of America to the outskirts of its great cities. There were no road maps to help guide these intrepid pioneers across the expanse of now fallow potato fields, parceled out estates, and undeveloped woodlands, but they kept on coming. In their Chevrolets they came, and their Fords and their Oldsmobiles, like an endless winding ribbon of Conestoga wagons across the wilderness to a land of untold promise and opportunity.

In the earliest days, suburban living came without an instruction manual, and few signposts showed the way. This eventually gave rise to the need for role models to assist kids like me in becoming properly socialized into this new cultural paradigm. Growing up on the Crabgrass Frontier, as suburbia came to be known, was as much a matter of indoctrination as it was physical and emotional maturation. Adults made certain to surround us with helpful archetypes whose purpose was, one suspects, to instill in us a desire to set higher standards for ourselves, to aspire to become something other than what we already were.

Among the earliest of these role models that I remember were the grade-school wunderkinder, Dick and Jane. Viewed by many as examples of the perfect suburban progeny, they were difficult for kids like me to identify with because they seemed totally devoid of any identity of their own. Dick and Jane had no last name; they never argued, talked back, or misbehaved; they never watched TV, read comic books, or went to the movies. Indeed, they seemed to lack most of the irksome and wearying qualities normally associated with children, making them unlikely candidates for emulation.

Take something as simple as a weekend outing, when Dick and Jane's family went for a drive to the park, the zoo, or Grandma and Grandpa's house in the country. During these highway escapades, everyone was always happy, excited, and forever blurting out things like "wow!" and "gee whiz!" Dad never lost his temper, shouting "Don't make me stop this car!" Mom never questioned her spouse's driving skills or expressed doubts about his sense of direction. The kids never forgot to use the bathroom at each rest stop, never asked repeatedly in a whiny tone of voice when they would reach their destination, and never puked all over the backseat. The car itself never suffered a mechanical failure of any kind, not even a flat tire. These kinds of things always happened on our car trips, and sometimes all on the same trip. Theirs was a difficult family to relate to.

As we grew older, our models became more sophisticated, but few captured our boyhood dreams and aspirations as well as the Hardy Boys, Frank and Joe Hardy, who became synonymous with the kind of bold and adventurous lives we often daydreamed about for ourselves. The duo enjoyed the respect and admiration of everyone from the mayor and chief of police to the local bank president. We longed to join them as they went speeding down a country road on their own motorcycles or expertly navigated a speedboat through a perilous storm on Barmet Bay.

What made them ideal role models from an adult perspective was that along with their respectful, clear-eyed maturity, the boys were quick to acknowledge all grown-ups as their moral and intellectual superiors. They did not drink, smoke, swear, talk back, lie, cheat, or disobey, and they usually found chasing criminals far more inviting than chasing girls, a choice we found increasingly odd as we grew older.

Adults sometimes tried to shape our thinking by using models with whom we already identified. It wasn't unusual for us to see Superman or even Batman and Robin appear in a special publication masquerading as an everyday comic book, only to find our superheroes extolling the virtues of good citizenship, proper grooming habits, and a positive attitude in school instead of battling the likes of Lex Luthor or The Penguin. This duplicity rarely succeeded; we were usually able to see past this ruse and separate these cardboard champions from the real thing.

One of the more popular, albeit primitive, means of educating millions of newly minted GIs and factory workers during World War II, as well as trying to mold their behavior in the process, was the humble filmstrip, the ancestor of today's ubiquitous PowerPoint presentation. Produced by the thousands, filmstrips covered every topic imaginable, from the cleaning and maintenance of an M1 rifle or the use a rivet gun to the preemptive marvels of proper condom use. After the war, filmstrips received a warm welcome from educators, who, while less concerned about condom use among their young charges, did find it necessary to remind us how important it was to stand up straight, stay in line, drink our milk, get plenty of exposure to direct sunlight, and never, ever put pencils up our noses.

Filmstrips were also a useful way of reminding us of just how much better things were here in the good old U.S. of A. Foreigners were often depicted as backward, gullible, superstitious, and generally clueless heathens whose biggest sin, apparently, was that they weren't us; and because they neither looked like us nor acted like us there was sufficient grounds for suspicion and/or derision. The term *foreigner* itself often took on an almost pejorative connotation, thereby encouraging us to adopt linguistic shorthand when referring to non-Americans. The French became Frogs; Italians were Dagos, Guineas, or Wops; the Polish, Polacks, and so forth. There was also an important distinction to be made between good foreigners and bad foreigners. Obviously, anyone who lived in a Communist country was a bad foreigner because on top of everything else, Communists were evil. Yes, citizens of non-Communist countries were also uncivilized louts, but at least they were our uncivilized louts.

There were certain unintended benefits of watching filmstrips that we were always prepared to exploit whenever the opportunity arose. The technology itself was usually enough to divert any teacher's attention long enough to allow us a few moments of unsupervised bliss, at least until he or she finally figured out how to thread the strip of celluloid through all those sprockets, get the lens focused properly, lower the thick, heavy window shades, and turn out the lights. In most cases it was enough time to get a credible spitball fight or funny face contest started among the reprobates and ne'er do wells who occupied the back row of every classroom in America. Furthermore, the chances of getting caught while engaged in some unseemly activity decreased in direct proportion to how dark the classroom became.

As we grew out of short pants and pinafores and became more worldly, adults had to employ increasingly sophisticated technologies to direct the course of our social development. Soon the stilted and unimaginative images of the filmstrip gave way to the more sophisticated and clever use of a movie genre known as the educational or instructional film. Produced specifically for the classroom, these now classic cautionary tales of everyday life were considered an indispensable tool for social engineering. The dominant theme was simple: If you didn't fit in, all you could expect out of life was unhappiness, and in the most extreme cases mental illness or even death.

Consider poor sloppy, disorganized Barbara, for example, in the timeless masterpiece "Habit Patterns." Invited to a socially important after-school party at Ann Tolliver's house, Babs finds she has nothing clean to wear. In desperation, she throws on a stained blouse and attempts to conceal the soiled spot with a scarf tied around her collar. But this amateurish effort to hide her poor grooming habits proves unsuccessful and Barbara soon finds herself shunned by the rest of the partygoers. "It's a little late for tears, isn't it, Barbara?" mocks the deep, unsympathetic voice of an invisible narrator. "How quickly you can be left out by the crowd. People are going to talk," taunts the voice. In the final scene, we find pitiful Barbara alone in her room, tears streaming down a face distorted with the pain of knowing she has become a social pariah.

For every Barbara there was also a Skip, Joe, or Bill—all very clipped Waspish names—who also had to learn his lesson the hard way. If it wasn't Jerry sitting outside the principal's office waiting to be suspended ("He refuses to listen to anyone with authority"), it was Jimmy the bicycle clown ("He has a foolish and dangerous it won't happen to me attitude") being carted off by an ambulance or wise-guy teen drinkers like Jack who, even after going to jail for killing his girlfriend in a drunk-driving accident, continued to drink upon his release and eventually wound up on skid row. It was a dangerous world out there for any boy or girl who failed to properly conform to the prevailing attitudes about behavior.

The middle of the twentieth century brought with it an explosion of technologies that, when they weren't being used to smite the totalitarian hoards, could be used as effective weapons in the war against nonconformity. Chief among these was television.

In 1926 an American by the name of Philo T. Farnsworth successfully scanned an image using a beam of electrons. This accomplishment, which came when Philo was twenty-one years old, led directly to the development of today's modern television technology. Sadly, my own crowning achievement by that age was to successfully pass a 7:30 A.M. college English Lit class through two swollen, bloodshot eyes that were usually not fully open until midday, which suggests that Philo may have been a bit of an overachiever.

However, television had a long way to go from Philo's first halting experiments before it was able to gain much traction as a commercial enterprise. In 1939 RCA televised the opening ceremonies of the New York World's Fair (not that there were an awful lot of viewers around to watch), including the first, although regrettably not the last, TV appearance by a president, Franklin Delano Roosevelt. The same year, RCA, having bought the rights to Philo's patents, also began to broadcast regular programming, including the first televised sporting event, a baseball game between Princeton University and Columbia University (Princeton won in ten innings by a score of two to one).

The outbreak of the Second World War pretty much put the brakes on any further commercial development of television, as companies like RCA began to retool and devote all of their resources to the war effort.

Immediately after the war, commercial development of television started to gain serious momentum. In 1945 a demonstration of its marvels drew 25,000 people to the Gimbel Brothers Department Store in downtown Philadelphia. Two years after the war ended, hundreds of stations had filed license applications with the FCC and the total number of TV sets in America had grown to 44,000 (as compared to 40 million radios); on December 27, 1947, "Buffalo Bob" Smith first uttered the immortal words "Hey, kids, what time is it?" It was Howdy Doody time, of course.

Not everyone was enamored of the burgeoning television industry, however. As David Frost since put it, television is an invention that allows you to be entertained in your living room by people you would never allow in your living room in the first place. Some critics were certain it spelled death for the art of conversation. Others claimed it would destroy eyesight, create an epidemic of lower-back pain, destroy the moral fiber of the nation's youth, and erode American values. Despite these threats, TV continued to thrive, and by 1954, when my family finally joined the television age, the number of sets in use had exploded to an unbelievable 32 million and the country was on the cusp of what would become known as The Golden Age of Television.

I don't remember much about our first television except that it was mammoth with a six-inch screen that forced me to sit no more than three or four feet away from it if I had any hope of seeing anything at all on the screen. Like all TV sets at the time, it seemed to take forever to warm up because of the prehistoric technology on which it relied to operate, a technology best remembered for its rows of glowing orange tubes and miles of multicolored wires.

There were a lot of makes and models out there to choose from, as companies like RCA, DuMont, GE, Philco, Olympia, and Sears all grabbed for a piece of the exploding television market. Dad, however, was not inclined to make hasty decisions when it came to any major purchase (or minor one, for that matter) and we ended up with a "starter" set he bought used for $95. As enthusiastic as we were about it, it compared poorly to the seventeen-inch Silvertone Bobby Craig had at his house or the huge console model Felix and Eddie Lauer enjoyed, with a twenty-one-inch screen that hid behind two sliding wooden doors. By today's standards a television was cheap—anywhere from $195 to $500. However, with the average American household income at around $4,800 a year and the minimum wage at seventy-five cents an hour, it was still a significant investment.

Television sets received picture signals from a huge scarecrow-like antenna mounted on the roof, and regardless of how big the picture screen, the image itself, such as it was, required constant and careful adjustment. Even a passing airplane—there was no shortage of those, living as we did just outside metropolitan New York City—could send the image reeling and tumbling, or simply obliterate it entirely in a cloud of "snow."

Today television is so specialized and the market so segmented that viewing has become an individualized experience. Eventually, I expect programming to become so specialized that every viewer will have his or her own personal channel. Television didn't start out that way—quite the contrary because, like radio, television began as a wholesome family affair, with Mom, Dad, and the kids all settling in to watch the same shows together. Advertising was of course geared toward grown-ups, particularly the man of the house, since that's where the money was, and the notion that kids, or any other demographic segment of the population, for that matter, might be a market unto themselves had yet to be fully realized or exploited.

By the time TV made its debut in our house, the mainstay of afternoon viewing was something called local programming. All local programming followed the same basic format: Start by having "local talent" dress up as a clown, cowboy, or spaceman (think Al Roker as Bozo the Clown—not hard to do); toss in a few oddball sidekicks of either human or puppet persuasion (think Bob Keeshan as Clarabelle the Clown); bring in a studio audience of kids ages five to eight; toss in a few cartoons and, voila, you had a local children's show. In Chicago it was the *Ray Raymond Show,* with Minerva the Mermaid, a human sidekick, and two puppets named Baron Barracuda and Triggerfish. In western Massachusetts it was *The Admiral and Swabby Show,* with a studio audience of kids called The Wicky Wacky Cloud Club. Philadelphia had Bertie the Bunyip with Fussy and Gussy and Sir Guy de Guy, while kids in Houston had *The Captain Don Travis Show,* with Seymour the space alien; kids in San Francisco had Charlie Horse and Humphrey Hambone; kids in Chicago had Garfield Goose, Bauregard Burnsides, and Macintosh Mouse; and kids in the Washington DC area had Pic Temple, Captain Tugg, and Ranger Hal.

The only reason local stations produced programs like these was to fill in empty time slots between network programming. It was Engineer Bill, Johnny Jupiter, and Milky the Clown, or a test pattern, and test patterns generated no ad revenue. Better the local anchor should look like a putz in a goofy costume and have the station make a few bucks than it was to lose viewers (and money) to the station across town with its own goofy-looking putz.

Sadly, local programming was a relatively short-lived phenomenon. As the networks became increasingly sophisticated in their ability to create programs—quiz shows, soaps, westerns, drama, news and information, variety, and classic comedies—that drew bigger and bigger audiences, which national advertisers supported with more and more money, local stations slowly began to die off, leaving behind little to mark their passing except pleasant memories in the minds of an entire generation of children.

In the evening, television programming was given over to a new genre called the family sitcom. Shows like *Leave It to Beaver, Father Knows Best, Ozzie and Harriet, The Donna Reed Show* were created to do more than merely entertain, they were also created to provide a baseline, a standard against which to measure the success of our own evolution as first-genera-tion patio pioneers. We loved watching these shows because they gave us a chance to laugh derisively at a bunch of wretched little miscreants whose pathetic lives were by all appearances even more screwed up than our own. Our parents enjoyed watching these shows because they relentlessly flogged the same values to which we were expected to aspire, including the most important rule of all: Obey your parents. In many respects, each episode of every show was a formulaic mini–morality play in which one of the young stars strayed from the path of parental righteousness. This, predictably, landed the malefactor in a heap of trouble, who then had to be bailed out by an unfailingly benevolent, patient, good-hearted adult.

Take young Theodore (aka The Beaver) Cleaver in a riveting episode of *Leave It to Beaver* titled "The Ring." Despite parental instructions to the contrary, Beav decides to take a ring that is considered a sacred family heirloom to school in order to show it off to his pals. He justifies his actions by hanging it from a piece of string tied to a belt loop, thereby circumventing his parents' prohibition against "wearing" it to school. At one point while showing it around to his classmates, Theodore puts the ring on his finger and, of course, it gets stuck. After several attempts to remove the ring by himself or with the help of his friends, the school nurse is consulted. When even she can't remove it, Mrs. Cleaver is brought into the picture and becomes aware of her youngest son's perfidy. The episode ends with a lecture that is both predictably firm and oozing with parental love and understanding. No voices are raised, fingers pointed, or punishments meted out. In other words, the whole thing was entirely unrealistic.

In a somewhat similar experience, I also borrowed an item I found tucked away in the drawer of a small desk both Mom and Dad used to perform a variety of household administrative tasks like paying bills, writing notes to the milkman, and so forth. Granted, I didn't ask permission, but it seemed like such a small matter, I figured why bother my Dad with something so trivial. The item in question was an ashtray made of molded metal and decorated on one side with the outline of a stooped old man standing next to a buxom young woman sporting a startled facial expression. Only when the ashtray was turned over did the reason for her astonishment become clear as the old codger had lodged his hand up the back of her skirt in order to fondle her buttocks. To a seven-year-old, this represented the cutting edge of humor, so I took the ashtray to school one day for show and tell. Unfortunately, because my first-grade teacher, Mrs. Lester, did not share the same level of sophistication as my friends and me, my presentation was cut short and my mother contacted. Needless to say, the outcome was extremely un-Cleaveresque.

Critics of early television often contend that shows like *Leave It to Beaver, Make Room for Daddy,* and *Father Knows Best* created false memories of postwar America because of the idealized fashion in which society and its institutions were portrayed. At some point, or so detractors claimed, reality and idealism were confused to the point where characters like Ward and June Cleaver were viewed as prototypes rather than stereotypes. However, that was immaterial to us, the young viewers, as was the entire pointless cultural debate that raged around us. We knew why that giant eye in our living room existed—it existed solely to entertain, amuse, and distract us, and we had every intention of making the most of this resource.

But television turned out to be more than merely chewing gum for the eyes, as Frank Lloyd Wright insisted, because the images on the screen took people who might otherwise have had very little in common and began to link them in ways that rendered moot the effects of distance and culture. We were on the road to becoming a global village, and the world began to shrink at an exponential rate.

The endless search for ways to promote conformity and social orthodoxy went even further and, in my estimation, reached its zenith with organizations like the Boy Scouts. Imagine a club created solely for the purpose of fulfilling every preadolescent boy's fantasy. Who among us didn't dream of surviving in the wilderness by our wits alone, stalking wild game, bedding down under a canopy of stars, and living off the bounty of the land? This—along with uniforms, badges of honor and rank, solemn pledges, secret handshakes, sacred oaths, and hallowed traditions—was pretty much all we could ask for out of life, and this is what the Boy Scouts of America promised us.

Unfortunately, instead of exploring the great outdoors, my own troop seemed to spend an inordinate amount of time in the basement of Mr. Williams, our scoutmaster, who didn't strike any of us as the kind of guy who knew an awful lot about tracking wild animals or fording raging rivers. Actually, he looked more like an accountant (which is what he was) than a rugged woodsman.

But if he didn't exactly inspire confidence in us, he probably had some reservations about us as well, particularly in our ability to do anything more complicated than tie our own shoes correctly. In this regard, his concerns were not altogether misplaced.

Under the best of circumstances, attendance at our weekly troop meetings never exceeded more than about ten scouts, including the regulars like myself; Jimmy Williams, our scout leader's son; Danny Caprio; Timmy Wolfson; Felix Lauer; Bobby Craig; and Randy Katz, a new kid in the neighborhood. The meetings were held on Wednesday evenings because it was the one night of the week that didn't conflict with any of our favorite TV shows.

Because he was the new kid, Randy was something of a wild card. The only thing he ever seemed to think or talk about was sex, a subject in which we were all developing a burgeoning interest. His repertoire of filthy jokes was endless, as was his ability to fill even the most innocuous comment with sexual innuendo. He never tired of regaling us with tales of his alleged sexual exploits, just as we never tired of pretending we believed every lascivious detail.

Scout meetings usually lasted no more than an hour and began with the obligatory Pledge of Allegiance and Boy Scout oath, followed by a brief rundown of late-breaking news about scouts and scouting from around the globe. The remainder of our meetings was usually devoted to an abbreviated lesson in the development of some skill considered essential to the well-rounded scout, like knot tying, semaphoring, or whittling. The curtain came down on whittling almost immediately after Felix managed to slice open his thumb, although the incident did offer opportunities for those interested in earning a merit badge in first aid. Semaphore was interesting only for those of us paired up with Randy, who used his signal flags to send messages like "Timmy Wolfson is a homo."

The meeting scheduled for knot-tying practice turned into a fiasco when Mr. Williams, called upstairs to the telephone, left us with instructions to practice our half hitch, clover leaf, and square knots, which we did by tying Timmy securely to a chair and pelting him with whatever loose object happened to be handy.

Despite this somewhat lackadaisical approach to the entire scouting experience, there were a couple of things I did enjoy. For one thing, there was marching in the Memorial Day parade. The martial music, the spit-and-polish precision of the local Army Reserve unit and veteran's organizations, flags snapping and flying in the breeze—all made my pulse quicken. Only the most jaded among us could avoid a swelling sense of pride as we made our way down Main Street, followed, we were certain, by the admiring glances of so many girls.

I began my Boy Scout career with intentions of the highest order, sure that it was only a matter of time before I joined the likes of President Kennedy, astronaut John Glenn, and actor Jimmy Stewart in becoming an Eagle Scout, the highest rank attainable. Unfortunately, I would soon discover that this was a road cluttered with many unseen obstacles and unanticipated hindrances that proved impassable to even those with the best of intentions.

In the culture of the Boy Scouts, those at the bottom of the totem pole held the rank of tenderfoot. In army parlance this is the equivalent of a buck private, which means that although you've been accepted into the service, you have yet to become proficient at anything. In order to begin moving up in the Boy Scout ranks, we first had to memorize a bewildering number of membership oaths, mottoes, slogans, and laws. This was followed by learning basic competencies in a variety of different areas like hiking, canoeing, first aid, and fire safety. We did this by completing a set of minimum requirements that resulted in being awarded merit badges.

Felix, Bobby, Randy, and I decided that we would try for a merit badge in hiking first, because it seemed the easiest. Hiking, after all, was basically just walking, something at which we could all claim a minimum level of proficiency. One of the requirements involved memorizing some of the basic safety rules about hiking like 1) how to avoid getting lost in the woods and 2) what to do if you were not very good at number 1. We were amazed to learn that the proper thing to do if you became lost in the woods was, in effect, to stay lost: to remain where you were on the theory that your rescuers would find you … eventually. To my mind, this seemed highly irregular. How would anyone even know you were lost in the first place if you weren't around to tell them, and even if they did know, what assurance did you have that they would even care? If my older sister suspected I was lost and unable to find my way home, I knew she could be counted on to keep the information to herself indefinitely. But there it was right in the handbook, so we had little choice but to memorize it.

The practical requirements for earning a merit badge in hiking were fairly simple. On a predetermined Saturday, Mr. Williams would drop us off at a nearby wooded area, where we were expected to tramp around for a few hours before being picked up again. We set off one warm autumn afternoon, each with a backpack containing snacks, a first-aid kit, and a full canteen of water. Randy included something a little extra in his pack, a deck of playing cards adorned with "52 international artist's models in erotic poses," which he promised to share with us during each rest break.

We marched along a path made by thousands of young feet over the years through stands of fir trees, acres of scrub brush and brambles, and open rolling fields of wild grass. Eventually, we topped a gentle rise and found ourselves nearing a group of perhaps a dozen girls about our own age, all decked out in Girl Scout green. They appeared to be engaged in some fieldwork of their own, botany I assumed, under the tutelage of a woman I immediately recognized as Mrs. Van Gundy, mother of the young and beautiful Allison Van Gundy, the most recent object of my unrequited seventh-grade affections. Knowing Allison was among the group, I straightened my neckerchief and added a bit of martial pep to my step as we passed by. If she should glance in my direction, I wanted it to be clear that I took my scouting seriously. Avoiding eye contact, we continued on our way.

We took our first break a few minutes later near a huge boulder known as Shelter Rock because legend held that generations of Indians had used the site as shelter from inclement weather. Dropping our packs, we sprawled out in a variety of restful poses and collectively caught our breath. When his breathing had slowed sufficiently, Randy pulled a cigarette from his shirt pocket, stuck it in the corner of his mouth, and lit it with a flourish using his personally monogrammed Zippo lighter. Although not yet smokers ourselves, we could not help being impressed by his élan and self-confidence he exuded. After taking a few more moments to watch Randy dispense a string of flawless smoke rings, we began to clamor for the deck of cards in his backpack.

This collection of gravitationally challenged female flesh would cause nary a stirring in a young man's libido today, but to us it was a veritable cavalcade of forbidden fruit. What gave the collection its promised international flavor were a few props like the strategically placed sombrero or fur muff, a grass skirt, or a skimpy Indian maiden's outfit.

After passing them around for us to study, Randy returned the entire deck to his pack, promising us we could inspect it again at the next rest break. Besides, the afternoon shadows were beginning to grow longer and we still had a couple of miles to cover in order to complete the required distance.

Before we had gone very far, I happened, either by instinct or by dumb luck, to glance briefly over my shoulder and spied a wisp of smoke rising from the spot we had just abandoned near Shelter Rock. As I stood there, the smoke grew into a thin column and I could see small tongues of flame beginning to eat their way into an ever-widening circle in the tall, dry grass.

I let out a shriek, "*Shit!*" and began sprinting back to the growing circle of flames. I arrived in seconds with my companions close at my heels. By now the circle of flames had spread to about twenty feet in diameter. The four of us began to dance around wildly in an effort to stomp out the flames, but the outer edge of the circle continued to grow and more and more smoke poured skyward. We were about to flee in panic when suddenly the cavalry arrived and we found ourselves surrounded by a sea of green uniforms; it was Mrs. Van Gundy's troop of Girl Scouts. She quickly ordered the girls to remove their jackets and use them to beat the circle of flames into submission. They did so, and within seconds the last of the flames was reduced to a smolder. Mrs. Van Gundy then had the girls walk carefully around the perimeter of the circle and empty the contents of their canteens on any embers that remained. The entire effort took no more than two minutes, and by the time they were done, the smoke had dissipated, leaving us staring at a wide circle of blackened earth. Looking up, I saw a dozen or so pairs of unblinking female eyes staring at us accusingly.

Ever the con man, Randy immediately tried to gain the edge by commenting on how lucky it was that we had all spied the mysterious grass fire at the same time because "Gee, it could've burned the whole woods down if we all hadn't come along when we did. Boy, you guys were great the way you beat the flames out with your jackets, and ..." Realizing his audience was stone-faced, Randy's voice trailed off and died mid-sentence when Mrs. Van Gundy stepped forward and handed him a slightly scorched Zippo lighter emblazoned with the initials *RK*. "I believe this belongs to you, Mr. Katz," she said coldly. I dared a quick glance at Allison, whose own eyes shot daggers of steel in my direction.

Well, there really isn't much more to the story after that. Predictably, as a result of our little indiscretion, the merit badge in hiking never materialized, and by the time Christmas rolled around two months later, the blush was pretty much off the scouting rose altogether. But that didn't much matter because adults, although sometimes short on things like patience and forbearance, always seemed to have a surfeit of ways to shape us into model citizens of the Crabgrass Frontier.

CHAPTER 2

Friends and Foes

Juvenile delinquency and teenage gangs were hot topics throughout postwar America, but nowhere more so than in suburbia, where prewar principles and ideals ran headlong into the reality of taming a new and uncharted frontier. Throughout the 1950s and '60s, highly credentialed professionals—sociologists, psychologists, educators, clergy, and law-enforcement professionals—were intent on weighing in on the subject. Some blamed the problem on permissive parents, others pointed the finger at comic books and music, while still others were certain the problem could be linked directly to fluoridated drinking water, which many regarded as a Communist plot.

Hollywood helped stoke these fires by cranking out films like *Blackboard Jungle*, *The Wild One*, the infamous *Rebel Without a Cause*, and my own personal favorite, *Reform School Girls*, all of which portrayed kids as seething volcanoes of hooliganism ready to erupt into a frenzy of antisocial behavior at the slightest provocation.

Admittedly, my friends and I did have our darker side, and acts of the most heinous antisocial behavior possible were not uncommon. For example, after almost every snowfall, we would hide in the bushes waiting to ambush unsuspecting vehicles with snowballs as they passed by. Occasionally, we smashed pumpkins, stretched Saran Wrap over the toilet seats in the boys' bathroom, set fire to the occasional paper bag full of dog crap after placing it on some unsuspecting neighbor's front porch, and even meted out the random wedgie to smaller kids who earned our ire.

However, none of these could in any way be construed as gang-related. We shunned gang membership. Gangs relied on both a rigid hierarchy and a strict code of behavior, two things for which we had little patience. It was bad enough when our parents tried to overorganize and overstructure our lives; we weren't about to do it ourselves. We chose, instead, to live for the moment, and our associations were far too loose to qualify as anything more than goofing around.

These affiliations had no names, no titles, no leather jackets, no colors, no grisly initiation rites, and definitely no debs. Indeed, the bond between members was sufficiently tentative that they might best be described as clumps. A clump was pretty much what the name implies, a loose aggregate of boys who gathered every day after school only to disperse as dinnertime approached and our presence was required at home. Membership, and I use the word advisedly here, was generally a function of geographic proximity, age, sports acumen, and overall recreational interests. It also didn't hurt to own a much-needed piece of play equipment.

It goes without saying that only under the most unusual circumstances were members of the fairer sex ever welcome to participate in our activities. Chauvinism as we now know it was unheard-of, although I don't think it would have made much difference either way. Girls tended to go their own way and engage in activities that were far less physically taxing than those of their male counterparts, hopscotch and playing on the monkey bars being the exceptions. Boys, on the other hand, once freed from the confines of adult supervision were in a constant state of motion and appeared only as occasional blurs as they went by. Rarely did the two groups mingle, and if they did, it was only briefly and solely for the purpose of tormenting one another.

An implicit social contract binds together any group of playmates, and the terms of this covenant revealed themselves in the form of certain accepted conventions to which we all voluntarily adhered. A classic example was the prohibition against saying anything bad about someone else's mother, which was considered an unseemly breach of etiquette although slurring the good name and reputation of your own mother never went out of style.

Squealing was another proscribed activity, unless it was required in self-defense. We never expected our friends to bite a fatal bullet with our name on it. By the same token, neither did we offer information too freely even when it was solicited. Because of parental injunctions against it, we didn't lie outright so much as completely disassemble the truth, rearrange it more to our liking, and rebuild it in a fashion that better suited our needs. There is nothing more impressive than a grade-school boy trying to explain something in excruciating detail to an adult while at the same time not revealing one scintilla of factual data.

There was always a certain amount of cross-pollination between clumps, and it was quite acceptable, even necessary, to belong to more than one clump at a time depending on individual circumstances. Because several of my friends at school lived all the way on the other side of town, they could not be part of my neighborhood after-school clump. Conversely, because a number of neighborhood playmates attended the local Catholic school instead of the public school, they could not be part of our playground clump.

Certain universal laws govern the group behavior of all preadolescent boys, and each member has a clearly defined role. It was a comfort to know that regardless of whom you happened to be playing with at the moment, even if they were mostly strangers, certain recognizable duties remained the same. For instance, there was always an alpha male, the undisputed leader of the group who directed its activities through the use of friendly physical and psychological persuasion. In most cases, the leader was someone we would try to emulate anyway because he possessed some attribute we admired. In addition to his great physical prowess on the baseball field, Steve Brodsky also had an uncanny knack for imitating the voices of many of our teachers with amazing fidelity, so much so that we were forever trying to convince him to showcase his talents over the school PA system. To his credit, Stevie always declined even in the face of a double-dog dare. He was, after all, the alpha male and not required to prove anything to the rest of us.

Like every pack of wild animals, kids were forever posturing and challenging one another in an attempt to improve one's status within the group hierarchy. As is the case in nature, these challenges—growling, baring teeth, and bristling of hair, or in our case pushing, shoving, and tripping—were more for show than anything else, as any real violence might have decimated the pack and endangered the entire species.

Sadly, nature requires that there always be someone who is low man on the totem pole, and it was this wretched soul who routinely got chosen last when the group split up into teams, tormented and teased about everything from his haircut to his clothes, and ditched by the rest of us when no other form of entertainment was readily available. Many of these individuals grew up to become employees of the U.S. Postal Service, where the years of humiliation sometimes exploded without warning into violent fits of rage.

Most every group of boys had someone in their midst nobody really liked but who was nonetheless tolerated and at times even deferred to because he possessed something other than personality, such as a tree house, a swimming pool, or just more and better toys than anyone else. This was nature's way of ensuring that even those on the fringe, those with a dearth of social skills, were not entirely excluded.

A critical role in every group of boys was the after-school equivalent of the class clown, a court jester of sorts who could routinely make us laugh. Among my friends it was Charlie Pendergast whose repertoire of jokes, sight gags, and rude noises and other obnoxious sound effects became legendary both in and out of school. His ability to move seamlessly from a Dirty Ernie joke to underarm fart noises to playing "Yankee Doodle Dandy" using a bizarre combination of cheek-popping, throat-tapping, and head-rapping made him the envy of jokesters everywhere. Charlie also knew that timing was just as important as the quality of the material itself and was quite prepared to demonstrate his skills when one of us had a mouth full of juice, milk, soda, Jell-O, pudding, ice cream, or any other food product that could pass easily through one's nasal passages. You haven't lived until you've snorted macaroni and cheese out your nose, as I have.

Every group of boys also seemed to have at least one kid who was prepared to push the envelope of preadolescent behavior further than anyone else by accepting any dare put before him. This was the kid you had to be careful about daring to do anything because in all likelihood he would do it. Occasionally, one of these daredevils would do something so outrageous that they failed to reach reproductive age, thereby permanently removing from the gene pool whatever faulty DNA was responsible for their behavior in the first place.

Unfortunately, there was one more figure who haunted our childhood, indeed haunted just about every childhood. This character was known simply as … The Bully.

Bullies held their own unique place on the periphery of our social hierarchy, not unlike a rogue elephant that has been remanded to the fringes of the herd. Accompanied by a variety of toadies who fed off whatever tidbits were tossed their way, bullies went through life surviving on the misery of others. We acknowledged them as members of our species, but just barely. It was at best a technical call.

My nemesis was Buddy Williams whose family had moved to our town from one of those square-shaped states out west like Wyoming or New Mexico shortly after the start of the school year. His five o'clock shadow strongly suggested an overactive pituitary gland, and made it difficult for my friends and me to believe he was the same age as the rest of us.

Buddy's real name was Bruce although I soon learned the folly of ever using his Christian name. Perhaps that's where the enmity originated. It must have been difficult to be a bully with a name like Bruce. On his better days, he enjoyed using me to demonstrate the proper execution of an Indian head rub or a bruising arm noogie, and although he relished tormenting many of my peers, he clearly favored me much the same way a dog favors a special chew toy.

At first I simply tried to avoid him, but our paths crossed too often during the course of a day for this to be an effective strategy. Besides, when we eventually did meet up, he seemed genuinely offended at the prospect I might have been avoiding him, which made the punishment all the more severe. For a short time, I attempted to enter his inner circle, but this proved just as futile because Buddy only took advantage of my availability to torment me further.

Leaving the movie theater one Saturday after seeing *The Amazing Colossal Man,* I became convinced Buddy's problem was that, like Air Force pilot Lt. Col. Glenn Manning, he had inadvertently been exposed to high doses of radiation and had begun to mutate. It happened to Manning when he accidentally flew his jet fighter into the restricted airspace of a top-secret military installation where nuclear testing was being conducted. Although he survived, Manning found himself growing larger and more cantankerous by the hour. Eventually, he ended up going completely crackers and in a fit of rage took out most of downtown Las Vegas. Manning was finally trapped and destroyed by the army high atop the Hoover Dam, despite the pleadings of his ever-faithful, normal-size fiancée.

Perhaps Buddy, who, after all, had come from a square-shaped state himself, which the military seemed to favor when it came to testing its atomic toys, had ridden his bicycle too close to a test blast and become irradiated like Lt. Col. Manning? According to Hollywood, what had happened to Lt. Col. Manning in *The Amazing Colossal Man* was no isolated incident, and all manner of bad things—the sudden interest in our world by alien beings, human mutations, and animal mutations—were happening as a direct result of mankind's efforts to tamper with the atom. Fortunately, I had a secret weapon.

Standing in front of the bathroom mirror, I assumed the classic pose of a body builder and grunted in an unsuccessful effort to will some modest muscle definition in my scrawny arms and chest. Dropping my arms back down to my sides, I exhaled and glanced down at the magazine propped open on the edge of the sink in front of me. A large, colorful advertisement that led with the words "Hey, Skinny" told the story of a young man named Mac, who, tired of and embarrassed by a lifetime of being pushed around by bullies, sends away for a thirty-two page booklet that promises to transform him into a "complete specimen of manhood—all in the privacy of his own home and after only fifteen minutes of special exercise each day. This was my kind of program.

We all know how the story ends. A short time later, Mac, who by now has become a muscle-bound oaf himself, returns to the scene of his last humiliation and restores the scales of justice to their proper balance by beating up the bully and walking off with the girl, to the admiring glances of all the other beachgoers ("He used to be such a skinny fella!) My eyes returned to stare at the boy in the mirror, and I sighed glumly to myself, "It'll never happen."

Every boy who ever lived has at one time or another felt the way Mac did when that bully kicked sand in his face. This alone probably explains the wild popularity and staying power of Charles Atlas and his amazing "Dynamic Tension" bodybuilding system, which even today attracts as many as 70,000 new customers a year. It spoke to the "Mac" in all of us.

Born Angelo Sicilano in the small Italian village of Acri, in Calabria, the future model, bodybuilding icon, and businessman who arrived at Ellis Island in 1903 was himself less than the ideal specimen of manliness. Like his alter ego Mac, Angelo was plagued by bullies, including one who tormented him by kicking sand in his face on the beach at Coney Island. According to legend, his date became so embarrassed by young Angelo's unwillingness and inability to stand up for himself that she walked off in disgust (not arm in arm with the bully), thus adding to his humiliation.

A few days later, as the dateless Angelo sought solace and refuge among the animal exhibits at Brooklyn's Prospect Park Zoo, he found himself mesmerized by the sight of a lion whose muscles bulged and rippled as it stretched.

"Well," Atlas recalled in one of thousands of later interviews, "he stretched himself all over—you know how they do, first one leg, then the other—and the muscles ran around like a rat under a rug, I asked myself, does this old gentleman have any barbells, any exercisers? No, sir. Then what's he been doing? And it came to me. He's been pitting one muscle against the other."

Actually, what Angelo had observed was an example of what we today call isometric exercise, or the process of pitting one muscle (or group of muscles) against another. As a result, the young immigrant was able to build up his weight and develop sufficient strength and self-confidence that in less than a year, he returned to Coney Island and beat up the bully who had so humiliated him the previous year. While there, he happened upon a statue of the Greek god Atlas and decided, because his magnificent new physique needed a name to match, to adopt the name as his own.

How much of this story is true remains to be seen; however, what is true is that the newly christened Mr. Atlas became a highly successful model at a time when the so-called physical culture craze of the 1920s began to peak. In 1922, he entered a bodybuilding contest at Madison Square Garden and found himself crowned "The World's Most Perfectly Proportioned Man." The demand for his modeling services skyrocketed as artists and sculptors, particularly sculptors, found the former pip squeak's barrel-chested physique almost irresistible. Today the results of this interest remain evident in some seventy-five statues around the world, including that of George Washington in New York City's Washington Square Park; Alexander Hamilton in front of the U.S Treasury Building, in Washington, DC; and The Archer in front of the Brooklyn Museum in New York.

However popular he had become as a model, though, Charles Atlas really made his name and fortune as a businessman. In 1928 he met a young entrepreneurial guru by the name of Charles Roman, who helped package and market the bodybuilding regimen to the public by using the same Coney Island bully incident that was responsible for Atlas's remarkable physique in the first place. In so doing, he tapped into every man's inner fear that he, too, was a ninety-seven-pound weakling.

Roman was smart enough to understand that, in many respects, Charles Atlas *was* the product. He made sure Atlas remained active in promoting the revolutionary bodybuilding program until he was well into his sixties. This included many public demonstrations and publicity stunts, one of which involved having Atlas strip to the waist and pull a railroad car 144 feet across a Sunnyside, Queens, train yard using only a length of rope and his own brawn. In the 1950s the American Medical Association threw its considerable weight behind Atlas by enthusiastically endorsing his unique

Dynamic Tension program. Everyone, including sports heroes like Rocky Marciano and Joe DiMaggio, seemed to turn to him for advice on health. His face appeared on the cover of hundreds of magazines both here and abroad, including *Forbes,* which dubbed him "Super Salesman" and named him one of the top ten marketing success stories in American business.

Sadly, for many of us the whole thing proved to be a cruel joke because when the Charles Atlas booklet arrived, I discovered that the program was broken into twelve lessons and that each lesson took two weeks to complete. In other words, it would be at best nearly six months before I began to see some sign that the program was working. I was more than prepared to work at it for several days or even a few weeks, if necessary, *but almost half a year?* It just wasn't possible. Not only did I lack the patience, but Buddy did not appear to be in the least bit inclined to cease hostilities long enough for the metamorphosis to take place. Frankly, I could be dead and buried at the hands of this knuckle-dragging nitwit before help arrived.

And so barring divine intervention, which was highly unlikely given my somewhat spotty church attendance, the Charles Atlas program looked like my only hope. Setting my mind to it, I began the exercises in earnest. I even decided to ignore the instructions, and instead of devoting just fifteen minutes a day to the special program, I doubled, and on some days even tripled, my time in the hope of reducing the number of weeks it would take to become a full-fledged he-man. So committed was I to this accelerated regimen that, occasionally, I tried to perform some of the exercises surreptitiously during class only to earn odd looks from my teachers and classmates, who simply assumed I was too shy to ask for permission to go to the bathroom.

The showdown with Buddy came on a clear, cold January afternoon during recess, well before I was able to complete the program, unfortunately. It had snowed the night before, not enough to declare a snow day but enough for the girls to make snow angels and for my friends and me to see how much white stuff we could stuff down one another's pants and shirt collars. Suddenly, the entire left side of my face exploded in pain, and it took a moment for me to realize I'd been hit with a snowball, which Buddy hurled directly at my head from close range.

As my face throbbed and reddened, I was reduced to dancing around in agony as melted snow ran down the inside of my shirt. Buddy and his coterie of cronies pounded each other on the back and laughed uproariously at my discomfort. Most of the other kids in the immediate vicinity stopped what they were doing and looked on. They knew the world was filled with lions and gazelles—the hunters and the hunted—and that the best thing for a gazelle to do in a situation like this was to simply freeze and hope he didn't attract the lion's attention. At least this is what Marlin Perkins taught us on Mutual of Omaha's *Wild Kingdom*.

As my ear continued to throb and tingle, I turned to my antagonist, pleading, "C'mon, Buddy, knock it off, that really hurt," which only made him laugh all the harder.

"Aw, what's the matter, little baby, afraid of a little snowball?" he taunted.

Most parents assured their kids that the only way to deal with bullies was to stand up to them because bullies were actually cowards at heart, an astonishingly ill-advised hypothesis.

I walked up to Buddy and looked him in the eye, hoping he could not see the fear on my face. This being the middle of winter on a school playground, there wasn't much sand to be had, so I improvised and kicked some snow in Buddy's direction and uttered the first words that came to my mind under these stressful circumstances, which, unfortunately happened to be a direct quote from the Charles Atlas ad: "Hey, skinny, yer ribs are showing." Buddy looked down at himself in confusion, and for a second I thought he might actually be slightly intimidated. Thus emboldened, I poked his enormous chest with my finger for added emphasis. The expression on Buddy's faced immediately turned dark and I knew I had made a serious miscalculation. The other gazelles looked stunned and for a moment time seemed to stop.

I didn't even see Buddy's fist coming, and when it hit me square in the face, it felt like a runaway freight train had collided with my nose. Anyone who has ever sustained a sharp blow to the head can tell you it really does produce a shower of stars. In this instance, however, it felt like an atomic bomb had exploded inside my skull, as the light of a thousand suns blinded me, followed by a blast wave of pain so intense my brain ceased to function normally. Every neuron fired off its own individual SOS signal advising the rest of my body that we had hit an iceberg and were going down fast. My legs got all wobbly, and although I managed to stay on my feet, the blow literally sent me reeling backward, my hands clutching my face. Never in my entire life had I realized that pain could be so, well, painful. Then an incredible thing happened. Suddenly, blood began to gush from both my nostrils in enormous quantities, pour through my fingers, and soak my clothes. Huge blotches of bright crimson splattered the fresh white snow all around me. The herd drew back, somewhere a girl screamed, and I opened one eye long enough to see Buddy standing there, almost in a daze. The scene was like something out of a slaughterhouse.

The next thing I knew, our school librarian, Mrs. Wedgewood, was at my side, telling me something about holding my head back, although I really couldn't understand what she was saying. My brain was still not capable of coherent thought. I saw her reach down for a handful of snow and remember thinking what an odd time she'd chosen to make snowballs, but the snow was for me, as she gently pressed it against the bridge of my still oozing nose. "Just hold that there," she instructed. It felt wonderful on my battered face, which by now had begun to pound fiercely.

Before long, both Mrs. Balducci, the school nurse, and Joe the custodian were also at my side, each gently taking an arm and guiding me step by step toward the school building. Even though only a couple of minutes had passed, the blood on my face and clothes was already starting to freeze into a stiff, brittle coating that crackled and flaked as we went. Hearing a commotion behind me, I tried to turn my head, but Mrs. Balducci wouldn't let me. "You just keep your head tilted back and keep that ice against your nose," she cautioned. Out of the corner of my eye, I saw Mrs. Wedgewood half pull, half drag Buddy toward the principal's office. His feet barely seemed to touch the ground and he didn't look anywhere near as tough as he had a few moments ago.

Needless to say, my mom almost had a cow when the school called and told her there had been "an altercation." She rushed me home and immediately called our family physician, Dr. Connell, and asked him to stop by during his afternoon round of house calls. Meanwhile, I tried to get myself cleaned up as best I could, but my clothes were covered in what was now brown dried blood and my nose was swollen and red. Mom got me upstairs, peeled away my clothes, layer by sticky layer, and hustled me into a hot tub to soak. Mom thought soaking in a hot tub could cure just about anything that ailed you. In this case, she was right.

That evening, Buddy's parents stopped by to apologize. They assured me that nothing like this would ever happen again and that Buddy was going to be severely punished. I didn't say anything, but I found myself wondering what form the punishment would take. Maybe they planned on taking away his daily steroid supplements. I also found myself thinking how odd it was that Buddy's parents looked so, well, normal. They could've been anybody's parents. I'm not sure what I expected, maybe that they themselves would be oversize hulks, but they weren't. They were just regular parents.

True to their word, that was the end of my Buddy problem, but I think it really had more to do with the fact that a few weeks later, Mr. Williams was transferred to Chicago by the company he worked for. I felt a little silly, actually. Had I known, I might have tried handling the matter with a bit more aplomb and saved myself a lot of aggravation. A number of onlookers later expressed surprise, even wistful disappointment, that my injuries were not more severe given the copious and dramatic loss of blood.

Sadly, this was not the last time I would be forced to deal with genetic mutants like Buddy, but like the threat of Commie spies, swarms of giant irradiated insects run amok, or the impending menace of puberty, it was just another normal day on the Crabgrass Frontier.

CHAPTER 3

A Cowboy's Best Friend

My very first pet was a goldfish, which is no surprise. On the Crabgrass Frontier, guppies, goldfish, turtles, and other non-mammalian species were common starter pets. From there we moved up to more complex life forms like parakeets, white mice, and the occasional guinea pig. I named my goldfish Phineas, after my favorite character on *The Howdy Doody Show*, Phineas T. Bluster, the trouble making Mayor of Doodyville. I won Phineas at the annual fundraising carnival run by the priests and nuns down at the local Catholic church, one of the few annual events non-Catholics like me were not only welcome but encouraged to attend. It wasn't really a carnival in the strictest definition of the term. There was no Ferris wheel, merry-go-round, bumper cars, or other rides you normally associate with a real carnival. It was mostly just games that appeared to involve some level of skill, like shooting basketballs through a hoop, knocking down a stack of pins with a softball, and tossing a Ping-Pong ball in the hope that it would drop inside one of a bunch of milk bottles.

We suspected that most of the games were rigged in some way so that winning was far more a matter of chance than skill. Only years later would I learn that the basketball hoop was replaced with one that was slightly smaller in diameter than a regulation-size hoop, making it much harder to sink a basket. The wooden pins used in the softball throw were actually weighted at the bottom, so unless you hit them in exactly the right spot, at least one always remained standing. It was fun to watch as the older boys, boys in their teens, tried to impress their dates at a game they believed utilized a skill at which they felt some prowess—like the basketball throw or the softball toss—only to spend every last cent trying unsuccessfully to win a stuffed animal for some moony-eyed girlfriend. Sometimes the person running the booth took pity on the poor dumb slob and forked over a consolation prize like a goldfish darting around inside a small plastic bag filled with water.

My best friend in second grade was Felix Lauer, whose older brother, Eddie, was a starting pitcher on the Junior Varsity baseball team. Everybody said Eddie had the makings of a great varsity pitcher. Obviously, Eddie fancied himself a sure winner at the baseball toss, but at ten cents a throw (three for a quarter), he managed to wipe out five bucks before quitting, red-faced with embarrassment and anger, particularly as his teammats razzed him mercilessly. The oily-looking game operator with a pencil-thin mustache who had egged Eddie on the whole time ("C'mon, Sport, try again, you almost had it that time") smirked knowingly before reaching into a box and handing him his consolation prize. Without saying a word, Eddie grabbed the bag and stalked away with his date—insisting she didn't really want that dumb old stuffed poodle anyway—and his teammates, still hooting and hurling insults, at his heels.

Before he'd gone very far, Eddie glanced at the plastic bag and scowled before tossing it into a nearby garbage can. And had Felix and I not been only a few steps behind, Phineas would have begun his unavoidable albeit predictable transformation into worm chow several days before he did. Fortunately, the force of his landing was softened by all the other trash—wadded food wrappers, crumpled paper plates and cups, and half-eaten hot dogs—that already filled the can. Picking it carefully from among the other detritus, I examined my prize with a practiced eye to make certain it had not suffered any undue damage and was relieved to discover the small goldfish darting feverishly within the confines of its small plastic home, clearly startled at this undignified turn of events but apparently no worse for the wear.

I was not the only kid wandering around the fairgrounds holding a plastic bag containing a goldfish. Everywhere you looked, people, young and old alike, seemed to be holding one or more such prizes, but I saw very few people loaded down with stuffed animals or any of the other bigger prizes that were promised, which suggested to me that there were a lot more losers than winners. The worst part, however, was the rumor that shenanigans were afoot between the parish priest and Mr. Wallace, owner of Wallace's Pet Emporium in the center of town.

According to my source, a casual playmate who attended the local Catholic school, Mr. Wallace and the priest had an arrangement in which the former provided all the goldfish the latter wanted as consolation prizes at no charge to the church. Obviously, any kid who got one would need to set up an appropriate home for the little fellow, which invariably required a trip down to Wallace's Pet Emporium, the only such store in town, for a fishbowl, colored gravel, food, and a few underwater knickknacks necessary to create the proper environment for a new fish. This could easily set parents back several bucks. But what were beleaguered parents supposed to do? It's not like they could say "No, throw the damn thing away, we'll just have to flush it down the toilet in a couple of days" to a kid who'd just won a new pet goldfish at a church bazaar. After all, churches were the very institutions where the sanctity of all living things was held in high esteem, were they not? So down to Wallace's went a weekend-long parade of elated children and grumbling parents.

The kicker, however, was that Mr. Wallace apparently had promised to donate twenty-five percent of any money he made selling goldfish-related merchandise that weekend back to the church. I was no math wizard, but even I could figure out that everyone concerned made out quite nicely as a result of this cozy little arrangement, except perhaps for the goldfish themselves.

The problem with having a fish as a pet is that they are not, generally speaking, very interesting or talented. It's not like you can pet them, take them for a walk, or teach them to fetch a stick. Consequently, our interest in them waned fairly quickly; usually, within a day or so, they were forgotten if not already dead. Once all the necessary equipment had been purchased and set up in some carefully chosen spot in our bedroom; once we were done tapping the side of the bowl or pressing our lips against it to gain the attention of the newest family member; once we had experimented with a variety of additional accoutrements like a battalion of green plastic soldiers or a few Matchbox cars; once we had emptied half a container of food into the bowl because it was the only thing the damned fish seemed even remotely interested in; once we had exhausted all of the possibilities for amusement short of actual fishicide (Billy Baxter used to entice his fish to the surface with a few flakes of food before zapping them with a beam of sunlight focused through the lens of a big magnifying glass), we pretty much forgot the whole thing, at least for a few days until an odd odor announced the fish's passing.

This was exactly what happened to Phineas, and although I don't recall being overly affected by his demise, I was aware that for the younger brothers and sisters of some of my friends, the occasion could be quite traumatic. And why not? For most it was their first brush with the cruel reality of death, which usually could only be assuaged by conducting a formal funeral service befitting a well known head of state, although most famous dignitaries are not, to the best of my knowledge, flushed down the toilet, as was Phineas.

The next step in the pet hierarchy was often something like a small turtle. Turtles were also nice because they were cheap and extremely low-maintenance. In most cases, a turtle's home consisted of a shallow plastic bowl with a little island in the middle, sporting a fake palm tree where the tiny amphibians could sun themselves. That and a few pieces of lettuce every few days seemed enough to keep them happy. Unfortunately, there was still the problem of their potential for amusement, and, like goldfish, they were generally acknowledged as yet another fairly unexciting if not downright boring choice as a pet. Still, for a time they were pretty popular and we tried to make the best of it.

One immediate advantage turtles had over goldfish was the fact that they could be removed from their habitat without our having to worry that they'd flop around and die within the first few minutes. We knew turtles could live both in and out of water, and we used this information to our advantage when it came to utilizing them for the purposes of entertainment. Unfortunately, this sometimes came to a less than satisfactory conclusion—for the turtle anyway.

Bobby Craig had read somewhere that turtles were very strong, relatively speaking, particularly their shells, which could withstand a great deal of weight. His little brother had a turtle named Tommy (its namesake being a once favored pull toy, also a turtle), and one day while hanging around with nothing much else to do, Bobby suggested we engage in a bit of scientific inquiry by seeing how much truth there was to this bit of turtle lore. We began by removing Tommy from his little plastic turtle lagoon and placing him on the kitchen floor. Fashioning a tiny harness out of string, we hitched the turtle up, tied the other end to a Matchbox car, and placed a bit of lettuce on the floor several inches away from his nose. Tommy blinked slowly once or twice, as turtles do, looked around dully for a moment, and then much to our delight and amusement made his way toward the lettuce, dragging the tiny car behind. Although it took some effort—his feet clawed for traction on the slick linoleum—he eventually made it and settled down to a well deserved lunch.

Not yet satisfied that we had explored all the endless possibilities for Tommy or fully plumbed the depths of scientific investigation, we forged ahead. Moving to the living room rug, where he could get better traction, we hitched Tommy to a large yellow metal Tonka truck. Unfortunately, it proved too much even for him, and after struggling mightily for a minute, he finally gave up and just sat there blinking. He even tried to tuck his head inside his shell, but the harness made it difficult, so he eventually just sat there inert, and no amount of lettuce or encouragement on our part could get him to move any farther.

Bobby and I felt we had pretty much exhausted this particular line of inquiry, and I moved on to another. This time we decided to see just how much weight a turtle could actually support and began by slowly stacking ever-increasing amounts of weight on his back until such time as we were satisfied the young amphibian had reached its limit. Frankly, we had given little thought to how we would know when this had occurred precisely, which unfortunately although predictably proved to be Tommy's eventual undoing. Without going into gruesome detail or pandering to the need for gratuitous violence, suffice it to say that after the Tonka truck, a frying pan, and a complete four volume set of Reader's Digest condensed books were all piled atop Tommy, there came a disquieting "crunch" followed soon thereafter by a slowly spreading puddle of what can only be described as turtle juice on the kitchen floor. Bobby and I moved quickly to remove all the objects we had piled on the now ex amphibian and return them all to their proper place while disposing of a now much flatter turtle in the trash.

Of course, Bobby's little brother had a fit when he got home and found Tommy missing, immediately divining that Bobby and I probably had something to do with it despite our repeated protestations to the contrary. Bobby's mom also seemed to suspect our involvement but after only a cursory grilling seemed amenable to letting the matter go and promising her youngest a replacement of some sort. Bobby's ears immediately perked up at that point because this promise opened the possibility that the replacement pet might by some miracle be the one and only pet a boy really wanted: a dog.

As every boy knows, a dog is far more than merely a pet. A dog, a real dog—not one of those yappy, hairless little rat faced things women of a certain advanced age seem to fancy—was a brave and fiercely loyal companion, even more so than all but the closest of our human friends. You never hear stories about a boy and his goldfish, a boy and his turtle, a boy and his parakeet, or a boy and his hamster because there simply aren't any. Dogs could be counted on in even the direst of circumstances, which was a lot more than could be said of many people.

Our drive to be paired with a devoted canine companion started at an early age. There was Buck, from Jack London's *Call of the Wild,* Balto and Togo, two of the famous sled dogs most responsible for carrying a supply of diphtheria antitoxin across the frozen wastelands of Alaska to Nome, thereby savings hundreds of lives; and of course Old Yeller himself, a dog that personified loyalty and courage.

Movies soon became a centerpiece for man's best friend, including one of the most popular celluloid canines of all time, Rin Tin Tin.

At the risk of being looked upon as a nitpicker, I never said anything to my friends about the fact that I found the name Rin Tin Tin—Rinty to his closest associates—mildly annoying because it didn't seem to mean anything. If you were going to go to all of the trouble of having a dog, I felt it should have a name that said something about the character of the animal itself, like Wolf, Killer, or Destructo. Even some of the more traditional names (Rex, Spot, Bowser, Wags, or Fido) would've been better; at least they were recognizable, but Rin Tin Tin? What in the world was a Rin Tin Tin?

Actually, as I would discover many years later, there was a perfectly reasonable explanation for Rinty's name, one that stretched all the way back to World War I Europe, when an American corporal by the name of Lee Duncan, a hardware store clerk by trade, came across a bombed-out dog kennel in Lorraine, France, and discovered a female German shepherd and her litter of ten-day-old pups. Fascinated by the uncanny intelligence of trained shepherds used by the German army, Duncan decided to take two of the pups, a male and a female, for himself and try his hand at training them on his own. He named them Nannette and Rin Tin Tin after two of the tiny finger puppets French children often gave American GIs for good luck.

His fascination soon turned to an admiration bordering on awe as the training progressed, and when Duncan learned that the officer in charge of the bombed-out kennel where he'd discovered the pups was imprisoned in a nearby Allied POW camp, he went to visit him to learn as much as he could about this breed.

After the war Duncan returned to America with both pups in tow, but before they arrived home in California, where he planned on returning to his job in the hardware business, poor Nannette succumbed to distemper. Duncan's growing interest in dogs, particularly German shepherds, compelled him to begin attending dog shows, where people were constantly amazed at Rinty's abilities. In 1922 a man by the name of Darrell Zanuck happened to be at one of the dog shows Duncan attended, trying out a new camera. He offered the former army corporal $350 to allow him to film the dog in action. Duncan accepted and decided then and there that he and his canine companion were destined for fame in the burgeoning film industry. This proved a lot more difficult to accomplish than Duncan expected. He and Rinty were turned away by every major film studio they approached. Reduced to knocking on the door of any second-rate studio they could find, the duo one day found themselves on the lot of a little known company called Warner Brothers watching a film crew shoot take after unsuccessful take of a scene in which a wolf was the central character. Duncan approached the film crew and advised them that his dog could do the scene flawlessly in a single take. It took a while to persuade the director to give the unknown dog a shot, but Duncan persisted and the director finally acquiesced; as promised, Rinty did the scene in one take.

It wasn't long before Rinty was one of the most beloved (and powerful) stars in all of Hollywood. His arrival is credited by many for saving the nearly defunct Warner Brothers studio. At the peak of his career, which spanned more than a decade, Rinty was one of the highest-paid performers in Hollywood and received as many as 10,000 fan letters a week, most of them from boys and girls smitten with the dog's unwavering loyalty and heroic acts. He was also listed in the Los Angeles telephone directory.

On Friday, August 10, 1932, with twenty-five feature films to the dog's credit (Duncan had just signed Rinty to a contract for his twenty-sixth film with Warner Brothers, which was scheduled to begin shooting the following Monday), the beloved Rin Tin Tin suddenly died. Although both Duncan and Warner Brothers were despondent over the loss, Rinty lived on in a number of the offspring he'd sired. Indeed, so dedicated had Duncan become to his dogs that when his wife filed for divorce in 1933, Rinty Jr. was named as a co-respondent because her husband was alleged to have loved his dogs more than he loved her. The divorce was never granted.

As the new medium of television began to eat into more and more of the movie market, one of Rin Tin Tin's great-grandsons was hired to play the lead in a new adventure series called appropriately enough, *The Adventures of Rin Tin Tin*. In the first episode, which aired on October 15, 1954, we were introduced to a young boy named Rusty and his dog Rin Tin Tin (aka. Rinty), the only two survivors of an attack on their wagon train by a band of rampaging Apaches. Discovered by a cavalry troop led by the brave and handsome Lt. Ripley (Rip) Masters, the orphaned duo are adopted by the soldiers and taken back to the fort to live. Rusty is made an honorary corporal, complete with his own uniform, while Rinty had to make do as a private with only a kerchief tied round his neck. We were never told why Corporal Rusty insisted on wearing his hat sideways, with the brim facing front to back rather than side to side.

Another television show featuring the adventures of a boy and his dog—this was, of course, *Lassie*—but there were any number of reasons we preferred the former over the latter.

First, there was the setting of each show itself. *Rin Tin Tin* took place in the middle of our favorite era, the Old West, complete with savage Indians, gunfights, and other forms of traditional Wild West amusement. *Lassie* took place somewhere in pastoral present-day rural America. Along with Rinty himself, the cast of the Rin Tin Tin Show included a U.S. cavalry troop headed by the aforementioned Lt. Rip Masters, Sergeant Biff O'Hara (he was often called upon to provide the show's comic relief), the stouthearted Corporal Boone, and, of course, the orphaned Rusty. Lassie, on the other hand, had to share the spotlight with a slight, almost feminine looking boy named Timmy; his widowed mother, Ellen; his aging grandfather ("Gramps"); and an overweight best friend named Porky.

The story lines gave each show its own unique gestalt and were as different as night and day. It seemed that in almost every episode of *Rin Tin Tin,* young Rusty would invariably holler "Yo ho, Rinty!" which, loosely translated into doggie talk apparently meant "attack" because that's what Rinty did, thereby forcing the bad guy to drop his gun and start begging for mercy ("Please, get him off me, make him stop"). Regrettably, and much to our disappointment, Lassie rarely engaged in this type of mayhem because she was usually too busy trying to save one of the leading characters, often the luckless young Timmy or doddering old Gramps from one life-threatening predicament after another. For example, Timmy had a habit, or so it seemed, of falling down every well in sight. Saving him usually involved a good deal of barking until some other family member mysteriously divined what the dog was "saying" ("What is it, girl? You say Timmy went squirrel hunting, lost his footing and fell into a ravine, and now he can't climb out because he broke his ankle and there's a hungry mountain lion prowling nearby?"). It was a bit much even for a kid to swallow.

Finally, there were also issues involving gender, personality, and pedigree to consider. Whereas Rinty was unequivocally all male, Lassie was a boy dog playing a girl dog, resulting in if not some gender-identification issues, at least some androgyny-fueled confusion; whereas Lassie was friendly and easygoing, as evidenced by lots of petting and tail wagging, there was something almost sullen and standoffish about Rinty. Lassie came from a background of pampering and privilege—he was bred and raised specifically for stardom. Rin Tin Tin's roots went back to the harsh realities of war-torn Europe, where his descendants had to work for a living. When all was said and done, it was generally conceded among all my friends that in a fight, Rin Tin Tin would definitely kick Lassie's ass!

After the turtle incident, Bobby's mom did replace his little brother's pet, but it was not the dog he had hoped for. Instead, she opted for a small, harmless-looking chameleon housed in a small aquarium filled with sand and rocks and warmed with a heat lamp. Bobby's brother named him Godzilla in honor of the gargantuan, cantankerous celluloid antihero that flattened most of downtown Tokyo in the now classic 1954 horror film of the same name. Audiences made up of hundreds of preadolescent boys attempted to aid the military (the U.S. military of course, because Japan was still forbidden to rebuild a sizable army of its own, with the memories of World War II only five years old) by bombarding the screen with the only potentially lethal weapons immediately at hand: our stash of Good & Plenty, Milk Duds, Junior Mints, and Raisinets.

Although its cage was covered with wire mesh, the adventurous lizard soon made its escape, and for days thereafter made several brief, unexpected appearances in the most unlikely places. For instance, a sudden earsplitting shriek from the bathroom was a sure sign Godzilla had stopped by to say hello to Bobby's older sister while she was in the shower, a visit that was not entirely welcome. Sadly, after a week or two of these rare Godzilla sightings, he disappeared forever.

Tragically, I never got a dog either. Eventually, I would come to learn that the world is split into two very different kinds of people—dog people and cat people—and as luck would have it, I had the misfortune of being born into a family in which the latter outnumbered the former.

Our family feline took over the house just around the time I turned nine, and because she boasted four all white paws, she was naturally dubbed Boots. And as any true dog lover can tell you, cats are the antithesis of dogs.

Dogs are gregarious social creatures who like nothing more than to be surrounded by similarly minded animals regardless of species. Cats are loners and will go to great lengths to be left alone. Dogs continually seek the love and approbation of other family members. Cats couldn't care less. Tossing a stick for a dog to retrieve will have the animal quivering with excitement. Asking a cat to fetch a stick will earn you a look like you've lost your mind. Talk to a dog and it will listen intently in an effort to fully comprehend your every whim. Talk to a cat and it will yawn once or twice before sauntering from the room, tail raised high in the air to ensure you see its brown wink good-bye. Dogs can easily be trained to bring you your slippers and the evening newspaper. Cats are fond of retrieving dead things like small rodents and birds that have yet to master the art of flying and leaving them proudly at your feet. If your house catches fire, the family dog will bark until everyone is awake and out of danger. If your family happens to own a cat, it will generally sneak silently out the nearest door, leaving everyone else to fend for themselves.

Alas, there would be no Rin Tin Tin or Lassie to accompany me on my neighborhood adventures; and as for Boots, there was no interest in anything but food, sleep, and a clean litter box. In return, the most I could expect was an occasional hairball deposited neatly in one of my favorite sneakers. So much for loyalty.

CHAPTER 4

Crabgrass Entrepreneurs

Although they certainly never intended as much, the visionaries who first conceived of placing advertisements between the covers of the most popular reading material ever created for children, comic books, were at the same time creating one of the most essential yet unsung instruments of public service of the mid–twentieth century. With seemingly flawless intuition, the purveyors of lowbrow commercialism tantalized and enticed us with promises that the solution to some of our most vexing childhood problems—not to mention untold wealth, popularity, physical prowess, romance, and the admiration of our peers—could be had for mere pennies.

What made these claims so convincing was the bloated, overwritten copy and gaudy in-your-face design of the ads themselves; who among us in those days did not believe that if you saw it in print it must be the truth. These were truly "amazing," "sensational," "one of a kind," and "never to be repeated" offers of a lifetime.

Consider all the opportunities these ads made available to budding entrepreneurs both young and old, like William Bergstrom of Illinois, who made a small fortune without spending a cent of his own money after becoming a Mason Shoe salesman in his spare time. What made the claim even more believable was the fact that it told the entire story from beginning to end right there in cartoon format from the day Bill first saw his next-door neighbor Jim pull into his driveway in a shiny new car. "Gee, how can he afford a car like that on the salary he makes?" Bill asked himself.

Flashing a wad of cash in Bill's face, Jim helpfully explains how in his off hours he made eighty-eight dollars *that week alone* by becoming a "Mason Shoe Man." After talking it over with his spouse ("My wife was thrilled!"), Bill sends away for a sales kit. When it arrives, they both are amazed. "Look, Bill, a real air-cushion inner sole that customers can actually feel," marvels his wife. "And look at this," responds Bill enthusiastically. "Over 175 different styles! Dress shoes, sports shoes, and work shoes from width AAAA to EEEE."

We all know how the story ends. In the last panel, our hero is flashing his own wad of cash while his wife gushes over a new toaster purchased with the proceeds of their newfound wealth.

Although this particular ad was geared toward a somewhat older audience (who says comic books were just for kids?), there were moneymaking opportunities galore for kids of all ages. Take the amazing Plastikit, for example, brought to you by the folks at Plastic Enterprises, Inc., of Baldwin, New York, which allowed the business minded young boy or girl to produce "$100 worth of valuable plastic objects" that could be sold to one's friends, neighbors, and family members, and all for the unbelievably low price of just $1.98. Furthermore, for those who acted quickly, Plastic Enterprises, Inc., was prepared to toss in two valuable booklets on how to make the most out of your Plastikit *at absolutely no additional charge.* If you were still not convinced, the offer came with a full money-back guarantee if you were not completely satisfied.

If you wanted cold hard cash and valuable prizes, too, prizes like a "professional type junior archery set" and "official size, official weight professional basket ball," or a "full sized ukulele like the one played by Arthur Godfrey," then Uncle Harry of the American Seed Company of Lancaster, Pennsylvania, was the man for you.

"Everyone wants American seeds," promised Jack Benny–look alike Uncle Harry, "because they are guaranteed fresh and ready to grow." Seeds that were ready to grow—what a concept! Who could pass up an offer to buy a packet of ready-to-grow seeds for only fifteen cents? What's more, because he trusted us, Uncle Harry was prepared to send us a starter kit containing forty seed packets at no cost. Our part of the bargain was simply to sell all forty packets at fifteen cents apiece and of the six dollars made, we only had to send four dollars back to Uncle Harry and pocket the remaining two dollars for ourselves! "Free prizes are given for selling just one set of 40 seed packets. Many boys and girls sell their packs in one day and get their valuable prizes at once!"

If selling wasn't your thing, there was no need to worry. There were always other possibilities for personal enrichment and professional achievement like books on how to land a Hollywood movie contract or art courses that could land you a high-paying job in the field of commercial art within months. It was all there, the entire American dream crammed into a single garish ad that pandered to the dreamer in all of us.

Another nice thing about these ads was that, regardless of your age or gender, there was always something relevant. For smaller kids there were the ads touting some toy—a jet-rocket spaceship ("the most sensational toy in America!"), a satellite wrist flashlight ("It's out of this world!"), a set of Captain Video two-way radio communicators ("It's scientific, futuristic, and educational!), and even a jet-propelled speedboat ("It really looks, sounds, and runs like the real thing!")—that was guaranteed to make you the envy of the neighborhood.

If it was attention you were after, there was a wide selection of rubber masks to choose from, including the monkey, colored minstrel, and Satan masks, as well as the "luminous life like rubber skull mask," although I never fully understood how the skull of a dead person could be "life like." If these didn't make you the life of the party, the glow-in-the-dark necktie emblazoned with the words "Will you kiss me in the dark, baby?" surely would, because, as the ad copy assured us, "the girls cannot resist it."

Were you missing a lot of fun and dates like "poor Mary?" The answer was simple. All you had to do was send away for the complete Dean Ross

Piano Course, "complete with the PATENTED AUTOMATIC CHORD SELEC-TOR." No scales, no exercises, no dreary practicing: "You actually play the minute you sit down at the piano!" Once again, we knew it was true because in the last story panel, we see Mary seated at a piano surrounded by adoring boys and thinking, "No more wallflower stuff for me. Now I'm the hit of the party, the center of attention wherever I go." Who knew that such happiness and popularity could be had for just $1.98?

Nor did comic book ads shy away from addressing embarrassing personal problems. One could end forever, for instance, the shame, embarrassment, humiliation, social stigma, and discomfort of bed-wetting immediately without rubber sheets or electrical devices of any kind with "Dry Tabs." For only three dollars, the folks at the Gary Pharmaceutical Company of Chicago, Illinois, were prepared to send you a three-week supply of this "amazing new formula" that was, according to the ad, "developed after years of hospital and clinical research as revealed in medical literature."

Although not a bed-wetter, I did suffer that most universal of all adolescent problems: zits. Fortunately, help was close at hand. For blackheads there was the remarkable Vacutex, which purported to extract the offending imperfection by means of a gentle vacuum action that drew it out. You knew it worked because the ad included before and after cartoon faces; while the first was covered all over with unsightly black dots, the second face was clear as silk.

Like many of my friends, rather than subject myself to embarrassing criticism or lost popularity due to ugly, dirt-clogged pours, I sent my one dollar to the Balco Products Company of New York, New York, for my very own Vacutex. It was easy to spot a Vacutex user at school because although it did not remove a single blackhead, this nifty little invention did leave a visible red ring around it, leaving our faces looking as though they were covered with tiny bull's eyes.

If you were beyond the blackhead stage like most of us and your face had the appearance of a lunar landscape, there was still hope because Clear X, a scientifically formulated cream, promised to "improve your appearance with the first application" and dry up any imperfections entirely within three days. "Love can be yours again," the ad promised. "You can't blame him [her] for not wanting to kiss you if your skin is oily and defaced with ugly pimples and unsightly blackheads and acne." Unfortunately, the only thing this product did was further highlight the already embarrassing blemish with a dried crusty substance that routinely drew more stares than the zit itself.

Despite the extravagant guarantees and the repeated failure of these products and promotions to live up to the promises inherent in the overblown prose and dramatic art of the ads, they remained an indispensable part of our suburban heritage. We liked them. They spoke to us directly in a language we understood. Eschewing subtlety, they remained unrepentant about the absence of any high-handed Madison Avenue marketing strategies, which they more than made up for with the zealousness, titillation, and prevarication that attracted us in the first place. There was no equivocation or hedging. Contrary to all that we'd been told by our parents, teachers, and other adults, the things that really mattered most in life could be had by means other than hard work and following the rules. Sometimes the things that really mattered in our lives, like being the envy of others or the center of attention, popularity, and material wealth, could in some cases be had merely for the price of a postage stamp.

CHAPTER 5

Tupperware Tribulations

My mom became a Tupperware Lady in 1957, when I was eight years old. I think Mrs. Lester from down the street recruited her along with several other ladies in the neighborhood. Tupperware seemed to have appeared out of nowhere and taken over our neighborhood overnight, like something out of *Night of the Living Dead*. One minute the icebox was full of glass bowls covered with aluminum foil and wax paper—many of which ended up shattered on the kitchen floor, the victims of greasy hands or just plain clumsiness—and next minute they'd been replaced by neat stacks of lightweight, pastel-colored plastic containers, each with its own airtight lid that actually "burped." I really liked the burp.

In the days preceding her first Tupperware party, Mom started acting pretty weird. She cleaned, scrubbed, dusted, vacuumed, waxed, polished, mopped, and wiped our house from one end to the other until it gleamed—and then did it all over again. You would've thought the president was coming to visit. She spent hours making lists of all the things she had to prepare, fretting over the menu, and worrying about whether or not we had enough chairs for all the guests. She was forever wiping invisible specks of dust off every flat surface.

The day of the party was even worse. Up at the crack of dawn, she got out the good china, the stuff we used only on holidays, and washed it repeatedly before stacking it all—the cups, saucers, and dessert plates—neatly on the dining room table. By the time my sister and I came downstairs for breakfast (Dad had had sense enough to leave for work early that morning), Mom was polishing the silver like a woman possessed and muttering to herself about picking up the linens from the cleaners before noon.

Small social gatherings—cocktail parties, barbecues, bridge luncheons, and the like—were not uncommon at our house, but I had never seen her get so worked up over the preparations. It was almost as though her reputation as a hostess was about to be tested and everything, absolutely everything, had to be just right. The fact that most of the invitees were her friends from the neighborhood, the same people she gabbed with on the phone, in the grocery store, and over the back fence, made the entire exercise all the more strange.

When I returned home from school that afternoon, I knew immediately that Mom had gone round the bend completely, as evidenced by the menu she was in the midst of preparing, including three or four different home-baked cakes and pies, a huge platter of deviled eggs, another platter of those little triangle-shaped sandwiches, the ones with the crusts neatly cut off, and a platter of little cubes of cheese, each skewered with its own little decorative toothpick. Never had Mom gone to all this trouble to prepare for a social event. Her agitation seemed to grow inversely to the amount of time remaining until the first guests were expected to arrive. When I innocently inquired about the status of dinner that evening she looked at Dad—glared, actually—and suggested we all take in dinner and a movie. My sister and I cheered at this unheard-of departure from our normal weekday routine and ran to get our coats. Clearly, something had gone terribly wrong with the sweet and adorable woman Dad had married.

On the way downtown in the car, after arguing with my sister briefly about what movie we should see, I turned to Dad and asked him why Mom was so testy.

As he started to mutter something in reply under his breath, my sister suddenly chimed in, "Because, stupid head, it's her first Tupperware party and she wants everything to be just right, that's why." Under normal circumstances, a reply like that would've prompted Dad to caution my sister against any further name calling, but in this instance he continued driving, his eyes staring straight ahead as though he had not even heard us.

Still not satisfied, I pushed on. "I still don't get it. What's the big deal?"

Finally, Dad broke his silence. "Here's the big deal," he said. "Your Mom and her friends are getting together to sell each other plastic bowls."

At first I thought he was joking, but when I turned to my sister, she only nodded her head in silent agreement. This was a bit much for my eight-year-old brain to fully comprehend, so I simply sat back in the car seat silently for a moment before muttering, "You gotta be kidding." He wasn't.

Tupperware was the invention of a grumpy, taciturn New Englander by the name of Earl Silas Tupper. Tupper was born in 1907, in a small Massachusetts town where, after graduating from high school in 1925, he went to work for a local nursery. In 1928, after taking night classes in horticulture, the twenty-one-year-old Tupper opened his own business as a tree surgeon. Although Tupper Tree Doctors did well, Tupper closed up shop in 1936 in order to devote himself full time to his first love: inventing.

Tupper was an inveterate tinkerer, a trait he no doubt inherited from his father. Although generally sober-minded, like most inventors he was also something of a dreamer, and this occasionally led him to pursue ideas that might best be described as ill-conceived—like the medical instrument Tupper patented for performing appendectomies through the patient's anus.

A year after his business folded, Tupper went to work for the plastics division of DuPont Chemical and became obsessed with a material invented by the British in 1931 called polyethylene, which was basically a waste by-product of the oil-refining process. Although polyethylene was generally considered a poor substitute for more common manufacturing materials, Tupper became fascinated with the new substance and began to experiment with it. A year later he quit DuPont and opened his own plastics company, the Earl S. Tupper Company, which did quite well during World War II making various small parts for military equipment.

During the war Tupper continued to experiment, and in the early 1940s came up with a cleaner, stronger variant of polyethylene he called Poly T (for Tupper); as soon as the war was over, he began using it to manufacture his own line of kitchen bowls he called "Wonderlier Bowls." What made them even more unusual was the special lid Tupper developed to cover them. Designed to fit like the lid of a paint can in reverse, the cover helped ensure that the contents remained fresh without the aid of products like tin foil. However, the pièce de résistance was the sound a bowl made when one pressed down on the small raised button in the middle of the lid. According to the company, this was referred to as the product's "burp and seal" feature, although my friends and I preferred to liken this modest expellation of air as a fart.

With all it had going for it—Tupperware was unbreakable, leakproof, lightweight, sleekly designed, and came in an assortment of eye-pleasing pastel colors—it would have been easy to understand why the new containers flew off the store shelves if that was indeed what had happened, but it wasn't. In fact, even after receiving the nod from no less prestigious a publication than *House Beautiful* ("Fine art for 39¢"), sales of the newest thing in household convenience continued to languish until a young Chicago divorcée by the name of Brownie Wise entered the picture.

Raised in poverty by her mother, a traveling labor organizer, Brownie Wise was an unlikely future candidate for the cover of *Business Week* magazine. By the time she turned twenty-four, Wise was herself a divorced mom living in Detroit with very few prospects. In an effort to make ends meet, Wise began selling various home goods door to door, including the newest thing in kitchen containers, the Wonder Bowl by Tupper Plastics, Inc. She turned out to be very good at it, and eventually the owner of the company, impressed with the young woman's soaring sales figures, invited her to his headquarters in Massachusetts. In her meeting with Tupper, Wise explained that the secret to her success was the "Tupperware party," a small, intimate gathering of women in one of their homes, where the benefits of the "bowl that burps" could actually be demonstrated. Wise insisted that Tupper pull his products off retail shelves and use his own customer base—housewives—as a sales force.

Tupper was captivated by the flamboyant, energetic Wise and hired her, a single, divorced mother with no corporate experience, on the spot to head up the company's entire sales effort. Eventually, she was given her own company, Tupperware Parties, Inc., to run, as well as 1,000 acres of Florida swampland on which to build her new headquarters.

Wise didn't waste a moment and immediately began recruiting and hiring an army of middle- and lower-middle-class women—housewives and mothers with little advanced education—to begin spreading the Tupperware message: "Tupperware will change your life—for the better." Wise offered women more than a job; she offered them a calling as apostles of a new religion that promised them a better life, not to mention a few hours a month away from the demands of domesticity. By 1954 sales figures for Tupperware topped $25 million and Wise appeared on the cover of *Business Week* magazine, the first woman ever to do so.

Sadly, the more celebrated Wise became, the more it seemed to rankle Tupper, even though she was largely responsible for the company's remarkable success. He became irritated at her flamboyance, high visibility, and lavish spending. By 1958 Tupper had had enough and fired Wise, giving her a mere $35,000 in severance. A few months later, Tupper sold the company to the Rexall Drug and Chemical Company for $16 million, divorced his wife, gave up his United States citizenship, and bought a small private island off the Central American coast, where he lived as a recluse until his death in 1983 at age 76. The patent on Tupperware itself expired a year after the inventor.

Despite the sudden turn of events, Tupper's dream lived on and today, more than sixty years after its invention, the company continues to thrive on international sales of more than a billion dollars a year; it's been estimated that a Tupperware party takes place every 2.5 seconds somewhere in the world.

Brownie Wise's dream likewise lives on as companies selling everything from jewelry to perfume, clothing to linen, and tattoos to Botox injections embrace her "party" method of home-demonstration sales. Indeed, the practice has become so pervasive that even the sex-toy industry has gotten into the act with so-called passion parties. The idea for the latter came to Anita Wildermuth, a sex-shop owner near Zurich, Switzerland, after listening to patrons who lived outside the city complain about how difficult it was to find the kind of erotic accessories she stocked in her store. Soon Wildermuth was on the road hawking various lingerie, massage oils, edible lubricants, and a dizzying array of sex toys—these included a line of dildos with names like The Monster, Tickle Her Pink, and The Feather Torturer—to eager participants. Clearly, these were not your mother's Tupperware parties.

When we arrived home several hours later, the last of Mom's guests were on their way out the door twittering the usual nonsense about what a lovely affair it had been. I headed straight for the refreshment table in an effort to scrounge whatever goodies might remain only to discover that the ladies had all apparently arrived with very healthy appetites because other than a solitary deviled egg sitting lonely and forlorn in the middle of a huge empty platter, its yolk now beginning to crust over slightly, the repast so lovingly prepared by my mother just hours earlier had all but vanished as though attacked by locusts—at least that's what Dad suggested under his breath.

Although exhausted, Mom appeared to have regained most of her usual cheerful demeanor even as she was now faced with the prospect of cleaning up after a wild evening of Tupper mania. I watched as she proudly, almost reverently, carried her new purchases into the kitchen and stacked them on the counter. She seemed particularly pleased with the two "free" gifts she received for hosting the event: a plastic butter dish and a couple of ice cube trays. I could tell by the look in her eyes that she'd been bitten by the bug, and for a time she became quite a successful Tupperware Lady in her own right. It ended, however, after Dad tripped for the umpteenth time over one of the scores of boxes of Tupperware products that seemed to have taken over the house. That was okay with Mom, though; she seemed to have tired of the epic cleaning sessions, cooking marathons, and locust plagues that came with the bowls that burped.

CHAPTER 6

A Cowboy Christmas

Jingle bells,
Khrushchev smells,
War is on the way.
(Cold War ditty, circa 1962)

Once upon a time, there was a special holiday on the twenty-fifth day of the last month of each year known to its celebrants as Christmas. Although comparable in many respects to a similarly named festival observed to this day, anyone who lived half a century ago would be hard-pressed to find much in the way of a resemblance between the two.

An obvious dissimilarity is the interlude between the beginning of the holiday period and the end. Fifty years ago any overt preparations for the upcoming festivities prior to finishing off the last of the turkey leftovers from Thanksgiving was unheard-of, in sharp contrast to today, when the Christmas season seems to begin shortly after the last Labor Day hot dog has been digested.

Strange as it seems, there is some historical justification for using Thanksgiving as the official start of the Christmas season. In 1817 the New York State Legislature established a statewide Thanksgiving Day, and by mid-century many other states had followed suit. As most children know from their history books, in 1863 Abraham Lincoln designated the last Thursday of November as a National Day of Thanksgiving, which is when it was celebrated for the next seventy-six years. In 1939, however, much to the dismay of retailers nationwide, the holiday happened to fall on the last day of the month. The business community became so disgruntled at the prospect of losing several days of potential Christmas shopping that they petitioned FDR to move the Thanksgiving holiday up a week by presidential fiat, which he did. The change was made permanent in 1941, when Congress passed legislation officially moving the holiday from the last Thursday to the fourth Thursday of November.

As the twentieth century made its way past the midway mark, the manner in which homeowners opted to decorate their property for the holiday was nothing like the competitive sport it has become today. In my neighborhood most outside decorations had yet to evolve beyond the most primitive stages: An evergreen wreath on the door and a simple string of colored lights around the doorway or shrubbery was about as sophisticated as it got. None of the lights blinked, flickered, or interacted synchronously; no phony icicles hung from the eaves; and there were definitely no figures of Santa, his sled, eight grazing reindeer, a phalanx of elves, wooden soldiers, or candy canes, lighted or otherwise, parading across the lawn. By today's standards it was all very bland and uninspired, and the concept of covering the exterior of one's home with enough wattage to distract unwary airline pilots on final approach to nearby LaGuardia or Idlewild airports was an unknown phenomenon.

Ours was usually among the last houses in the neighborhood to be decked out and festooned in anticipation of Santa's arrival; it remained dark and unadorned usually right up until a few days before Christmas itself. There were two reasons for this. First, my dad was what in polite society is often referred to as parsimonious. When I was about seven years old, I overheard Mom telling Mrs. Lutz, a lady who lived across the street, that there was a picture of my dad in the dictionary next to the word *cheap*. Upon hearing this, I excitedly ran into the house and grabbed the dictionary off the shelf to see for myself, but I found nothing. Later that evening during supper, I started to question Mom about this when suddenly she smelled something burning in the kitchen, so I never did get to see the picture.

Second, Dad strongly believed that it was irrational to purchase something that was by definition already in the process of dying before you even bought it, the same reasoning he used to justify his reluctance to buy Mom flowers on special occasions like anniversaries and birthdays. He also held that tree vendors were little more than a pack of brigands preying upon those rendered simpleminded by the spirit of the holidays.

Every year Dad would wait until the very last minute to buy a tree in the mistaken belief that this ensured him a much better price, when the only thing it really ensured was that he came home with the scrawniest of the few remaining trees on the lot.

What followed once the tree made it home is as common a Christmas tale to most families as is the story of the Three Wise Men. Dad made several trips to the attic, where the decorations had been stored the previous year. One by one he searched each box until he found the tree lights. After carefully untangling each string, he then plugged them into the nearest electrical outlet and, of course, most of them remained dark. Fixing the older lights was pretty easy. You simply unscrewed the big colored bulbs and replaced them with new ones, just as you would a regular lightbulb. The same company that made regular tree lights (Noma was the most popular brand) also made liquid filled lights shaped like little candles that would bubble when you plugged them in as well as some of the earliest blinking lights.

Unfortunately, these sturdy, reliable, trouble-free American tree lights began to get competition from overseas, where the Japanese, of all people, a nation we had practically nuked back to the Stone Age not ten years earlier, began making Christmas-tree lights that were smaller, cheaper, cooler, and much safer to use. They also had a maddening flaw my dad was convinced had intentionally been engineered into the product by what he referred to as "those inscrutable little Japs," which was that when one light went out, they all went out and the only way to find out which of the dozens of tiny delicate lights was at fault was to *check each and every single light in the entire fucking string!* This could and often did take hours and required everyone in the household, including Grandma and Grandpa to get down on their hands and knees and examine each light one by one until the culprit was located and replaced. The process was inevitably accompanied by an embarrassment of richly inventive colloquialisms from Dad before the problem was finally remedied. This was a ubiquitous tableau that occurred repeatedly throughout the neighborhood and was simply accepted as another one of the many rituals that accompanied the season.

Once the lights were on the tree, the rest was pretty anticlimactic. Ornaments were carefully unwrapped from tissue paper and strategically hung on each branch, garlands were strung, and several pounds of silvery tinsel were distributed liberally around the tree. The final act involved Dad unfolding a stepladder and crowning the entire glorious affair with the same handsome figure of an angel that had adorned the top of every family tree since he was a boy. Only then did we step back and allow ourselves to become enveloped by the sense of warmth that accompanies the first full viewing of a freshly decorated tree. Even I had to admit that despite the crooked trunk, oversize bare spot, and ever-shedding pine needles that made the tree appear so hopelessly sickly at the lot, we had once again successfully transformed it into a thing of garish beauty.

The Crabgrass Frontier fostered a number of other interesting holiday traditions that were all somehow uniquely consistent with the era itself. For instance, in the late 1950s, while dialing the telephone number of a local department store where kids were promised they could speak directly to Santa, a young boy accidentally telephoned the combat headquarters for the joint United States and Canadian missile defense system (NORAD) in Colorado Springs. Instead of a jolly old elf, the youngster found himself talking to the commander of the entire North American missile defense system, who had at his fingertips the ability to obliterate the entire planet just by pushing a few buttons. Fortunately, the Director of Combat Operations quickly realized that the United States was not under attack and, legend has it, assured the youngster that NORAD would track Santa's progress throughout his journey on Christmas Eve to ensure that nothing untoward interfered with the Jolly Old Elf's appointed rounds. From this a tradition was born, and each year we could listen on the radio as the combat center followed Santa's progress. Occasionally, a flight of military aircraft was dispatched to provide visual confirmation of the "target" as well as to provide air cover for him and his sleigh.

In 1966 another tradition was born that managed to combine custom and technology when a local television station in New York, WPIX Channel 11, began airing a picture of a burning Yule log accompanied by familiar Christmas carols. The idea was the brainchild of the TV station's manager, who thought it might be nice if the city's millions of apartment dwellers were allowed to share, at least vicariously, the warmth and joy of a flaming hearth of their own. Although my friends and I, who by that time were well into our dyspeptic teens, found the entire concept of staring at a televised fireplace idiotic, the WPIX Yule log proved to be so popular that a number of TV stations across the country, particularly in urban areas, began televising a Yule log of their own. And although the WPIX log was finally doused in 1989, it was rekindled again in 2001 and managed to sustain a Neilson rating sufficient to keep it burning ever since, for at least a few hours each Christmas day.

Television truly ruled the roost at Christmastime, and the airwaves were awash in specials with everyone from Ralph and Alice Kramden to Ozzie and Harriet Nelson, Lassie and Timmy to Johnny Desmond and Bing Crosby, and Perry Como to Judy Garland helping us get into the holiday spirit.

Although the holiday was keenly anticipated all year, one of the things that confused me as a child was how it had segued from what was supposed to be a religious celebration into one involving a fat guy all decked out in a red suit who ran around willy-nilly delivering gifts to the good little boys and girls of the world in a single twenty-four-hour period. Clearly, the emphasis on behavioral rewards (those boys and girls who failed to make the cut in terms of proper conduct were alleged to receive a lump of coal) had parental fingerprints all over it, and by all appearances it was yet another lame attempt at social engineering. Indeed, a quasi-scientific analysis once determined that in order for Santa to successfully deliver his entire payload in a single night, the gifts would have to be distributed at the rate of more than 800 per second; in order to achieve this prodigious rate of distribution, the Jolly Old Elf would have to travel at 3,000 times the speed of sound, or 2,250,000 miles per hour, at which point Santa, his reindeer, his sleigh, and all of its contents would instantaneously burst into flames.

Regardless of how secularized Christmas became, the holiday was not without its theological conundrums. For example, biblical tradition acknowledged Joseph as Mary's husband, yet that same tradition held that he was not the father of Jesus, a role credited to none other than The Almighty himself. This raised a host of interesting questions, not the least of which involved a desire to more fully understand the precise biological mechanics leading up to Mary's pregnancy. The best grown-ups could come up with was a somewhat muddled hypothesis called the Immaculate Conception, which, when boiled down to its essentials, required us to suspend every commonly held scientific principle regarding the procreation of our species that we had been taught thus far, if we had been taught anything at all.

Furthermore, grown-ups had a special name for women who engaged in procreative acts with anyone other than their lawfully wedded spouse. I knew this from sneaking a few hurried glances at some of the more lurid paperbacks (*Love Cheat, A Woman Must Love, Born to Be Bad*) hidden in the back of the local stationery store. Besides, wasn't there a specific religious admonition promulgated by The Almighty himself against such goings on? What was a confused Crabgrass Cowboy to think?

These theological fine points mattered little, however, because when all was said and done, the only thing that really mattered about Christmas was devising an effective strategy for convincing Santa that we were truly deserving of the one special gift that was sure to make the holiday memorable. Consumption of the last remaining turkey croquette was universally hailed as the official start of the holiday season and the point at which it was no longer considered premature to start lobbying in earnest for the one gift we coveted most. By today's standards the Crabgrass Frontier didn't even qualify as low-tech—it was more no-tech—when it came to finding sources of inspiration for that all-important Christmas wish list. Although learning quickly, Madison Avenue was still in its infancy in the 1950s and had yet to fully blur the line between entertainment and product promotion as it has today, so that the two are virtually indistinguishable. Despite this shortcoming, young patio pioneers like me had at our disposal the world's most comprehensive compendium of all the finest toys imaginable. It was called the Sears, Roebuck & Co. Christmas Wish Book, and it was in the 1950s and '60s what shopping malls would become in the 1970s, specialty catalogs would become in the 1980s and 1990s, and online shopping has become in the twenty-first century.

First published in 1933, this eagerly awaited publication was usually timed to arrive around September of each year and was acknowledged as the earliest known indicator of the upcoming holiday season.

One section of the catalog was considered gender neutral and included toys that were appropriate for both boys and girls. Board games fell into this category, as did amusements like the View Master, Etch a Sketch, Cootie, and the first toy ever advertised on television, Hasbro's Mr. Potato Head. Many of these toys were geared toward younger children, for whom differences in gender were neither as obvious nor as consequential as they would become in the years ahead.

Among my earliest personal favorites was the Winky Dink Magic Television Screen, which was nothing more than sheet of Saran Wrap–like plastic and a package of "magic" crayons we used while watching the *Winky Dink Show,* hosted by Jack Barry. Barry, who went on to host a number of popular game shows (*Tic Tac Dough, Twenty One, Concentration*), played second fiddle to the star of the show, an animated little boy by the name of Winky Dink, and his dog, Woofer. In every show young Winky found himself in one set of unfortunate circumstances or another and only we, the members of his viewing audience, could help him out by placing the plastic over the TV screen and using our crayons to draw some object—a ladder, key, or fire hose, for example—as instructed by the show's host. Many parents, my own included, first came to know the *Winky Dink Show* by the sudden appearance of Crayola artwork directly on their television screens put there by eager youngsters who failed to appreciate the role of the sheet of plastic in the whole process. Before receiving my Winky Dink Magic Set, I personally spent the better part of five minutes one evening attempting to improve upon the dour visage of Edward R. Murrow by decorating his face with a set of horns, a scar, glasses, and a thick, bushy mustache using a few carefully chosen Crayolas purloined from my sister's room. Just as I was finishing up with a few special effects (I thought smoke billowing out of Mr. Murrow's ears was an especially nice touch), Dad happened by and the project was hastily terminated.

A number of toys came into being during my childhood as a direct result of technology developed during the dark days of World War II. In 1943, while participating in the shakedown cruise of a new battleship, naval engineer Richard James was trying to come up with a way to use torsion springs to measure horsepower as well as dampen the effect of engine vibration on various nautical instruments when he accidentally knocked one of the springs to the floor. James was fascinated with the way the spring kept moving after it fell onto the deck. He picked it up and stared in fascination as it wobbled back and forth in his hands. After returning home, James told his wife, Betty, about his discovery and convinced her that they could turn the idea into a marketable children's toy. She eventually came up with a name for their new invention after thumbing through the dictionary for ideas and came across the Swedish word *slinky,* meaning "sleek and sinuous." The Jameses introduced the Slinky at Gimbels department store in Philadelphia just as the first postwar Christmas holiday got into full swing. James was so nervous, he talked several friends into buying the toys; within ninety minutes every one of the 400 toys had been sold. Shortly thereafter the couple founded the James Spring & Wire Company and later James Industries to mass produce what was fast becoming a wildly popular toy; about 250 million have been sold since.

Regrettably, in 1960 Richard was bitten by the same bug that apparently bedevils eccentric, self-made millionaires and Richards swapped his wife, six children, and a multimillion-dollar business enterprise for the life of an ascetic in some small unknown Bolivian religious cult, leaving Betty to save the company from near bankruptcy.

Silly Putty was another classic toy that sprang from America's war effort. Due to a shortage of rubber (most rubber came from the Far East and was under Japanese control), the War Department pressured U.S. companies to come up with a cheap synthetic alternative. James Wright, a chemical engineer at General Electric, tried his hand at it by mixing boric acid and silicone oil, but the result was a flop. The substance he produced could be stretched, molded, and bounced, everything, it seemed, but replace rubber; it was shelved. In 1949 an advertising consultant and entrepreneur by the name of Peter Hodgson happened upon a sample of the odd flesh-colored substance at a Christmas party and convinced one of his clients, a New Haven, Connecticut, toy store owner, to try selling the glutinous goo through her catalog. She did, calling it simply Bouncing Putty because that's what it did. It immediately outsold everything else in the catalog except a fifty-cent box of Crayolas. Hodgson was so impressed, he bought the rights to Wright's invention. After repackaging it in red, plastic egg-shaped containers, Hodgson named it Silly Putty, and the product debuted at the 1950 Toy Show, where it was an instant hit. It was not until 1957, however, after being endorsed by none other than Howdy Doody himself, that Silly Putty reached actual fad status. Playing against type, although worth $140 million, Hodgson lived a quiet life with his wife, Margaret, and son, Peter Jr., at their home, known as Silly Putty Estates, until his death in 1976.

Perhaps the nicest thing about our toys was the fact that they were designed and manufactured solely for the purpose of youthful entertainment. They existed so that we could have fun, although from a parent's perspective, I suppose, the flip side of this coin was the fact that the more engaging and entertaining the toy, the longer it kept us occupied and out of their hair. It was a classic win-win situation and, I suspect, the chief motivating force behind why so many parents often went to such great lengths to fulfill their children's most fervent Christmas wishes. That some toys might, while in the process of amusing us, quite accidentally enhance our cognitive abilities, eye-hand coordination, or other developmental skills was irrelevant, as far as we were concerned. Besides, there was an entire subspecies of juvenile plaything known generically as the educational toy—globes, word games, and jigsaw puzzles of the United States all fell into this category—created expressly for this purpose. Generally speaking, anything that sought to expand our knowledge or enhance a skill as its primary goal, and did so secondarily in a manner that we might find mildly entertaining (or at least slightly more entertaining that the daily classroom grind), was by definition an educational toy. Kids universally eschewed these efforts to suffocate their leisure-time activities by attempting to slip in some socially redeeming feature. We knew intuitively that educational toys were to toys what educational films were to films, and no amount of guile or camouflage could alter that fact. If a gift was in any way practical, utilitarian, or instructional, it was not considered a toy.

Another nice thing about our toys was the fact that no one ever tried to describe or promote them by invoking the word *safety*, and terms like *kid friendly*, *childproof*, and *mom tested* had yet to invade the popular lexicon. Our toys were chockablock full of the very things that today would cause an immediate erection in any self-respecting personal-injury attorney—jagged edges to cut little hands, sharp points to puncture small bodies, tiny removable parts to lodge in narrow throats—yet I can't recall a single instance in which a childhood friend was either killed or maimed by a Christmas gift, excluding the occasional broken tooth from one of Aunt Clara's deadly homemade holiday fruitcakes.

Next in the Wish Book came the section devoted entirely to all of the predictable fare you would expect little girls to covet, like the Chatty Cathy and Betsy Wetsy dolls, Kenner's EZ Bake Ovens, tea sets, and cowgirl outfits. I was barely eleven years old in 1959 when the girl's toy market was suddenly and permanently turned on its ear by the appearance of a young teen from Willow, Wisconsin, named Barbara Millicent Roberts (aka Barbie). Until then toy makers believed most little girls preferred to play with infant or child dolls because doing so allowed them to develop their nascent mothering skills, an obvious goal for every female regardless of her age. Then along came Ruth Handler, who divined that perhaps what young girls really wanted was a peer, a friend, someone with whom they could share the slings and arrows of childhood. At first the executives at Mattel, every one of them a male, scoffed at the idea, saying the doll not only lacked broad marketing appeal but also would be too expensive to manufacture profitably. Handler didn't flinch and continued to refine her idea, using as a model a popular European doll named Lilli, until Mattel finally gave in and approved the project. Named Barbie after Handler's own daughter, Barbara, the pint-size, post-pubescent plastic prototype first appeared at the 1959 American Toy Fair and was an instant hit, selling a total of 351,000 in the first year alone.

But the most astonishing (alarming, to some) thing about the new upstart was her quasi–anatomical correctness. Young Barbie sported two very palpable protuberances where none had ever existed on any doll any of us had ever seen before. Obviously, this required further investigation, which generally proved all too disappointing, if not downright confusing, when Barbie was fully disrobed; the oft-quoted dimensions of a human equivalent (39-18-33) proved to be a cruel hoax. Not only were Barbie's chest ornaments merely hard plastic nubs with no apparent features or purpose, as opposed to the soft, warm pillows we were just beginning to consider with rising interest, but also things below the waist got just plain weird; the hard, flat surface was nothing like what I recalled from the early days of playing doctor and "I'll show you mine if you show me yours" with many a neighborhood girl.

As far as my friends and I were concerned, anything in the Wish Book that did not speak directly to our needs as boys—as builders, space explorers, warriors, inventors, train engineers, heavy-equipment operators, superheroes, athletes, or champions of the Old West—was just filler, and we breezed past it with hardly a second glance. So emblematic of our childhood did some of our favorite toys become that even today, a half century or so later, we recall them with a mental clarity usually reserved for our earliest feats of sexual prowess.

I still remember quivering with excitement when I came down the stairs on Christmas Day 1957 and first spied a Lionel steam locomotive circling relentlessly around the tree, over and over again, pulling half a dozen freight cars behind it; afterward, never did I come across the pair of bared breasts, even those belonging to Debbie Neilson, with whom I took my first trip to second base, that could successfully reproduce the thrill of that moment. My new Lionel locomotive gave off a shrill whistle and emitted tiny puffs of smoke from its smokestack. Let's see Debbie Neilson's tits do that!

Speaking of models, like many an aspiring cold warrior, I went through a phase where I attempted to faithfully reproduce scale models of some of the nation's finest military hardware, particularly fighter jets and navy vessels, using kits sold by the Revell Company. In the early 1950s, the practice of building models made of balsa wood had given way to the newer and cheaper models made of injection molded plastic. Unfortunately, like thousands of other young boys born in an era in which the words *attention deficit disorder* were still unknown, I found that in order to build one of these models properly—meaning, the final product bore some vague resemblance to the picture on the box the product came in—required a degree of patience and concentration, not to mention meticulous attention to detail, that was unheard-of among my friends. Upon receiving one of these kits, our initial excitement usually began to wane the minute we opened the box and saw to our dismay that, aside from perhaps the fuselage and the wings or the hull, in the case of, say, a battleship, the box was filled with hundreds of tiny, unrecognizable pieces and a folded set of lengthy instructions. All of the pieces were attached to plastic frames and had to be carefully snapped off one by one and organized in a way that allowed the model builder to access the proper parts in just the right sequence. Absent this painstaking level of organization, the project quickly began to degenerate and eventually deteriorate into utter chaos. Eager, glue-stained little hands quickly became magnets that attracted any small pieces of plastic—not to mention dirt, lint, scraps of paper, and anything else they happened to brush against; while acres of newspaper so carefully spread out on whatever flat surface had become the designated work space was soon reduced to a shambles as the project devolved.

The first time I tried to build a model, I knew within seconds I'd been hoodwinked because, according to the instructions, proper assembly required approximately four days to complete. I still find it astonishing that the folks at Revell believed there existed a race of eight-year-olds with enough forbearance to devote four full days of their busy lives to building something that when finished they technically weren't even supposed to play with. Models, we were told, were for display purposes, which means you were only supposed to look at them. The only person I knew who actually built airplane models purely for exhibition was Artie Kessling, whose bedroom had several display cases filled with the *crème de la crème* of his collection. He even had several reproductions of World War II–era airplanes suspended from the ceiling frozen in mock aerial combat; so exacting were his efforts to accurately capture every tiny detail that if you looked closely enough inside the cockpit canopy of the Japanese Zeroes you could just make out the epicanthic fold of the pilot's eyes.

To the best of my knowledge, Artie Kessling never experienced or succumbed to the frustration and rage that eventually stymied all of my efforts to complete a model-making project as directed by the manufacturer in the instruction booklet. By the same token, I'm pretty certain that neither did Eddie ever experience the same unbridled thrill as did my friends and me when we took several sloppy, half-built model warships—battleships, cruisers, destroyers, and even aircraft carriers—and after covering them from stem to stern with lighter fluid, lit them and set them adrift in Pollywog Pond, watching as one by one they slid, hissing and smoking, to their fiery graves beneath the surface of the scum-covered pond.

When all is said and done, it was the obligation of every young patio pioneer to maintain law and order on the newly tamed Crabgrass Frontier. For this reason we were drawn inexorably to the figure of the classic American cowboy and frontiersman, and our play attempted to mimic their heroic adventures as we had come to know them through stories, television, and comic books. This was no mean feat because despite the well-scrubbed *Leave It to Beaver* exterior, the Crabgrass Frontier could be a dangerous place for the unwary youngster. Raccoons, the occasional skunk, and other assorted remnants of original neighborhood wildlife; as well as rapacious developers and the omnipresent Communists, were at hand wherever we turned, and quite prepared to supply our lives with an unexpected bit of nastiness. It was far from the idyllic and worry-free environment portrayed to the outside world.

Consequently, we looked for guidance and direction to the cowboys, pioneers, settlers, and other frontier heroes who not only had extensive experience settling a wild, untamed environment but also had the equipment—the clothing, armaments, and other hardware—necessary to get the job done right, people who had already exterminated a satisfying number of those who would stand in the way of Manifest Destiny.

One of the nicest things about how the American West was settled was the total absence of any moral ambiguity. Did Gene Autry, Hopalong Cassidy, Roy Rogers, Matt Dillon, Wyatt Earp, Maverick, the raffish Palladin, or the mysterious Lone Ranger ever scratch their heads quizzically regarding matters of political correctness or ethical certitude? I think not, and we weren't about to, either. Good was good, bad was bad, and like Supreme Court Justice White said on the subject of pornography, while he couldn't necessarily define it, we certainly knew it when we saw it. Even if they did not as a group choose to sport all-black apparel, those who would perpetrate evil were easy to spot. They were chiefly Indians, greedy railroad barons, claim jumpers, slick eastern dandies, some Mexicans, and a few drunken louts like Mike Fink the infamous river boater. Occasional exceptions had to be made, as in the case of the Lone Ranger's ever faithful Indian companion, Tonto, born *not* Jay Silverheels, the name the former professional Canadian lacrosse player adopted after he took up acting, but Harold J. Smith.

It never crossed my mind to question why thousands of seemingly normal, intelligent people would be inclined to give up all their earthly possessions (except those you could fit in the back of a Conestoga wagon and on the backs of a few pack animals) and all of life's creature comforts for a dangerous life on the edge of civilization. Likewise, it never crossed my mind to question the veracity of how those lives were popularly portrayed in the movies and on television. Even if my friends and I had been told that the motivation for our relentless expansion westward was often greed, or that western towns welcomed the arrival of a cowboy in its midst with about the same gusto one usually reserves for an outbreak of head lice, it would've made no difference. Our heavens were filled with the light of a million frontier heroes, a light that haloed them all into a single, mythical whole.

Our efforts to emulate these heroes knew no bounds. If they rode horses, we had to ride horses too, even if ours were made of hard plastic mounted with heavy springs to a steel frame, or merely a broomstick with an imaginary horse's head attached to one end. We straddled both with equal zest and galloped across the plains in a cloud of dust and a hearty "Hi ho, Silver!" We preferred clothing that any self-respecting queer-eyed guy would be mortified to wear today: cheap vinyl chaps, flamboyant western-style shirts with decorative piping and ersatz mother-of-pearl snaps, elaborately tooled boots, and, of course, splendid, handsomely decorated wide-brimmed cowboy hats. Finally, we fully accessorized with cowboy lunch boxes, toothbrushes, guitars, dartboards, wagons, sheets and blankets, plastic dishes, and an ancestor of today's action figure, the windup toy.

All of these things paled, however, in comparison to the awe and reverence we reserved for the weaponry of the Old West. Never in the noble and highly regarded history of toy making had this much thoughtful consideration been given to replicating so many of the very instruments that had originally been created solely for the purpose of slaughtering other members of our own species.

The standard was, of course, the gun that is said to have won the West in the first place: the venerable six-shooter. In the estimation of true aficionados like me, the best of these was a highly sophisticated model called the Shootin' Shell Fanner 50, made by Mattel, which allowed us to fire the weapon in more than one way, including the traditional method (by pulling the trigger) or by repeatedly "fanning" the hammer with the edge of one hand while holding the gun in the other. This, along with a couple of dandy special effects—it used exploding caps and ejected plastic shells—and a low-cut holster to facilitate a lightning-quick draw, made it a highly desirable piece of hardware for the savvy Crabgrass Cowboy.

Unfortunately, I never owned a Fanner 50 of my own because, although it was considered the champagne of toy guns, I came from a family with beer-drinking tastes. Consequently, I had to settle for one of the many die-cast, metal-alloy country cousins that were also available. It could've been worse. A number of my friends had to accept the lowest of the low-end models, a cast-iron six-shooter made by Hubley that was so cumbersome, many smaller cowpokes in the neighborhood had to use both hands to lift it, thereby all but eliminating the quick draw from their repertoire of gun-slinging strategies.

In the constant struggle for playground dominance, we were always looking for a competitive edge over the bad guys, even if it meant occasionally turning to gimmickry, a need toy companies were more than willing to address. For example, one short-lived novelty was the secret one-shot belt-buckle derringer, which could be fired by flexing your stomach muscles. Unfortunately, it had some rather obvious shortcomings, like the fact that it required reloading after every firing, making it of only limited use when we were under attack by more than one bad guy, as was usually the case. Furthermore, it was a weapon that blurred the line in terms of strict adherence to the Cowboy Code of Honor. Attributed to Gene Autry, the Cowboy Code of Honor held that a good cowboy never took unfair advantage of an enemy, this notwithstanding the fact that, by definition, our enemies were free to employ whatever cheap, underhanded tactics were necessary to gain the upper hand with us. As a result, most of us took the stand that the Cowboy Code of Honor was best viewed as a set of general behavioral guidelines, not hard-and-fast rules, because we recognized intuitively that a good cowboy had to be situational in his ethics. This was particularly true given some of the other individual guidelines, guidelines that smelled vaguely like one more shabby attempt to engineer our social behavior since they called upon us to: 1) tell the truth, 2) respect our parents, 3) avoid religious and racial intolerance, 4) work hard, and 5) always be gentle with other children, the elderly, and animals.

A few of my friends also danced briefly with weapons in which the familiar exploding caps were replaced with some mysterious internal mechanism to provide the appropriate sound effect, like Ric-O-Shay Rifle, which made a strange whining sound (*ka zingggggg*) every time you pulled the trigger. But the attraction of this and every other Johnny-come-lately eventually waned because there was nothing that could replace the satisfying "*snap!*" that accompanied the firing of a traditional cap gun.

Obviously, for the whole cowboy thing to work properly, we also needed bad guys, and they were usually in short supply because, after all, who in their right mind wanted to be an Indian? Tough times sometimes called for tougher measures, and, distasteful as it was, we occasionally had to permit a small number of girls to join our game if for no other reason than to provide us with an enemy we could then annihilate. Girls were good because they were more easily bossed around than most boys and their dolls were easily taken hostage if they ever became recalcitrant. They were also far more willing to wear those stupid feather headdresses that were the staple of most Indian costumes.

When no girls were available, we then turned to those boys who ranked lowest in terms of dominance in our pack, which invariably included Timmy Wolfson, who never seemed to mind wearing a feathered headdress. Despite his placid, easygoing demeanor, Timmy could be a savage opponent, as we learned in one particularly hair-raising battle when, while armed with a toy bow and arrow, arrows tipped with red suction cups, Timmy set about shooting every one of us in the nuts at least twice. Rather than allow the outrage to continue, we finally tackled him and, after tying him to a tree, de-pantsed him and filled his underwear with leaves. Frankly, had the roles been reversed, I would have struggled to free myself a lot harder than did Timmy. It wasn't until many years later, when Timmy arrived at our fortieth high school reunion with Benjamin, his domestic partner and date for the evening, that I fully appreciated the reason for his acquiesce

These were the issues and concerns in the minds of young lads like my friends and me as we gazed longingly at the visual feast paraded before our eyes on every page of the Wish Book and argued vociferously over the relative merits of one toy over another like theologians debating the fine points of how many angels could dance on the head of a pin. In this way, we were eventually able to whittle down our own personal wish list to the one single item we wanted most desperately to greet us from under the tree on Christmas morning, which brings to mind one of the most commonly held misconceptions about the largesse children of the Crabgrass Frontier are alleged to have experienced solely because our parents came of age during the Great Depression.

According to the myth, so traumatized were our parents by the aching want and deprivation of the 1930s that they were helpless to withhold anything from us and sought only to shower us with every material thing our little hearts desired and fulfill our every wish. Apparently, somebody dropped the ball around our house because my parents never got the memo on this or anything even remotely like it. In fact, not only my parents but also just about every parent on the planet (or so it seemed) held to the belief that deprivation was actually a good thing. We were told it built character, whatever that was, and were assured that the longer our deepest desires remained unfulfilled (at least insofar as those deepest desires involved the expenditure of their money), the better a person it made us.

We all knew the drill ("When I was your age, we were so poor we had to brush our teeth with dirt"), and we were helpless against it. Consequently, we all knew that wish lists were basically a waste of time because the most we could hope for on Christmas Day was one A-list toy, a few smaller toys from the B- or even the C-list, several new pairs of underwear and socks masquerading in gaily wrapped packages as gifts, and a crisp new one-dollar bill from one of the Grandmas. This was the dreary reality we faced each Christmas, which is why we spent so much time choosing just the right toy and put so much effort into maneuvering our parents into a position where they fully understood the life-and-death importance of our choice.

We all had our special strategies for accomplishing this goal. Sensing his parent's heightened awareness of neighborhood status, Bobby Baxter tried to stress the fact that whatever gift he was haggling over was generally considered the *sine qua non* of holiday gifts that year, one that would certainly impress all his friends to the point where they were sure to share these feelings with their own parents. Others managed to find some way of repeatedly making casual references regarding their toy of choice no matter what the topic of conversation happened to be. I was convinced that subtlety was the best strategy, so rather than ever ask for a particular toy directly, I made certain to place hints in a variety of strategic locations around the house. I might, for example, leave a copy of the Wish Book on the back of the toilet in the upstairs bathroom open to the appropriate page, perhaps even circling the item in crayon and adding a few pithy observations like "Wow!" or "Neat!" to make certain even a casual reader got the point. I made sure to cut out any ads for the toy I wanted from the newspaper and post them around my bedroom, even leaving them on my unmade bed, where Mom was sure to see it when she got around to cleaning up my room. If an advertisement appeared on TV, I quickly turned up the sound so loud both Mom and Dad could hear it regardless of where they happened to be in the house at the moment, a tactic not without risks and potentially counterproductive (*"Turn down that goddamn TV!"*).

Yes, while Christmas was certainly one of the most exciting times of the year, it was also exhausting for kids because it required of us a level of guile and cunning normally reserved for only the direst circumstance during the other 364 days of the year.

In 1955 little debate was needed in terms of choosing our most preferred toy from among the plentitude of those available because of our frenzied desire to own anything even remotely related to Disney's megahero Davy Crockett, and even the most diehard cowboy aficionado found himself genuflecting before the altar of this great frontiersman.

The craze actually began a year earlier, on December 15, 1954, when Disney aired the first episode ("Davy Crocket, Injun Fighter) of a three-part series starring a handsome twenty-seven-year-old newcomer by the name of Fess Parker. The second episode ("Davy Crockett Goes to Congress") aired a month later, and the third ("Davy Crockett at the Alamo"), a month after, that making it one of the earliest known miniseries; with this Crockett-mania exploded in the consciousness of America's preadolescent youth.

Parents began shelling out millions for all manner of Crockett paraphernalia, including $10 million for coonskin caps alone. Indeed, the demand for this furry headgear became so great that within months it had driven the cost of raccoon pelts from twenty-five cents a pound to more than eight dollars a pound, thus forcing manufacturers to substitute cheaper squirrel and rabbit pelts for the real thing ("Honey, have you seen the cat?"). Another $300 million was spent on other forms of Crockett-alia, including "b'ar" rifles, powder horns, flashlights, wallets, rugs, moccasins, and even underwear; not to mention a recording of the show's theme song, "The Ballad of Davy Crockett," which was translated into twenty-six different languages and sold 7 million copies in the first six months of 1955 alone. It's been estimated that at the height of the craze there were almost 3,000 different Davy Crockett products available and that approximately 10 percent of all children's wear sold in America was Crockett-related. Furthermore, Disney's efforts to patent the Crockett character and name as its own (a Baltimore federal court finally ruled that the name Davy Crockett was within the public domain) succeeded only in pushing the marketing frenzy to greater heights.

Unfortunately, by the end of the third and final episode, Uncle Walt had a problem on his hands. As most students of American history are aware, the Alamo was to Davy Crockett what the Little Big Horn was to General George Armstrong Custer. In other words, Disney bumped off his biggest star just as it was about to go supernova. As Walt Disney himself admitted years later, "We had no idea what was going to happen with Crockett. Why, by the time the first show finally got on the air, we were already shooting the third one and calmly killing Davy off at the Alamo. It became one of the biggest overnight hits in TV history, and there we were with just three films and a dead hero."

Undeterred, Disney did everything possible to keep the craze alive, first by pumping out new merchandise as fast as stores could sell it and then by hurriedly stitching together the first three episodes into a full-length feature film entitled *Davy Crockett, King of the Wild Frontier,* which was released in theaters just in time for the 1955 Memorial Day weekend. Disney also started production on two brand-new episodes, "Davy Crockett's Keelboat Race" and "Davy Crockett and the River Pirates," the first such prequels of their kind, that were scheduled to air in December 1955. Clearly, it was going to be a Crockett Christmas if Uncle Walt and Mickey had any say in the matter; and indeed it was.

As the holidays approached, my friends and I became crazed in our lobbying efforts, and any remaining hint of subtlety on the matter of what we wanted went right out the window.

Personally, my eyes were fixed on what many considered the pièce de résistance of the many thousands of pieces of merchandise available, the official hundred-piece Davy Crockett Alamo Set made by Marx, which allowed kids to re-create the famous battle over and over again. Stunning in its attention to detail, the set included a tin replica of the old Spanish mission along with several companies of Santa Ana's evil hoards, some on horseback and others on foot. Obviously, there was also Davy and his company of defenders, plus all the creature comforts of any well-appointed frontier fort, including a well, hitching post, cooking fire, special platforms to fight off any Mexicans who tried to climb over the walls, and cannon to blow their heads off if they stormed the front gate.

Nothing in my six short years on the planet had prepared me for anything like it, and from the moment the Sears Wish Book arrived at our house, my mind was made up—it was going to be Walt Disney's Davy Crockett, King of the Wild Frontier 100 Piece Play Set or nothing at all. It was a risky approach, and all my friends, while expressing admiration for my principled approach, counseled against it. "At least have a backup," they begged, but I wouldn't hear any of it.

As Christmas drew nearer, I began to second-guess myself and wonder if perhaps I wasn't being a bit nervy about the whole matter. Perhaps Santa, who would be the final arbiter in the matter, would not take kindly to being held hostage by some puny little six-year-old with a dead raccoon on his head. But I stuck to my guns. Let others run around the neighborhood with their faux powder horns and fake flintlock rifles. I was going to fight the battle of the Alamo my way, over and over again, or I wasn't going to fight it at all. And that's exactly what I told Santa during our brief annual exchange at Macy's that year. Furthermore, in order to avoid any possible confusion or misunderstanding, I followed up by reiterating my wishes in my annual letter to Santa, which my parents assured me was sent to him directly at the North Pole.

I sweated out the last few days before Christmas, and while my friends bubbled merrily about the universe of possibilities awaiting them under the tree, I had reduced my own future down to a single choice. It was all or nothing, and I had only one roll of the dice remaining. Christmas Eve had the makings of a long night.

The rule in our house on Christmas morning was that my sister and I had to stay in our beds until at least 6:00 AM. This was at best a technical rule because there was nothing forbidding us from making as much noise as possible, thereby disturbing whatever additional rest my parents had ever hoped to achieve. Consequently, by virtue of both the din as well as whatever residual excitement an adult might still harbor on this magical morning, things usually got under way closer to 5:30.

Mom usually went down first to crank up the old stovetop coffee percolator. Dad, an avid 8-mm filmmaker, went down next to plug in the tree and prepare his equipment in order to capture that thrilling moment when my sister and I made our way down the stairs gazing in wonder at the delights awaiting us under the tree. By the time I was about four years old, however, the filmmaking efforts had defaulted to a much less candid re-creation of the event several hours after the actual moment had passed. This came to pass as we began to understand that without at least one cup of coffee and three or four unfiltered Lucky Strikes, Dad's filmmaking efforts were about as watchable as Federico Fellini's.

It seemed to take forever to make our way through the piles of gaily wrapped gifts, and even as everyone oohed and aahed as each was opened, my eyes carefully patrolled the remaining packages to see if any matched what I thought would be the appropriate size and shape of a Davy Crockett Alamo set. I barely acknowledged my mom when she came over and kissed me in an overzealous show of appreciation for the gift I gave her, a quart-size bottle of perfume (*"parfum"*) I'd discovered at Nassau Stores, the local department store acclaimed to have at least one of everything ever made somewhere within the confines of its dark, narrow, dusty aisles. My gift to Dad was equally successful: a pencil sharpener bought only a few doors down at Wright Hardware, another personal favorite because it had creaky wooden floors, a high tin ceiling, and floor-to-ceiling shelves that could only be reached by a ladder mounted on tracks running along each wall.

As one by one the gifts under the tree began to disappear, my stomach grew queasy and my confidence began to wane. Perhaps I'd miscalculated Santa's willingness to have his arm twisted by a six-year-old? It wasn't that I had not gotten some nice presents, I had. I got a Whizzler, which was basically just a top with a hole poked in the side so that when you pulled the string and sent it spinning across the floor, it also gave off a satisfying shrieking sound; a new sled to replace the one I'd destroyed going down Suicide Hill the previous winter; and a Presto Magic Set, "with more than a hundred baffling magic tricks" that would allow me to "earn money by giving thrilling magic shows." This last gift offered some interesting possibilities if along with everything else it promised I could figure out a way to make my sister disappear.

Eventually, when the last gift had been opened, I was forced to accept the tragic reality of my situation and acknowledge the fact that I had gambled and lost; and my dream of re-fighting the historic siege of the Alamo in my bedroom simply evaporated. Frankly, it took a Herculean effort to keep my disappointment from showing, and, except for a few brief moments when I couldn't quite keep my lower lip from quivering, I think I kept it together pretty well. That is, until I heard Dad call from the front hallway, "Hey, what's this? Looks like Santa left something in the coat closet instead of under the tree. Let's see who it's for."

My heart leaped into my throat as I jumped to my feet and raced to see what my dad was talking about. Could it be possible? I said a hurried silent prayer, a prayer so pure and unvarnished it could only have come from a child, as I made my way through the knee-high drifts of crumpled wrapping paper, ribbon, and discarded gift boxes that now filled the living room. As I turned the corner, Mom and Dad both stood there grinning, itself a rare occurrence this early in the morning, with one last remaining package, which they extended in my direction. For a second I stood frozen in place until my sister's voice—"Well, don't just stand there. Open it, stupid"—broke the spell and I reached out reverently, half expecting my parents to pull it away at the last second, shouting gleefully "Just kidding!"

With the gift safely in my grasp, however, my fingers quickly turned to talons as I tore away the wrapping. In seconds it lay open in front of me, looking exactly as I had imagined so often over the past two months. It was mine, the "*Official* Walt Disney Davy Crockett, King of the Wild Frontier 100 Piece Play Set" was all mine. Finally, after more than a century, the wrongs of history could be righted and the scales of justice properly balanced once and for all.

Obviously, I didn't know it at the time, but the lunacy surrounding Davy Crockett was already on the wane because even if the show's hero had not been bumped off in the third episode, the nation would soon begin to turn its attention to a new frontier: outer space. Soon astronauts, rocket ships, and ray guns began to crowd out cowboys, covered wagons, and six-shooters for room in our imaginations. We began to realize for the first time that we were living in our own heroic era, one with its own daring and intrepid pioneers who engaged in their own bold adventures.

In light of the degree to which I'd once given my heart over to Davy so completely, perhaps a brief postscript is in order regarding my efforts to rewrite history. As it is with any new toy, my interest in the Davy Crocket Play Set followed a fairly predictable arc from the moment I received it on that memorable Christmas morning to its final demise six or seven months later.

Part of the problem was the fact that one of the toy's most appealing features was also one of its greatest drawbacks, and little by little the much-touted hundred-piece set began to shrink, first to ninety-nine pieces, then ninety-eight, ninety-seven, ninety-six, and ninety-five pieces. It seemed like every time I opened the box, another piece went missing. At first it was just some of the smaller accessories, a cooking fire here and an andiron or butter churn there, nothing too noticeable, until I couldn't find one of the cannons belonging to Davy and his men, a serious blow to their ability to defend themselves.

Admittedly, it was sometimes my own fault, like the time I left everything set up in mid-battle and turned my attention to a favorite television show instead. When I returned I discovered too late that our cat, Boots, who until that day had shown interest in only two things—eating and sleeping—apparently shared my interest in history, as evidenced by the fact that she had gnawed rather extensively on a number of plastic figures, including three defenders of the Alamo. Fortunately, Davy was not among them, much to my relief. For a while I tried to incorporate the now disfigured heroes into the story line by pretending that they had been captured by the evil Mexican General Santa Ana and his men and managed to escape his clutches, but only after having had to endure horrible and disfiguring torture. When this no longer satisfied my imagination, I simply tossed them out and brought in reinforcements from among my hundreds of green molded plastic World War II soldiers. Of the three replacements, one was armed with a bazooka, another with a fifty-caliber machine gun, and the third with a flamethrower, which helped restore some balance to the level of firepower available to each side.

And so it went, little by little the once proud set became over time a hodgepodge of pieces from several different places, although the centerpiece remained the still proud Alamo itself.

The end came on a hot but otherwise unassuming summer afternoon the following July when Ritchie Pagano joined me for yet another go at the famous battle out in the garden behind our house. From the very first, my friends were pleased to find how generously I was willing to be in terms of sharing the joys of my new play set with them. Anyone desirous of joining me, however, had to first accept three nonnegotiable provisos: 1) they always had to accept the role of Mexican attackers, 2) the attacker always lost, and 3) Davy Crockett himself could never be killed off. He could be wounded, maimed, knocked unconscious, taken captive; he could even, as one of my more creative playmates determined, be felled temporarily by blood poisoning and left reeling, stuporous, in the hot Texas sun, but he could never be killed outright. My friends took these restrictions in stride at first, if only to be allowed to play for a single joyous afternoon with what was generally conceded to be the finest Christmas gift anyone had received that holiday season, at least in our neck of the woods, and for once it was mine.

As the winter turned to spring, and spring became summer, I observed among many of my friends a noticeable decline in the level of interest displayed when invited to join me for an adventurous afternoon with Davy. I'm not entirely certain, but this may in part have had something to do with the fact that over time the play set began to lose some of its luster at the same rate as it lost parts. And so, arguments about who would play whom and by what rules became increasingly commonplace until that fateful afternoon when Ritchie, apparently angered at the prospect of having to be on the losing side once again, decided to take matters into his own hands and break the longstanding rules in a decidedly unsportsman-like manner. He loaded up the remains of Santa Ana's army into the back of an oversize yellow Tonka truck and attempted to crash through the north wall of the Alamo. Although momentarily taken aback at this whole-sale breach of etiquette, I soon came to my senses and determined that the only way to address this treachery was to place the entire matter in the hands of the Lord. He responded, as any just and loving God should, by pummeling the truck and its cargo of miscreants with an extremely rare meteorological occurrence: a shower of asteroids in the form of fist-size rocks that stopped the attack in its tracks. Undeterred, Ritchie called upon his own just and loving God (Ritchie was Catholic, which meant he had a different God), who with the help of a nearby garden hose, unleashed another uncommon weather-related occurrence, particularly in the semi-arid regions of mid Texas: a Category 5 Hurricane, that successfully lev-eled half the fort and drowned many of its occupants. Enraged, I called upon my imagination and transformed myself into the gigantic, fire-breathing scourge of downtown Tokyo, Godzilla, and proceeded to stomp what remained of Davy's enemies into the ever-growing puddle of mud. Suddenly, I was under attack from above, not by Ritchie, for he was by now a distant memory, but by yet another of the many megablights (no doubt still more karmic comeuppance for having attacked Pearl Harbor) to strike downtown Tokyo in the mid-1950s: Rodan. Soon the two behe-moths were rolling around in the mud, roaring and grunting in mock bat-tle until an even louder roar, this one coming from my mom, who ordered us out of the garden. Ritchie was sent home and I, now a much humbler prehistoric monster, was dragged wincing and protesting by the ear to the bathroom, where Mom stripped off my mud-stained clothes.

"What on earth is wrong with you?" she demanded.

I knew from experience that this was a trick question and chose my response carefully, starting with the traditional "It's not my fault" defense in an effort to shift the lion's share of responsibility to my playmate.

"Besides," I protested. "Ritchie did it first."

The second the words escaped from my lips I knew I had made a tactical error because it opened the way for the classic parental parry, "Oh, and I suppose if Ritchie Pagano decided to jump off the Empire State Building you would've done that, too?"

I held my tongue because I knew that the real answer to that question—it all depended on whether or not Ritchie had superpowers or a parachute when he jumped—was not likely to gain me much ground in the debate.

An hour later I was freshly scrubbed, dressed in clean clothes, and sent back out into the hot summer sun with orders to "stay out of the dirt." I wandered to the garden where the final epic battle had taken place earlier in the day to see what remained, but frankly there wasn't much, I'm afraid. The tin walls of the fort were twisted and bent beyond repair and most of the fighters, attackers, and defenders alike had been scattered about or ground into the mud. Kneeling beside the battlefield, I reached out tentatively towards one of the figures in the hope it would be Davy himself but quickly withdrew my hand as Mom's unequivocal admonition rang in my ears. I could've continued and later made the argument that while I had indeed been prohibited from playing in the dirt nothing had been said about mud. Letting discretion be the better part of valor, however, I withdrew entirely with only mild regret. Davy, after all, had served me well, but as the Good Book admonished, it was a time to turn from the playthings of a child and move on. So I did.

CHAPTER 7

Duck and Cover

"This is a test. This station is conducting a test of the Emergency Broadcast System. This is only a test."

(Screeeeeeeeeeeeech!)

This has been a test of the Emergency Broadcast System. The broadcasters in your area in voluntary cooperation with federal, state, and local authorities have developed this system to keep you informed in the event of an emergency. If this had been an actual emergency, the attention signal you just heard would have been followed by official information, news, and instructions. This concludes our test of the Emergency Broadcast System. This was only a test."

By the time I was seven years old, my sister had me convinced I was personally responsible for the Cold War. Although she never suggested a direct causal relationship, she made it clear something beyond merely coincidence connected my birth with the events that followed, and a preponderance of evidence seemed to support her position.

For example, less than three months after I was born, the Russians exploded their first atomic bomb; two months after that, the Communists took over all of mainland China. The next year, 1950, the Korean War began, followed by the arrest of Julius and Ethel Rosenberg who were tried, convicted, and executed as Russian spies. Senator Joseph McCarthy, meanwhile, warned America that more spies (he was a little hazy on the exact number) had infiltrated the highest levels of our government; the U.S. detonated the very first H-bomb; the Russians detonated one of their own; and a bellicose Nikita Khrushchev took off his shoe during a session of the United Nations General Assembly and while pounding it repeatedly on his desk bellowed that he would bury us.

The evidence was so compelling and the logic so flawless that for several days I was firmly convinced of my own unwitting collusion in these events until a kindly teacher assured me that this was not the case; that I was no more responsible for the fearsome and unsettling events unfolding around us than was someone born on Saturday, December 6, 1941, responsible for starting World War II. Upon hearing this news, I was so relieved, I celebrated by gluing together a stack of my sister's favorite 45 rpm records.

Even though I grew up during the Cold War, neither my friends nor I even knew such a thing existed. Global tension was just the way things were, and as the Cold War progressed, we began to adapt our play to more accurately reflect the vicissitudes of the day. Clearly, catching spies was a priority when we weren't otherwise engaged in playing kickball, building forts out of scrap lumber, or flipping baseball cards.

In order to catch a spy, the first rule of thumb was to recognize that they had an uncanny ability to blend into the community but that, over time, even the best spies invariably gave themselves away by revealing subtle differences from the rest of us. An accent, a poorly kept yard, unusual habits, even the way a person dressed, could give him or her away. For all these reasons, our neighbor Mrs. Bender became a prime suspect.

A quiet, withdrawn woman, Mrs. Bender was rumored to have lived in Eastern Europe, where she married an American serviceman during the war. After the war the newlyweds returned to this country and settled down; but Mr. Bender suffered a massive heart attack and died shortly thereafter, leaving his widow to fend for herself in a strange country where she knew practically no one and had very little in common, including the language, with the people around her.

My stalwart friends and I were not fooled by this clever ruse. Obviously, the woman married a red-blooded American soldier with a heart problem, if indeed that was the *real* cause of his death, in order to infiltrate an all-American town like ours and spread the seeds of the most heinous of all political dogmas, Communism. She was a foreigner who spoke with a thick, unfamiliar accent, a serious black mark on her patriotism, and who had come from a country now under Communist control. Her dress was plain and colorless, no one ever saw her shop at the local stores, and, to the best of our knowledge, she did not attend church. My friends and I agreed it was pretty suspicious and worth looking into more closely.

For almost an entire Saturday we staked out her house and kept copious notes on her every activity: *1:33 PM—Suspect sets up observation post at kitchen window. 1:39 PM—Suspect digs in garden, possibly attempting to bury something. 2:17 PM—Suspect returns to house.*

That night, we snuck into Mrs. Bender's garden and did some digging of our own, but to our great disappointment found nothing, although we did manage to uproot a number of plants that appeared to have been only recently put in the ground.

Eventually, Mrs. Bender disappeared, and we were never quite sure if she had just moved away or if the FBI had finally caught up with her.

Throughout our childhood we learned to live with the fact that a cloud, a fiery, mushroom-shaped cloud, hung over our heads at all times, and it could incinerate us instantly if we did not take the proper precautions, like those we learned from Bert the Turtle.

Bert the Turtle was a cartoon civil-defense mascot who taught us how to duck and cover at the first sign of a nuclear explosion. The moment we saw the brilliant flash of an exploding atomic bomb, presumably over downtown New York City only twenty-five miles away, we were to throw ourselves to the ground and place our hands over the back of our necks. This, we were assured, would protect us from the 5,000-degree heat of the bomb's fireball and the 1,000-mph winds of the blast wave that followed.

Throughout our childhood signs of the growing Communist menace continued to haunt us. On October 7, 1957, the Russians launched the first man-made moon, called *Sputnik,* into orbit, followed by a dog named Laika, and eventually the first man. The Russians also threatened to over-run Berlin, shot down an unarmed American U-2 spy plane, and stormed out of a summit conference with the United States. Because of the grow-ing tension, no effort was spared to prepare us in both body and mind for the anticipated conflict, even at school.

Our first line of defense in the classroom was a civics magazine called *My Weekly Reader,* which contained mostly propaganda for the grade-school set. Each issue hammered home warnings of the ever-increas-ing threat we faced from unchecked Communist expansion.

Once our minds were properly prepared for the coming conflagration, we then honed our survival skills by preparing for surprise air attacks by the Russians. If an enemy bomber or ICBM missile crossed the famous Arctic DEW (Distant Early Warning) line, the nation was immediately alerted. At school this set off a frightening clamor of bells. Instantly, with-out fear or fanfare, our teachers directed us to close our study materials, form two neat rows, and proceed directly out to the hallway in an orderly fashion. They brooked no talking, giggling, or horseplay of any kind. Once in the corridor, we turned away from the row next to us and faced the wall, dropped to a crouch clasping both hands behind our heads, and waited. Sometimes, if I thought I wouldn't get caught, I lifted my head to peer down the hall at the strange sight of all these children stacked neatly side by side like Lincoln Logs, and strained to catch the distant roar of high-altitude bombers as they approached our school. It made me queasy to think that at any moment I might be blinded by the light of a million suns as the windows of our classrooms exploded inward from the blast. There was always a sense of relief when the short, sharp all-clear bell sounded and we could resume our daily routine.

So intent were community leaders on raising our consciousness of the threat we faced from the perils of Communism that one day in the fall of 1960 amid the hoopla of a presidential election, the school held a special event called Red Menace Day. The purpose of the event was to further instruct us on the evils of Communism by allowing us to experience it firsthand, or at least experience it as it existed in the popular imagination. Therefore, the school day was adapted to more closely mirror what school officials imagined would be the Communist way of life were it suddenly imposed in our small suburban community. It was a noble effort. The day was filled with martial music, special assemblies, and a mock execution of our least favorite teacher, Mr. Delvecio, for attempting to teach us the now banned Pledge of Allegiance. When the ersatz gunshot marking his demise sounded from the public-address system, my classmates and I roared our approval and demanded that the entertainment portion of the day continue.

My friends and I assumed that the ubiquitous nuclear testing that was part and parcel of the Cold War was also responsible for producing what we considered two of its most egregious side effects. The first was Unidentified Flying Objects, or UFOs. What else could explain the sudden outpouring of interest in our tiny little planet tucked away in a relatively small galaxy called the Milky Way in a modest little corner of the universe? UFOs were by no means a modern phenomenon, there being recorded sightings going as far back as 3,400 years ago in Egypt during the reign of Pharaoh Thutmose III. Indeed, more than one self-made popular scientist has suggested that everything from the pyramids to Stonehenge to the mysterious statues of Easter Island were built with at least some extraterrestrial assistance.

The modern age of UFO mania began on June 24, 1947, in the sunny skies over Washington's Cascade Mountains when a private pilot out of Boise, Idaho, by the name of Ken Arnold reported seeing nine silver-colored oblong-shaped objects flying in a tight formation, at speeds he later estimated were in excess of 1,200 mph. He believed the objects to be around forty to fifty feet in diameter and traveling in a manner unlike any known commercial or military aircraft. In reporting the incident, an eager journalist referred to the objects as "flying saucers," and a myth was born.

In the weeks following Arnold's Mount Rainier sighting, the skies across America seemed alive with flying saucers. Two days later a group of tourists visiting the Grand Canyon said they saw a "huge silver globe" gliding across the rim of the canyon. Two days after that, on July 28, an Air Force pilot reported a formation of six glowing discs over Lake Meade, Nevada. For days similar sightings seemed to come from all around the country. On more than one occasion, these sightings proved to be either MFOs (misidentified flying objects) or the work of pranksters from our own planet rather than aliens from outer space. On July 1, 1947, The San Antonio *Light* reported that a resident of Hot Springs, New Mexico, had successfully chased down a flying saucer only to find it was actually a large piece of foil that had been carried aloft by the wind. The following day the same newspaper carried a photograph of an Ohio woman holding pieces of what later proved to be a weather balloon. Two flying saucers were found on July 11, the first in Black River Falls, Wisconsin, and the second in Twin Falls, Idaho. The former turned out to be constructed of two soup bowls fastened together with glue and the latter, a set of cymbals held together by stove bolts.

The pièce de résistance, however, occurred late in the evening of Independence Day 1947, when a loud explosion in Corona, New Mexico, awakened rancher Mac Brazel. Investigating the next morning, Mr. Brazel found a large field of debris in one of his pastures, including wire, scraps of metal, lightweight pieces of some plasticlike material, and scraps of metal foil. Mr. Brazel also reported seeing strange writing on some of the material.

Like any good citizen who finds the remains of a flying saucer in his backyard, Mr. Brazel packed up some of the debris and took it to the nearby Army air base at Roswell, New Mexico, whereupon military officials descended *en masse* on the hapless rancher's pasture, collected the remaining debris, and returned to the air base. An Air Corps intelligence officer by the name of Maj. Jesse Marcel is reported to have commented that the material was "unearthly," and as if to confirm his observation, a few days later officials at Roswell issued a press release stating that "the Army Air Force here today announced a flying disc has been found." Later the same day, the military issued a second press release retracting the first and claiming that what had been found was actually pieces of a radar reflector from a weather balloon, and in doing so gave birth to a conspiracy theory second only to that surrounding the assassination of JFK or the legendary mythical passing of Beatle Paul McCartney.

At some point the facts of this or any one of the other hundreds of sightings become irrelevant. The term *flying saucer* had by now become a permanent part of the American lexicon and the phenomenon itself, be it fact or fiction, officially entered popular culture for good.

Things on the saucer front seemed to quiet down for a while as the new decade began, but 1952 erupted in a new frenzy of sightings. Everywhere you turned someone, including trained observers like commercial and military pilots, claimed to have seen something of an unusual nature, and hundreds of bits of scrap metal were turned over to authorities as possible wreckage from a flying saucer. The flap peaked in July 1952, when radar at Washington DC's National Airport tracked up to twelve unidentified "objects" the Air Force later said resulted merely from a temperature inversion, an assertion contradicted by numerous civilian meteorologists who said no such inversion existed at the time and in the place the objects were sighted.

Actually, official explanations for these phenomena were a dime a dozen, and if blaming them on temperature inversions didn't work, there was always another, like cloud formations, ball lightning, swamp gas, or misinterpreted sighting of various planets from Venus to Jupiter. An Australian physiologist went so far as to suggest the sightings were merely "the effect of red blood corpuscles passing in front of the retina." These explanations did little to assuage a wary public already anxious about a world that seemed to grow more menacing everyday. Despite efforts to publicly downplay these odd occurrences, the U.S. government was concerned not so much out of fear that we might be under attack by space aliens, but that these occurrences might represent some as yet unknown technological leap by the Soviet Union. After the plethora of sightings in 1952, the military rekindled its UFO investigation, calling it Project Blue Book. Even the CIA got into the act by convening its own covert science advisory committee, called the Robertson Panel.

As usual, Hollywood did its best to firmly affix saucer mania into the hearts and minds of an America already overdosing on paranoia, and by the early 1950s theater screens were ablaze with tales of alien skulduggery, many of which were simply thinly veiled allegories for the growing tensions between the U.S. and the U.S.S.R. Confirmed saucer heads like my friends and me continually debated whether the influx of extraterrestrials would ultimately prove itself a boon or a bane on the future of humankind. Most of us leaned toward the philosophy that alien beings were malevolently inclined and sought to dominate the human race or, worse, to eliminate it altogether. Hollywood seemed to support our position, if films like *The Thing from Another World, Earth versus Flying Saucers, Mars Attack,* and *Invasion of the Saucer Men* were any indication. Clearly, these interplanetary interlopers were in need of interstellar *lebensraum,* or living space, which could then be used to colonize the rest of the solar system.

A minority opinion argued that these visitors were actually quite benign and concerned only with the well-being of the planet and its human inhabitants, as evidenced by the wise and kindly Klaatu, as played by Michael Rennie in the movie *The Day the Earth Stood Still.* Klaatu pops up on the South Lawn of the White House one day in his flying saucer to warn humankind that the combination of its aggressive nature and its advanced nuclear technology was a recipe for self-extinction if we don't get a grip on ourselves. Unfortunately, all Klaatu gets for his troubles is a case of lead poisoning, and had his robotic sidekick, Gort, been unable to reanimate his protoplasmic space companion (*"Gort! Klaatu barada nikto!"*), things could have quickly turned ugly for us earthlings.

If semi-hysterical news accounts were not enough to convince us of the existence of UFOs, there was also an explosion of popular magazines, both fiction and those that claimed to be nonfiction, as well as an avalanche of books written by a variety of self-proclaimed experts. From the point of view of the saucer heads, the three most important were all written by one of the patron saints of UFOs, USMC Maj. Donald E. Keyhoe (retired), who penned *Flying Saucers from Outer Space, The Flying Saucer Conspiracy,* and *Flying Saucers—Top Secret,* which together were considered the Talmud of saucerology.

Keyhoe first came to public attention in 1950 with an article published in *True Magazine* entitled "Flying Saucers Are Real." It is Keyhoe who claimed that the U.S. government knowingly kept the entire UFO business under wraps for fear that wide-scale panic would result if the truth ever became public. Picked up by radio and television, the story created a sensation and ultimately led to Keyhoe's appointment as chairman of the NICAP (National Investigations Committee on Aeriel Phenomena) several years later. If government officials hoped that naming Keyhoe to head the committee would allow them to better control him, they were sadly mistaken. During a live television appearance, Keyhoe, frustrated by the heavy-handed editing of his script by Air Force officials, began speaking extemporaneously on the subject, but because his comments included information that had not been authorized by his military handlers, the audio portion of the broadcast was suddenly cut off. The Air Force later claimed it was for reasons of national security.

By this time saucer mania had become firmly entrenched into our patio culture. Store shelves were filled with comic books, toy ray guns, trading cards, coloring books, Halloween costumes, lunch boxes, puzzles, windup toys, and, of course, the granddaddy of all flying saucers, the Frisbee. This last item had its humble utilitarian beginnings as a simple pie tin made by the Frisbie Pie Company of Bridgeport, Connecticut. At some point curious and presumably hungry college students discovered the pie plate had certain unique aerodynamic properties when properly tossed, and a recreational amusement was born. Years later a Los Angeles building inspector by the name of Walt Morrison designed a plastic version of the Frisbie Pie Company's pie plate, which he named the Pluto Platter in an effort to cash in on the burgeoning flying-saucer craze. Morrison went on to patent his invention, eventually selling the rights to a newly formed toy company called Wham-O. So interested was the U.S. government in Morrison's design that it spent almost half a million dollars studying it, using special high-speed cameras, wind tunnels, and a specially built prototype flare launcher.

Additionally, magazines like *Popular Mechanics* began to speculate on the feasibility of designing and building saucer-like vehicles for both public transportation and personal use, and building architects, interior designers, and product designers began taking cues from the sleek lines and smooth surfaces so evident in both terrestrial and extraterrestrial space-age transport systems.

The censorship of Keyhoe's comments was enough to make a believer out of my friends and me, and with all the zeal of those boys who fifteen years earlier had searched the horizon for hints of German high-altitude bombers or stood on the shores of Jones Beach looking for the appearance of submarine periscopes, we spent many a warm summer night searching the skies for signs of extraterrestrial activity. Unfortunately, the only thing we ever saw were civilian airliners on final approach to nearby LaGuardia or Idlewild airports.

Imagine how discouraged we were to find out that, what with nuclear annihilation, *Sputnik,* puberty, wrathful older siblings, bogeymen, permanent school records, playground bullies, relatives who gave clothes instead of toys at Christmas, broccoli, and Spam (just to name a few), not only was our own world often an inhospitable place to live, but there was also an entire universe out there, presumably hostile and filled with beings that could not wait to get their gooey protoplasmic appendages on us. Was it any wonder we couldn't sleep at night?

Our ongoing hanky-panky with the atom during the Cold War resulted in some additional and quite disagreeable side effects inasmuch as the earth became, according to Hollywood and writers of popular science fiction, suddenly awash in life forms that had mutated in a variety of unpleasant ways. Giant irradiated ants took over much of the Los Angeles sewer system in the movie *Them.* Displaced by a nuclear test in the Pacific Ocean, an angry oversized mollusk tears apart the Golden Gate Bridge in *It Came from Beneath the Sea.* Another ill-advised test conducted near the North Pole in *The Beast from 20,000 Fathoms* loosed a cranky prehistoric monster, so put out at being disturbed from its icy slumber that it wreaks havoc on, of all places, the amusement park at Coney Island. Even humans were not immune to the mutating effects of radiation, like the hero of *The Incredible Shrinking Man,* Scott Carey, who comes in contact with a radioactive cloud from a nearby nuclear explosion and shrinks to only a few inches in height and is still shrinking as the movie ends. And Lt. Col. Manning thought he had problems.

Cold War images became so predominant that we hardly noticed them. Local store owners and businessmen adopted names like the Atomic Undergarment Company, Atomic Termite & Pest Control, and Atomic Car Wash. The movie theater featured titles like *Invasion, US, The Day the World Ended,* and *Panic in Year Zero.* We could listen to the "Atomic Bomb Blues," by Muddy Waters and Homer Harris; "Thirteen Women (and Only One Man in Town)," by Bill Haley and the Comets, or "Jesus Is God's Atom Bomb," by the Silvertone Singers. There were toys (Atomic Bomb Ring—"Squint into the secret lens and zowie!"), there was candy (Atomic Bubble Gum—"It's a Blast"); there was even a burlesque act called The Atom Bomb Dancers.

If one icon of that frenzied era stood out from all the rest, it was the fall-out shelter. I first became aware of shelters during a visit to the Village Hall. Mom and I were walking up the steps to the building when I noticed an odd looking sign. The design was simple, depicting three bright yellow inverted triangles superimposed over a black circle, and at the bottom was an arrow pointing down toward the basement. I asked Mom about it and she said it meant there was a fallout shelter in the basement of our Village Hall. She explained that the basement had been stocked with army surplus cots, bedding, medical supplies, and field rations. In the event of an attack, as many citizens as possible would crowd into whatever cramped space was available for at least two weeks. I asked her if this was where we would come if a war broke out, but she told me not to worry about it; a silly answer when you consider that worrying about such things was pretty much *all* we did in those days.

Over time, similar signs sprouted up on public buildings all over town and even our school became a designated shelter. Far from frightening us, the fact that our school had been chosen as a safe haven from nuclear obliteration struck most of us as pretty neat. There were even plans afoot to mount a secret expedition to locate the shelter, but these were quickly put to rest when our principal, Mr. Brunner, made an announcement that any unauthorized visits to the school basement would be grounds for detention.

As far as I was concerned, however, the absolute pinnacle of shelter technology was achieved with the development of private shelters for the home.

Several of my friends had basement shelters. Even at our house my parents kept canned goods, batteries, an old set of Melmac picnic plates, plastic water tumblers, and a first-aid kit in the basement. My friend Jimmy had an elaborate shelter in his basement built of cinderblocks and sandbags that was actually a room within a room, and during the winter that's where Jimmy's parents stored the family camping equipment.

The backyard shelter, however, is what really tickled our fancy; a separate self-contained environment, a futuristic lifeboat in which the occupants could ride out the storm overhead. Until Armageddon arrived, however, we also found it served other uses as well.

Felix Lauer had a shelter in his backyard. Above ground, lying there on the lawn waiting to be buried, it looked like nothing more than a 20-foot section of drainage culvert about six feet in diameter, with a metal cap welded onto either end. Once installed, however, it became an instant kid magnet and our official headquarters for almost the entire summer of 1962.

Opening the heavy metal hatch and climbing down the steel ladder for the first time was an eerie experience. With no circulation, the air was hot and stale. With the hatch shut, the absolute darkness was oppressive, and the meager light thrown off by the candle we lit threw strange, flickering shadows against the corrugated steel walls of the shelter. The thought of living in this steamy, claustrophobic darkness for two weeks while the world above burned itself to cinders left me feeling queasy.

Eventually, after several visits, we could throw off our fears and enjoy the novelty and privacy afforded by our underground burrow. The fact that we were forbidden to be there made the experience all the more enjoyable. Our visits usually didn't last more than an hour, after which the space became too uncomfortable and we longed for fresh, clean air.

One day, about two weeks before the start of another school year, my seventh, Felix invited me to spend the night at his house under the sole supervision of his older brother Eddie. Eddie, a star outfielder on the high school baseball team, agreed to the arrangement under the proviso that Felix and I had to swear we would never tell his parents that instead of remaining home to supervise his younger sibling, he planned to spend the evening with his girlfriend, Sarah Jane Craig, whose bubbly, all-American-girl personality, coupled with her cheerleader good looks, left a trail of lovesick boys behind her wherever she went. Felix and I jumped at the deal, and later that night as Eddie prepared for his date with Sarah, we sat innocently in front of the TV, seemingly absorbed in our favorite Saturday-night western, *Have Gun—Will Travel.*

Warning us to stay out of trouble on pain of death, Eddie was soon out the door, and the moment Felix and I heard his old Chevy roar down the street trailing great plumes of black smoke, we were off like a shot. Our first stop was the kitchen, where we provisioned ourselves for the next hour.

"Oreos," I asked?

"Check," replied Felix.

"Milk?"

"Check?"

"Flashlight?"

"Check."

"Extra batteries?"

"Check."

"Comics?"

"Check."

We were ready.

Earlier in the evening, Felix had opened the shelter hatch to cool things off, and by the time we arrived it was quite comfortable, even a bit chilly. I went in first with Felix right behind me, closing the hatch as he came. He switched on the flashlight and we eased to one side of the ladder where earlier we had piled some wool blankets and pillows Mrs. Lauer kept stored in the shelter. We settled in and for the first few moments allowed ourselves to revel in a level of unfettered freedom kids rarely get to enjoy. We then dove into our supply of cookies, milk, and comic books.

At first we swapped story lines, traded boasts about our respective comic-book heroes, and nudged one another with our elbows whenever we wanted to draw attention to a particularly compelling element of the story line. Eventually, Felix began to fidget and finally announced he had to use the bathroom. He handed me the light and I used the beam to guide him up the ladder, where he eased opened the hatch. "I'll be right back," Felix promised as he eased the hatch closed again behind him.

For a moment I continued reading but then switched off the light to enjoy a moment of total and absolute solitude. It was so dark, it made no difference if my eyes were open or shut. Letting my imagination wander, I wondered what it would be like if World War III started right at that very moment; if almost nobody else in the world survived and when I surfaced two weeks from now, the only other person around was Susan Dahlman, a classmate whom nature had fated to blossom well before any of the other girls in our grade, thereby making her the source of considerable interest among the boys.

After a time my eyes grew irritated and I had difficulty keeping them open in the closeness of the shelter. Silently, I swore at Felix to hurry.

I didn't know what awakened me at first although I was pretty sure it had to be Felix returning to the shelter from his bathroom break. It wasn't.

"Are you sure it's safe?" said a muffled female voice from the other side of the hatch. "Sure, I go down here all time," replied Eddie. *Eddie? What was Eddie doing here?* my mind screamed. The hatch eased open with the now familiar squeal of metal and a blast of cool, fresh air washed over me, bringing me fully awake.

"My little brother and his dopey friends have been playing down here again," I heard Eddie tell his female companion, obviously Sarah. "If my dad ever finds out, he's dead," said Eddie as he started down the ladder.

Quietly, I ducked my head under the hot wool blanket as he made his way to the bottom, inviting Sarah to follow. "C'mon," he assured her, "I'm right below you." More shuffling and they were both inside, standing not four feet away from where I was hiding. They stood there a moment and exchanged a few short kisses followed by one that seemed to last forever. I was sweating like crazy.

"C'mon, Eddie, please turn on a light," urged Sarah. I'm dead, I thought to myself. There's no way they can miss me. I heard a click, then saw the feeble beam of a flashlight through the heavy blanket. To my surprise they turned away and shuffled a few careful steps to the other end of the shelter. They must have mistaken my hiding place for a pile of bedding! I risked a peek and took in great silent gulps of sweet fresh air as it poured down the hatchway. Glancing up, I glimpsed a circle of stars outlined in the open hatch just above my head. Freedom was so close! Could I get away? My heart was pounding!

But a new sound caught my attention. Eddie lowered a narrow sleeping platform attached to the wall of the shelter. Setting it in place, he unrolled a thin mattress, sat down, pulling Sarah with him, and resumed where they had left off at the foot of the ladder. Eddie switched off the flashlight, and once again we were thrown into total darkness. Then came rustling noises, followed by the sounds of more kissing, heavy breathing, and the occasional soft moan from Sarah. This was my chance, I thought. I would wait just a few more minutes until they were totally absorbed, and then ease my way up ladder into the night.

A couple of times I heard Sarah utter a halfhearted "No, Eddie" that seemed to go unnoticed. Then I heard the sound of a belt buckle. This was it! I eased myself out from under the blanket, barely daring to breath. The cooing continued, punctuated now by an occasional heavy grunt that, I assumed, came from Eddie. I took a step, but as I raised my foot it caught the edge of a box of kitchen utensils and the whole thing was sent flying with a thunderous crash. Falling forward, I reached out to catch myself and succeeded only in pulling two more boxes to the floor.

Terrified, Sarah let out a scream that was magnified tenfold in the enclosed space of the shelter. Eddie began to curse but was cut short when he fell off the platform bed and hit the floor hard. Suddenly, the beam of his flashlight momentarily cut through the darkness, illuminating Sarah with her blouse and bra bunched up around her neck. My eyes were immediately riveted to her fully exposed breasts.

"*Shut if off, Eddie, shut it off!*" Sarah screamed hysterically and we were again plunged into pitch blackness.

I couldn't wait any longer. Half blind, I jumped to my feet and shot up the ladder, slamming the heavy metal hatch closed behind me with a loud clang! I darted across the backyard to the sound of muffled screams and curses from inside the shelter. Quickly, I scooted in the backdoor, taking the stairs to Felix's bedroom two at a time. When I got there Felix was sound asleep on top of the covers. Without bothering to undress or even take off my shoes, I jumped into the bed next to his. My only chance was to pretend to be asleep when Eddie arrived, and from the sound of things he would not be long in coming.

Eddie, now out of the shelter, charged across the lawn like a runaway locomotive. The backdoor through which I had come just moments earlier slammed open and Eddie came stomping up the stairs. I mussed my hair and put my head down on the pillow in an attempt to feign sleep. Eddie exploded through the bedroom door and angrily slapped at the light switch until it came on. Felix sat up in bed bleary eyed, obviously startled by the intrusion. I rubbed my eyes and squinted, hoping my acting skills were believable. Eddie stood at the foot of the bed, clothes in disarray and fists on his hips, huffing through clenched teeth. His face was beet red with anger, but now he looked unsure. He paused. Time stood still. Clearly, this was not what he had expected.

"*You little twerps were playing in the bomb shelter again and forgot to lock it. Someone got in there tonight and tore it up!*" he bellowed. I waited for him to lunge, but he didn't.

"*I'm tellin' Dad when he gets home, and he's gonna skin your butt, but good!*" Eddie shouted, and with that he turned and stormed out of the room, slamming the door behind him.

He ran back down the stairs still cursing, and for the first time I allowed myself to think I might actually get out of this alive. I quivered with relief.

Felix stared at me goggle-eyed. He didn't have a clue what had just happened. Jumping out of bed, I switched the light off once again and raced to the window, where Felix now joined me. "What's going …," he started, but I cut him off. "Shhh," I whispered. We watched Eddie cross the yard back to the shelter entrance, where Sarah now stood crying in big heaving sobs. Eddie tried to slide a comforting arm around her shoulders, but she quickly shook it off and demanded to be taken home. "What the hell just happened?" whispered Felix. "Shhh," I shushed him again. "I'll tell you in a minute."

Once again Eddie's car roared to life and squealed down the street. When it got quiet, I sat cross-legged on the bed and began telling Felix what had just taken place in the shelter, while intermittently cursing him for abandoning me and almost getting me killed.

Our new clubhouse eventually lost much of its allure when reality intruded a few short months after my close encounter with Eddie and Sarah Jane. The end came on the evening of Monday, October 22, 1962, when President Kennedy went on national television to advise the country that the Russians had snuck nuclear missiles into Cuba, thereby placing a large part of the country in immediate danger of a Russian attack with little or no warning. President Kennedy assured us that the threat would not be allowed to remain, that the small island nation was now under a naval blockade and that any vessel, including those from the Soviet Union, attempting to enter Cuban waters would be stopped and searched even if it meant using force. The President also assured us that any nuclear missiles already in Cuba, some of which were already operational, would be removed.

My sister and I were sent to bed immediately after the speech ended. While my parents remained downstairs talking quietly at the kitchen table until late into the night, I lay in bed wide-awake, trying to understand what had just happened. I was scared.

The next morning it took me a moment to remember why I had awakened feeling so anxious. Even at school the tension was palpable, particularly among teachers and staff, who were often seen huddled in conversation.

Weirder still was the number of my friends and classmates who didn't show up for school at all. According to a mutual friend, Felix Lauer had been seen helping his parents and older brother Eddie lug several boxes from the house to the shelter. David Caprio showed me a note from his parents asking that he be excused for the remainder of the week because the family was leaving town to visit relatives in Ohio; both Bobby Craig and his older sister, Sarah Jane, were rumored to have left late the previous night, the family's Chevy station wagon piled high with camping gear, for a summer cabin up in the Pocono Mountains.

The next several days were strangely subdued as everyone else continued to follow their usual routines as though in some kind of trance. Each day fewer and fewer kids showed up for school, and even some of the teachers began to disappear. With few substitutes available, some classes had to double up.

Normalcy disappeared altogether on Friday, when during a special assembly each of us was called by name to the front of the auditorium, where we received a set of identification tags to wear around our necks. They looked like the ID tags soldiers wore, called dog tags, and we were instructed to wear them at all times. What we didn't know was that they were intended to identify our remains in the event of nuclear war, a nuclear war that now seemed almost certain.

Although we didn't realize it at the time, the crisis peaked that same Friday, October 26, when a Russian freighter was stopped and searched for quarantined materials, and again on Saturday, October 27, when a U-2 reconnaissance plane was shot down by a Russian surface-to-air missile and its pilot killed. Then suddenly it was over.

When President Kennedy again went on national television, it was to announce that the Russians had agreed to remove their missiles and bombers from Cuba and that the danger of mushroom clouds appearing over American cities had, for the time being at least, passed. Oddly, the general reaction was not one of victory but of relief that we had received a last-minute reprieve from an event that had until this point been simply theoretical.

Normalcy, always a relative term at best, took its time returning. Most of my friends were back in time to share information about their out-of-town adventures by Halloween. Felix reported that upon hearing the news about the U-2 airplane being shot down, the family had actually spent Saturday night in the shelter. Privately, he admitted to being frightened, as we all were, and that our former clubhouse seemed a far more joyless environment than the one we had experienced the previous summer.

A year after the Cuban crisis, the shelter was stripped of its contents, filled with concrete, and officially decommissioned. Fortunately, Eddie never did find out who was responsible for interrupting his blissful interlude with Sarah Jane that night, a night I would always remember because unbeknownst to anyone but me, I had robbed the star of the high school baseball team of a home run.

CHAPTER 8

Smoking

I did not start smoking myself until I was 9 years old and even then I was not constant. I was always ready to reform if I could see any profit in it, but the only profit I could see in it was the heavenly pleasure of giving up the reform and going back to smoking again.

—Mark Twain

I started smoking in 1961, when I was twelve years old, although it was not the first cigarette in my life. My first attempt came when I was about six and I was playing with a toy train set in the basement, keeping my mother company while she ironed. She had just lit a cigarette for herself and out of nowhere I asked if I could have one, too. She said sure and even offered to light it for me, a gesture I very much appreciated since I was not permitted to play with matches. Before doing so, however, she showed me exactly what to do with it. She took her own cigarette (it was an L&M, if my memory is correct), brought it to her lips and drew in, making the tip glow brightly. I watched in fascination as she slowly inhaled, drawing the smoke deep into her lungs, held it a moment, then released a long plume of gray smoke into the air. Placing her own cigarette in an ashtray at the end of the ironing board, she took another one from the half empty package and handed it to me. I placed it awkwardly between my lips, as I had seen both of my parents do a million times, while Mom pulled a match from one of the packs they gave away by the handful at every store, carefully close the cover, and slid it against the sandpaperlike strip until a small flame burst to life.

"Remember," Mom reminded me, "once you get a mouthful of smoke, just inhale like you were filling your lungs with air." I acknowledged her with a nod, thinking the whole experience was pretty neat, and wondered why I had never thought of asking to smoke before. Probably because it seemed like something only adults did, and if only adults did it then it must be fun, and if it was fun we would surely never be allowed to engage in the activity ourselves. Obviously, I was wrong, I thought, as Mom brought the flame nearer to me. Either that or I had simply misjudged how permissive my parents might be under some circumstances. Either way, here I go, I thought as the flame touched the tip of my cigarette and I puffed a little to get the thing started then sucked on it enough to fill my mouth with smoke.

I inhaled quickly and deeply, whereupon my lungs immediately sent a special-delivery message to my brain, advising it that a bomb had just exploded down there and it had better do something quickly. My brain responded by sending me reeling across the basement family room in paroxysms of coughing, choking, gagging, retching, spitting, heaving, and hacking up what little bit of lung tissue remained. Between gasps I looked to my mom for support, but she just kept on with her ironing, her own cigarette dangling from her lips as though her only male child was not on his knees in front of her, face beet red, and preparing to asphyxiate.

It took several more minutes for my respiratory system to return to something approximating normal. My lungs and chest continued to burn, as they would for hours, and the tears from all that coughing still ran down my cheeks. Mom took another pull on her own cigarette and slowly placed it in the ashtray. Setting down the iron, she then turned to me, face impassive, and asked, "Want another?" What a stupid habit!

Fast-forward six years, where I can be found huddled behind the junior high school library with several schoolmates, each puffing away on our favorite brand of cigarette, shooting the breeze while waiting for the first homeroom bell to announce we had three minutes to get to class. Yes, we were smoking, although as neophytes we had yet to perfect the art of actually inhaling the toxins directly into our lungs; this would come with time and practice. Eventually, we would get over the nasty irritation and actually come to enjoy the sensation. Once we perfected this step, we could move on to some more sophisticated smoking-related mannerisms like blowing smoke rings and the ever-popular French inhale, in which one allows the smoke to drift from the mouth and draw it in again through the nostrils, a sign that you had truly mastered the art.

Why did we smoke, particularly after so many of us had experienced similarly unpleasant episodes like my own? For four very good reasons. First, cigarettes were relatively inexpensive and very accessible. Second, our environment was saturated with cues that led us consciously or unconsciously to the conclusion that smoking was a good thing. Third, it was a cool thing to do, so by extension we became cool by doing it. Finally, and perhaps most important, most of us lived in households where at least one and quite often both of our most influential roles models, our parents, smoked.

As difficult as it may seem today, for the patio pioneer of any age, it was impossible not to be influenced by the overwhelming amount of positive reinforcement that accompanied smoking. As if to underscore our naïveté, smoking was still considered a social custom rather than a habit resulting from chemical dependency. Thumb through any publication and you could easily find half a dozen of America's best-known celebrities—Phil Silvers, John Wayne, Rock Hudson, Lauren Bacall, Jack Webb, Lucille Ball—all extolling the virtues of their favorite brands, including Camel, Pall Mall, Winston, Marlboro, L&M, Old Gold, and Lucky Strike.

Furthermore, there seemed to be an overwhelming amount of scientific evidence in support of smoking. Some, like the folks who made Camel cigarettes, touted the psychological benefits, saying, "It's a psychological fact that pleasure helps your disposition. That's why everyday pleasures, like smoking for instance, mean so much. So if you're a smoker, it's important to smoke the *most pleasure-giving cigarette* ... Camel."

Others, like the manufacturers of Chesterfield cigarettes, had immutable medical evidence suggesting that "nose, throat, and accessory organs are not adversely affected by smoking" their brand and could prove it with a study they conducted themselves, using a "responsible consulting organization" and "a competent medical specialist." Still others, like the folks who produced Old Gold cigarettes, went so far as to invoke the U.S. government, which, according to the company had proven that "no other leading cigarette is less irritating, or easier on the throat, or contains less nicotine than Old Gold."

The testimonials were endless and came from celebrities, medical experts, military leaders, and a host of other easily recognizable public figures, and all reached the same conclusion. Not only was smoking not a bad thing, it was actually a good thing, almost as though it was a practice to which one should aspire. So we did.

As if this were not enough, there were other very clear messages we received via cigarette advertising, messages that suggested smoking provided other benefits that were terribly important to any adolescent: The people who smoked in these ads were all attractive, self-confident, talented, smart, funny, well liked, and wise to the ways of the world. Clearly, even if we knew we were none of these things, perhaps if we took up smoking, others might be fooled into thinking we were. It seemed worth a try. Besides, not only were the two people in our lives who had the most direct effect on us, our parents, in all likelihood smokers themselves, so were most of our other relatives, not to mention every other role model from teachers to policemen, from the local mayor to the president of the local bank.

That these same individuals, particularly our parents, also prohibited us from smoking ("Do as I say, not as I do") was just another one of those pesky inconsistencies we had grown accustomed to. The fact that it was a pleasure forbidden us made it just that much more attractive.

Although Winstons did taste good like a cigarette should, I was prepared to fight rather than switch from my Tareytons. Some of my friends were prepared to walk a mile for a Camel; others preferred Kent with the micronite filter; a few agreed that L.S.M.F.T meant more than Loose

Straps Mean Floppy Tits; and some of my friends just wanted to be Marlboro men.

Regrettably, nothing so glamorous could last. As far back as the 1920s, some studies suggested a link between smoking and a variety of health problems, but it was not until 1964, a mere two years after I had finally perfected the art of inhaling without choking, that the U.S. Surgeon General's Office dropped the hammer on smoking by issuing a report linking the habit to a variety of unpleasant diseases, which in turn led to even more unpleasant forms of death. The news deterred few smokers. To kids the concept of mortality was something that barely registered, and even then it was only as a hypothetical. Nonetheless, it loosened the first pebbles in what over the next several decades would become the antismoking avalanche.

Today little remains of the glory days of smoking. I used to get a pack of smokes for a quarter from one of the ubiquitous cigarette vending machines you could find in almost every store and business in town. Now they cost up to eight dollars in some places, much of the increase due to the federal, state, and local sin taxes that have been added to the price; the cigarette vending machines themselves have disappeared altogether, along with almost every other trace of social acceptability, such as much of the advertising, convenient public ashtrays, and free matches with every purchase. People still smoke, of course, not because it is glamorous but because, as we now know, cigarettes contain ingredients more addictive than heroin. Most municipalities have banned the practice in public places, cigarette packs are required to include warnings of the dire consequences that accompany use of the product, and most smokers have been reduced to huddling in doorways, where they puff furtively in small, forlorn groups. It was by all appearances one battle the Indians had finally won.

CHAPTER 9

Demon Rum

The first time I got drunk, I was seven years old and on my way to Sunday school. Getting drunk wasn't what I had in mind when I drained the contents of all those cocktail glasses scattered about the living room, the ones left over from a particularly festive neighborhood get-together my parents had thrown the night before. It just sort of happened.

When my older sister and I came downstairs to fix ourselves breakfast early that morning, there was debris—ashtrays overflowing with cigarette butts, crumpled napkins, cups half filled with cocktail peanuts, a bowl crusted over with dried onion dip, empty glasses—strewn almost everywhere we looked. From a purely social standpoint, the gathering had clearly been a success, a fact I already knew from lying in bed and letting the ebb and flow of party sounds—music, voices, laughter—lull me to sleep the night before.

Although dressed and ready to leave for Sunday school while Mom and Dad slept off the effects of their merrymaking, I paused long enough to inspect the damage while snacking on a few leftover potato chips and carefully examining the contents of a glass that was almost, but not quite, empty. It smelled kind of like lemonade, so I took a sip. Thus emboldened, I emptied the remains of all the glasses into one before quaffing it down in two or three hefty swallows. Yuck. My lips puckered at the unfamiliar taste, and I quickly joined my sister in the kitchen for a quick Pop-Tart and a glass of milk before we both headed out the door for church.

The first sign of trouble came just as we entered the twin glass doors leading into the education wing of the church, when my body began to rebel against even the simplest instructions from my brain. As I stepped through the doorway, my foot caught on some invisible trip hazard and sent me stumbling into a display of religious tracts entitled "Why Christ and Communism Don't Mix."

"Knock it off, twerp," my sister hissed, thinking I was goofing around. Before I had a chance to respond, she veered off to join her fifth-grade classmates in pre-Confirmation class and I was left to fend for myself.

By now I was beginning to feel decidedly woozy, and this, combined with my diminished motor skills, made navigating the crowded hallway an increasingly dicey proposition. The floor had taken on a decided slant, and for the first time I noticed that the door to my classroom had begun weaving around. I waited, and when it came around in my direction again, I plunged through it, dropped into the nearest seat, and immediately broke into a cold sweat. Folding my arms in my lap, I lowered my head, but even with my eyes closed, the room continued on like at the Tilt-a-Whirl. The room turned insufferably hot, the noise from my classmates became almost unbearable, and my stomach began to flip-flop like a politician at election time. I knew I was in serious trouble.

Startled by the soft touch of a hand on my shoulder, I jerked away quickly, a very poor exercise in judgment on my part because the sudden movement succeeded only in riling my already delicate constitution. I found the strength to raise my head and looked into the worried eyes of my Sunday-school teacher. Sensing danger, she immediately placed an arm around my shoulders and helped me up. My legs wobbled and the room spun as she carefully guided me across the hall to the men's room, and not a moment too soon.

Praying at the porcelain altar was a ritual that would become almost second nature to many of us as we grew older and our relationship with alcohol evolved from a mere nodding acquaintance to a full-blown love affair. At the moment, however, all I cared about was rinsing the awful taste of bile from my mouth. "Everything okay in there?" asked an anxious voice. I muttered something only half intelligible as I wiped a few bits of recycled Pop-Tart from my shirt. The door closed again, but I heard several adult voices engaged in hurried conversation on the other side. "I'm telling you, I smelled the alcohol on his breath," whispered my Sunday-school teacher.

"You mean he's drunk?" inquired another anxious voice, one I recognized immediately as that of our minister, Reverend Parker. There were more voices, but they all went silent the moment I opened the door. There was an awkward pause, then four heads swiveled in unison to examine me, each with its own unique expression: confusion, concern, incredulity, and something that looked like it might be the beginnings of indigestion.

Reverend Parker broke the silence first. "Are you feeling a bit better, son? Why don't we take a little walk down to my office so you can lie down while I give your parents a call?" I followed as he turned and walked down the hall toward his office behind the main sanctuary of the church.

There was a couch in the anteroom, and Reverend Parker invited me to lie down on it while he searched for something to cover me. I hesitated, knowing my shoes would probably leave dirt marks on the thick upholstery, but he didn't seem to mind, dismissed my objections, and instructed me to close my eyes and rest while he called my parents.

I had no idea how long I'd been dozing when the muffled sound of laughter awakened me. My eyes searched for the source just as the door to Reverend Parker's inner sanctum opened and several people, including my parents, stepped out. I quickly shut my eyes again, feigning sleep, as they made their way across the room where I lay. "C'mon, sleepyhead, time to get you home and into your own bed," said my mom as she gently shook my shoulder.

During the brief car ride home, my parents quizzed me about the events leading up to my sudden illness, thereby confirming what they already suspected. They recapped for me the unexpected phone call from an embarrassed church secretary and the somewhat awkward conversation that followed regarding the highly suspicious symptoms evidenced by their son during religious-education class. Even though Reverend Parker had been charming about the entire matter, my parents were obviously discomfited because it suggested that their absence from services was a direct result of having overindulged in alcohol the night before, a charge even I knew was preposterous because hungover or not, unless it was Christmas or Easter, neither one of my parents was likely to be anywhere near a church on Sunday morning.

An oddly similar incident occurred several years later when my parents—after discovering a secret cache of *Playboy* magazines hidden under my mattress—decided to punish me by removing the centerfolds and taping them all over the living room walls. Their intent was to watch me squirm with embarrassment when I returned home that evening. Unfortunately, it was the same evening Reverend Parker had targeted our house for an unscheduled pastoral visit and my sister, blissfully ignorant of the trap that had been set, politely ushered him inside the house. Caught flat-footed by his appearance, Mom and Dad stumbled over each other to explain why it was that the living room was plastered wall to wall with pictures of bare-breasted women. When I finally arrived home a couple of hours later, although the centerfolds were gone, the humiliation of the moment was still fresh in their minds. Angrily, they demanded to know what I had to say for myself, which I should've immediately recognized as a trick question. My first impulse was to be honest by pointing out that *they* were the ones responsible for decorating the room with all that exposed female flesh, not me—and what did they have to say for themselves? I thought better of it, however, and instead suggested that the presence of the *Playboy* centerfolds probably added a much needed touch of panache to the overall decor of the room, an observation that only succeeded in getting me grounded for the next two weekends. Frankly, I don't think they really wanted my opinion in the first place.

My initial brush with demon rum raised a number of questions. For example, if the symptoms I experienced—dizziness, a diminution of basic motor skills, loss of speech, nausea, and vomiting—were all directly attributable to the consumption of alcohol, why in the world would anyone want to drink the stuff? And why did it have none of the more pleasant side effects I expected after watching adults drink it in quantities far greater than what little I'd dredged up from the bottom of a few leftover cocktail glasses?

Based on my own observations, adults in the embrace of alcohol were generally far easier to get along with than at most other times. They laughed, told jokes, sang, and seemed far more amenable to the presence of youngsters. Indeed, it was a well-known fact among kids that a parent who had one or two drinks under his belt was far more likely to fork over the ten cents necessary to purchase a toasted-almond ice cream bar from the Good Humor man than was a parent who did not.

Kids also knew that the price of all this collegiality was something adults called a hangover. It was a condition that usually set in the following day, one that left the celebrants generally tired, grumpy, slow-moving, and thoroughly dim-witted. Most of us learned at an early age to give any grown-up in the throes of this condition a wide berth. We also learned how to make our own breakfast.

Despite whatever downside might accompany the recreational consumption of alcohol, the fact remained that it was an activity firmly embedded in almost every facet of our emerging culture to the extent that few social activities were deemed complete without it. Some activities, like the cocktail party, appear to have been invented solely for the purpose of consuming alcohol—as if grown-ups needed an excuse. Judging from the complex customs and rituals associated with the use of alcohol, drinking was by all appearances a subculture all its own.

Like many houses back then, ours featured an all-purpose basement activity area, sometimes called a family room, as standard equipment. Decorated with the obligatory pinewood paneling and linoleum floor, this space served as, among other things, a place for the storage of alcohol and all of the accoutrements related to its use, as well as for informal adult social gatherings. Ours had a small wet bar, a set of four very futuristic stools, and a well-stocked supply of liquor I would come to know only too well in years to come. Behind the bar were a mirror and a dizzying array of glasses, including many with decorations—palm trees, pink elephants, and hula girls were particularly popular—painted or etched on the sides; as well as jiggers, shakers, stirrers carefully crafted in the shape of bosomy women, coasters, plastic fruit picks, paper umbrellas, ice buckets, ice tongs, corkscrews, strainers, and napkins imprinted with risqué cartoons. There were special decorative items like wall plaques announcing "Martini Spoken Here," as well as dancing quarter notes, treble clefs, and bass clefs made of black wire. There was also the hi-fi, or high-fidelity phonograph, and next to it a collection of 33 1/3 rpm records featuring performers like Patti Page, Vic Damone, and Johnny Desmond. And in the unlikely event these alcohol-fueled events ever got off to a slow start, there were always a few novelty recordings like Spike Jones and the City Slickers to loosen up the crowd.

I soon learned that alcohol came in so many different forms and could be combined in so many different ways with so many different ingredients that grown-ups found it necessary to keep a guidebook nearby with instructions on how to concoct any one of the many drinks—martini, zombie, daiquiri, Manhattan, piña colada, Collins, old-fashioned, stinger—so popular during these early booze-besotted Frontier days.

Both my sister and I found these bacchanalian festivities too irresistible to ignore, though we both were assumed to be sound asleep well before the first guest arrived. This was rarely the case because our house was equipped with the type of forced air heating system that allowed one to eavesdrop on conversations in other rooms, particularly during warmer months when the furnace was not in use.

Hearing the uncensored sounds of grown-ups at play in their natural surroundings was quite marvelous indeed, and made all the more so by the fact that we weren't supposed to be listening in the first place. Admittedly, my understanding of what I overheard was limited. For example, at one unusually raucous get-together the wife of a neighbor took aside the husband of another, and for no apparent reason that I could ascertain invited him to stop by the following week in order to cavort with the family dog—to pet her poodle, I believe is how she put it. Nonetheless, like an anthropologist, I was thrilled at the opportunity to be able to observe these magnificent beasts in the wild even though much of their behavior remained a mystery to me.

Like everything else adults reserved solely for themselves, the fact that we were denied entry into the enchanted world of alcohol simply made it all the more attractive to us, and like smoking or driving a car, we looked forward eagerly to the time when we too could imbibe in these magical spirits. Consequently, as we got older getting drunk for the first time was viewed as an important rite of passage into adulthood, and one we eagerly sought to fulfill. We also knew from advertisements for various alcoholic beverages that these products would make us smarter, funnier, more socially engaging, and far more attractive in much the same way cigarettes would, as promised in the ads for tobacco products. How could we *not* want to drink?

Once we began to experiment with the wonders of alcohol most of us successfully overcame our aversion to some its more distasteful side effects. We had to because despite the aftereffects, there was a period, albeit brief, in which alcohol actually did produce in us a feeling of confidence that we rarely felt under normal circumstances. We experienced a rush of warmth and camaraderie for those around us, even those whom an hour earlier we secretly loathed. Pluck and courage filled us to the point where we welcomed a physical challenge in order to prove our mettle. Jokes became a hundred times funnier no matter how many times we had already heard them. Our ability to think critically and debate issues logically—even those issues about which we knew nothing—was heightened to the level of sheer genius. Music was transformed, as was our capacity for improving just about any composition with the addition of our own complex harmonies and instrumental sound effects. In other words, for a few brief, shining moments, the entire cosmos was in a state of equilibrium, resulting in a sense of personal well-being that was the antithesis of the normal adolescent zeitgeist. That our ability to form coherent sentences or pronounce multisyllabic words became increasingly impaired was irrelevant, as was the fact that our brains found it increasingly difficult to handle the millions of complex electrical signals necessary to maintain proper muscular coordination, balance, and speech. Only after these things began to flee us like rats from a sinking ship did we realize that for the umpteenth time we had crossed the line and would have to pay the consequences.

As we grew older and stumbled deeper into the abyss of puberty, new and more compelling reasons for abusing alcohol began to emerge. Not surprisingly, many of these were directly related to our burgeoning interest in members of the opposite sex. For example, alcohol often allowed us to overcome the fact that when it came to communicating with girls, we lacked even the most rudimentary social skills. The more attracted we were to a particular girl, the more difficult it was to articulate even a modest salutation. Oh, how we longed for the good old days when all we needed to do to express our ardor for a girl was simply bean her with a rock or knock her to the ground. If she arose in tears and headed for the nearest teacher, we knew immediately our love was unrequited. On the other hand, if the object of our affection arose, dusted herself off, and reciprocated with some act of mayhem of her own, we knew it was true love.

For teenagers, the rules were much more complicated, and besides, somewhere along the line, girls had successfully amassed sufficient power over boys that even the suggestion of a rebuke or dismissal was sufficient to leave us feeling worthless and empty for days.

Fortunately, alcohol changed all that because to the savvy drinker it could provide just the right amount of bottled bravery necessary to overcome those nagging doubts and insecurities long enough to walk right over to the prettiest and most popular girl in the room, lean confidently against the wall or doorway, and utter what amounted to a stream of absolute gibberish like "Havet glee labsna ablu Beezldable, dit?" (translation: "Have you heard the new Beatles album yet") before sinking slowly to the floor in a sodden heap.

In brief, alcohol at least provided the illusion, or perhaps delusion, that in the presence of females we could be something other than the tongue-tied, inarticulate goobers we suspected ourselves to be.

Mixing boys, girls, and alcohol offered some other intriguing possibilities. I first became aware of these when as a sixth-grader I overheard part of a discussion between two high school boys in which one regaled the other with a recent triumph at the Town Dock parking lot, a popular destination for amorous teenagers.

"So she says to me, 'Where are the submarines?' and I say, 'C'mon, Peggy, it's only a figure of speech. Here, have another beer.'"

"And then what happened?" inquired the second boy.

"So, she finishes another can, and before I know it, *wham,* she's all over me. I mean she was hot, really hot!"

"She really wanted it, huh?" asked his companion breathlessly.

"Yeah, she wanted it," replied the first. "She wanted it bad!"

"So what did you do? Did you give it to her?" his friend demanded to know.

Unfortunately, they wandered out of earshot before I got to hear the end of the story, but I knew I had stumbled upon a very important piece of information, a piece of information that would no doubt prove invaluable once I figured out what "it" was.

I knew in all fairness that my experience at Sunday school that morning did not technically qualify me for membership in the demon-rum club because my condition was accidental, resulting merely from an innocent childhood experiment gone awry and not because I set about to render myself senseless via the intemperate use of alcohol. Intent was a key factor in such matters.

My official investiture into this bacchanalian brotherhood had to wait for another eight years when at age of fifteen, Bobby Hammond, Ronnie Shore, and I happened across a mind-boggling bit of scientific trivia while doing research in the library for a science paper.

Hey, listen to this, you guys," I said excitedly and began to read from the book. According to the author, it was not unusual for small wild animals like foxes, skunks, and raccoons to become slightly inebriated after feeding on partially rotten apples. The phenomenon occurred because in the course of decomposing, the fruit released enzymes that resulted in fermentation, which in turn produced some small quantity of alcohol.

The book went on to suggest a science experiment whereby yeast and sugar were added to a bottle of regular store-bought apple cider. Allow the whole mixture to sit and ferment in a cool, dark place for several days and the result would be a bottle of hard cider.

"You mean all this time we actually could be making our own booze?" asked Ronnie incredulously.

"Well, yeah," I responded hesitantly, "according to this we can," although in truth it seemed far too easy to be true.

Later that afternoon the three of us gathered up the necessary ingredients and hightailed it to Ronnie's garage, where we mixed them with the kind of care and finesse usually reserved for handling weapons-grade plutonium. We decided to hide the experiment in a minuscule body of water—a puddle with aspirations really, called Pollywog Pond, which got its name from the fact that it was a favorite breeding ground for frogs and every spring the water was alive with thousands of tadpoles.

When we were small boys, Pollywog Pond was a place of magic and adventure. We fished with poles made of tree branches, string, and a small safety pin. We caught frogs and hid them under our beds in old coffee cans until eventually they expired and began to stink up the house. We built rafts—pirate ships, really, to ferry us from one side of the pond to the other—and on those very hot summer days we'd simply lay on our backs in the shade and watch the ducks glide effortlessly back and forth looking for a handout and dragonflies as they darted over the surface of the water.

The three of us approached the pond and began to make our way around it slowly as Ronnie carefully eyed each of the large rocks that marked the water's edge. Finally, he hopped up onto one that stuck out into the water several feet. After pushing up the sleeve of his jacket he knelt down, leaned out over the edge of the rock, and carefully lowered the bottle into the pond until it rested on the shallow bottom, with the top four inches still poking above the surface. Carefully, he worked the jug down into the muck until it was entirely hidden from view.

"There," he said with obvious satisfaction. "Now all we have to do it wait."

The next three days seemed like an eternity, and I began to suspect that Ice Ages had passed with greater speed, but finally Saturday arrived. As darkness began to descend, we rendezvoused at the pond to retrieve our do-it-yourself chemistry experiment and test the results.

When the moment arrived, we stood by the edge of the pond in the growing darkness of a chilly early-spring night positively giddy with anticipation. In a repeat of our previous visit, Ronnie again pushed up his sleeve and reached into the cold water and groped around for the jug.

"Yuck, this stuff is gross," he said searching around in the muck for our prize.

I began to worry. "Are you sure this is the right spot," I asked?

"Yeah, I'm sure," he replied impatiently, still poking around in the rotted vegetation. "Just keep your pants on and gimme a minute," he said.

I continued to fret. "I mean, in the dark it's hard to tell one rock from the other. How can you be sure it's the same rock?"

Ronnie glanced over his shoulder and looked at me balefully. "Because it's the same rock where I felt up your mother," he responded angrily. Insulting someone's mother was a risky strategy, but considering the pressure we were all under, I decided to let it pass.

"Aha, gotcha," Ronnie blurted out suddenly, lifting the jug of cider from the water in triumph, the bottom half of it covered with black ooze from the pond. "Whew, this stuff really stinks," he added while trying to wash the worst of it off with his other hand.

We quickly made our way to a small group of trees surrounded by a thick growth of evergreen bushes, a spot we referred to simply as The Fort, which got its name back in the days when playing cowboys and Indians was the highlight of our day. We dropped to our knees in a small circle and Ronnie placed the cider jug in the middle. "Go ahead, Einstein, you made it, you open it," he commanded. I pulled the jug toward me, and while holding it firmly with one hand, I gave the cap a tentative twist, but it wouldn't budge. Grasping the jug more firmly, I tried again with a grunt—still nothing. Fearing insults from my friends, I wrapped one arm around the middle of the jug, wiped my right hand on my pants to make sure it was dry, and said, "Here goes" as I gave the metal cap one last mighty twist. I felt it give slightly, then suddenly—*whoosh!*—a geyser of fermented cider shot into the air drenching all three of us—hair, faces, clothes, everything. We were all so surprised, we just sat there motionless, not saying a word. I looked cross-eyed as a drop of cider made its way down the bridge of my nose and stuck out my tongue just in time to catch it as it dripped off the tip. I tasted it cautiously, then licked my lips before announcing, "Hey, this ain't bad."

I lifted the jug to my lips and took several swallows. Both Bobby and Ronnie grabbed for it and after a brief tug-of-war Ronnie jerked it out of Bobby's hands and proceeded to slake his thirst.

"Ah," he said after finally lowering the jug from his mouth and passing it to Bobby. "That is good stuff," he said, pounding me on the back to emphasize his sincerity.

The jug made several more circuits around our small circle until it was almost half empty. We paused to congratulate ourselves once again when Bobby, announcing the need to relieve himself, started to get to his feet only to fall unceremoniously back to the ground in an untidy heap. Both Ronnie and I found this extremely amusing and laughed uncontrollably at his misfortune. Grinning at his own awkwardness, Bobby finally made it up and walked unsteadily to a nearby tree, wrestling with his zipper and muttering the whole way. Ronnie and I applauded enthusiastically at his efforts.

Within a matter of minutes, all three of us began fighting a losing battle with gravity and the simple act of standing up became increasingly difficult without a considerable amount of concentration and effort.

The next thing to abandon us was our ability to speak, as the intricacies of the English language began to slip from our grasp. Finally, ideation itself, the ability to form coherent thoughts and thread them together in some logical fashion also flew the coop, and with it the last vestiges of sobriety. In a word, we were unapologetically, undeniably, unequivocally, and magnificently … drunk.

The question that faces every pilgrim once he or she finally arrives at that long-sought-after destination is—now what? I've spent all this time and effort to get someplace, but what do I do now that I'm here? I can't go somewhere else because, after all, this is where I wanted to be. For Ronnie, Bobby, and me the answer was simple—keep drinking—and so we did until the jug was empty. Little did we know as we polished off those last few tasty drops that events were already conspiring to make this the very least of our problems.

I think I was the first to notice, or at least verbalize the fact, that the earth's rotation was becoming increasingly noticeable and, quite frankly, more than a little bothersome. The sensation was compounded by the fact that my eyes were no longer willing or able to focus on fixed objects; much like in a cartoon, everything appeared in multiple images and all of them swimming in different directions. In desperation, I tried closing my eyes, but this only created the sensation that I was falling down a bottomless black hole. Eventually, my stomach began to rebel at this highly unusual and unfamiliar sensation.

"I don't feel so hot," I mumbled to no one in particular. The only reply was a horrible retching sound that came from a clump of bushes somewhere off to my right in the general direction I'd seen Bobby crawling on his hands and knees moments earlier. The noise suggested that he was attempting to rid himself not only of the contents of his stomach but of most of his internal organs as well. Soon the sound of someone else upchucking came from somewhere off to my left, and there was little for me to do but join my friends in their agony.

It took several hours for the anarchy that gripped me to subside to the point where basic thought processes and motor skills had a fighting chance to regain control of my mind and body. By this time it was well past my curfew and when I arrived home the house was dark and the front door locked. The only way in was to ring the doorbell, which I did. My dad, an imposing figure even in the best of circumstances, opened the door dressed only in his boxer shorts and glared at the bedraggled, vomit-stained excuse of a son who stood on wobbly legs before him. His only words as he opened the screen door to let me pass were, "Christ, you stink." Frankly, I was in no position to argue the point with him, so I just edged my way past him, stumbled my way up the stairs to my room, and was asleep before my head hit the pillow.

In the morning my first thought was that I had died and gone to Hell as the blazing sunlight tried to burn holes through my skull. Every sound was magnified to the point where I was certain I could even hear the cells in my body dividing. My entire body was covered with a hodgepodge of scrapes, scratches, and bruises; my hair looked like a bird's nest of dirt, twigs and leaves; and the inside of my mouth felt like something furry had crawled inside and died. All things considered, Hell probably would have been an improvement.

CHAPTER 10

The Dirtiest Word

Under certain difficult and trying circumstances profanity offers a relief denied even to prayer.

—Mark Twain

"You're fulla shit," was my response to Ritchie Dugan the day he tried to convince me that *fuck* was a dirty word. It couldn't be. It didn't sound even remotely off-color, as did some of the more popular entries in our modest yet ever-growing vocabulary of vulgarisms.

"Fuck, fuck."

Nope, no matter how many times I said it, the word sounded harmless, even silly, and the possibility it had sufficient power to affront seemed remote at best.

When I asked Ritchie what it meant, a sly grin spread slowly across his face, and without a word he formed a crude circle using the thumb and index finger of his left hand, then mysteriously began to piston the index finger of his right hand through the opening. Finally, he raised his eyebrows knowingly and a leer spread across his face, as if this settled the matter once and for all. Rather than risk the appearance of ignorance and in an effort to feign comprehension, I leered knowingly in return.

"Ah," I replied aloud while thinking, what the hell is *that* supposed to mean?

Upon further reflection, I was so sure Ritchie was trying to lure me into one of his infamous pranks, I decided to take the matter up with the one person who had always proven himself peerless in terms of knowing everything worth knowing: my dad. Was this not the man who taught me to ride my first two-wheeled bicycle, an evil-looking black Schwinn Panther? Had he not shown me how to capture invisible radio waves from the air by building a crystal radio set that required no electricity or batteries to operate, only an empty cigar box, a cardboard tube from an empty roll of toilet paper, some wire, and a few diodes? Did he not know how to make a nickel disappear from the palm of his hand only to then magically pull it from my ear? Who else would I approach to assist me at such moments? Fuck, indeed.

Unfortunately, what I didn't realize at the time was that the infallibility and omniscience of grown-ups was at best illusory and that my father, along with every other adult on the planet, was at that very moment growing quietly more dim-witted with each passing day. By the time I reached my early teens, it was quite apparent adults were universally clueless when it came to understanding issues of any consequence. Increasingly, even our most exacting and tightly reasoned arguments were met with senseless parental rejoinders like "Because I said so." Consequently, many kids, myself included, made a solemn pledge that upon entering adulthood, when it was time to shoulder the responsibilities of parenthood ourselves, we would never allow these same gratuitous utterances to pass our lips.

So it came to pass on an otherwise uneventful Sunday evening several days after Ritchie's attempt to broaden my lexicon of contemporary vulgarisms, as the family gather in the living room for a well established ritual known a TV dinner night, that I decided to put an end to the niggling issue regarding the word *fuck* once and for all.

I began to assemble a set of wobbly metal TV tables when Mom entered.

"Who's got the Salisbury steak?" she chirped brightly as she entered the living room with a small hot aluminum tray held firmly in each oven-mitt–clad hand. The tone of her voice made June Cleaver seem downright bitchy by comparison, but this bubbly demeanor was as familiar a part of these evenings as was the unusual presentation of the food itself; and why not? It was one of the few meals Mom had to prepare that did not require any cooking, at least in the traditional sense of the word. The only ingredient was the self-contained meal itself, which was easily identified among the growing number of frozen-food products on the market by its unique container, a box designed to look like the front of a television set complete with faux dials, knobs, and wood-grained cabinetry. Preparation required only a preheated oven, a forty-five-minute wait, and—*voila*—a complete, ready-to-serve dinner, all reasonably priced at around ninety-eight cents per person. No lengthy shopping lists to write, no measuring, pouring, sifting, stirring, or mixing; and perhaps best of all, cleanup was almost nonexistent. Was it any wonder moms everywhere embraced domestic innovations like the frozen TV dinner with such unbridled enthusiasm?

Not that frozen food itself was anything new. As far back as the 1930s, a number of these strange new products had begun to appear on the market, in large measure because a college dropout named Clarence Birdseye successfully parlayed his experience as a U.S. government researcher assigned to the icy wastelands of the Canadian Arctic into a patented method for freezing food in a way that didn't rob it of either its taste or its nutritional value. Anything, including food, was certainly easy enough to freeze if exposed long enough to temperatures below thirty-two degrees Fahrenheit, but it was Birdseye who figured out that the *faster* food was frozen, the better it tasted later on.

Birdseye asked himself, what do Eskimos know about freezing food that others don't? He began experimenting by trying to reproduce conditions similar to those the Eskimos experienced while preserving and storing the whale, seal, walrus, and fish meat that were the mainstay of their diet. Basically, all he needed was an electric fan to create a counterfeit wind chill and some table salt to replicate the briny medium that allows water to remain in a liquid form at temperatures below thirty-two degrees and that was the source of almost everything on the typical Eskimo menu.

If it was edible and not nailed down, Birdseye considered it fair game for his experiments, including, alas, one or two of his son's pet rabbits. Fortunately, given the speed with which rabbits reproduce, the loss was soon forgotten. History is silent on the subject of which other pets of Birdseye's children may have been sacrificed in the name of science.

Serendipitously, it was around the same time, the mid-1920s, that American industry began to discover the wonders of Freon gas, which eventually led to the invention of the refrigerated warehouses, trucks, railroad cars, grocery-store display cases, and, ultimately, home appliances that allowed frozen food products to be processed, transported, and stored. It didn't happen overnight. In fact, another twenty years would pass before these innovations had a significant impact on American eating habits—just in time for the boom in the number of hungry young mouths in need of feeding.

One can only speculate what role, if any, "intelligent design" may have played in these events. Could it be that the nearly simultaneous development of a commercially viable method for freezing and storing food, the invention of the La-Z-Boy recliner, *and* the creation of the first primitive television set was merely scientific Kismet?

What my mom had no way of knowing as she stood on line at the local A&P was that purchases like hers actually represented the leading edge of revolution in the retail food industry, a revolution that eventually helped transform the fabric of the American family not only by changing its eating habits but by changing the customs and rituals that accompanied those eating habits as well.

By 1945 the United States had endured almost fifteen years of privation resulting first from the Depression and then from the rationing of consumer products required as part of the war effort. Following World War II, however, Americans began looking for ways to indulge, even pamper, themselves. Soon mashed potatoes could be made in an "Instant," popcorn in a "Jiffy," and rice in a "Minute." Potato chips would eventually come stacked in cardboard tubes (Pringles); whipped cream would be pre-whipped (Reddi Wip,); orange juice, milk, and soft drinks would be made from powder (Tang, Kool-Aid, Carnation Dry Milk); and cheese came loaded in an aerosol can (Cheez Whiz). There was creamless cream (Coffee-mate), sugarless sugar (Sweet'N Low), baconless bacon (Bac-Os), and butterless butter (I Can't Believe It's Not Butter).

Eventually, these convenience foods became so packed full of additives, preservatives, and extenders that they had a far better chance of surviving a nuclear war than did the people they were designed to feed, which was fine with moms everywhere as long as it meant not having to face another sink full of dirty dishes.

After she placed my dad's Swanson Salisbury steak dinner on the TV table in front of him (he was the only one who dared indulge in what every cafeteria-savvy child in America recognized immediately as that dreaded concoction called "mystery meat"),Mom then turned to me.

"How about the turkey?" she inquired while looking at me knowingly.

C.A. Swanson & Sons had indeed found my soft spot with their mini–Thanksgiving feast complete with sliced turkey floating in a strange brown glutinous substance, a dollop of whipped potatoes, unnaturally green peas, and a bite-size portion of apple cobbler. Little did I know, as I cautiously pulled back the aluminum foil that covered my meal, that it was actually the result of a colossal miscalculation that had left Swanson up to its corporate keister in frozen gobblers in 1953. According to fast-food lore, someone that year had grossly overestimated the demand for frozen Thanksgiving turkeys, a mainstay of the company's product line. Consequently, with the holiday come and gone, the company found itself with 260 tons of unsold frozen fowls on its hands. The surplus birds had to be stored in refrigerated railroad cars and hauled back and forth across the country until somebody could figure out what the hell to do with them.

Enter Gerry Thomas, one of the companies more innovative young salesmen, who, even before the start of Swanson's turkey troubles, had begun toying with a few ideas of his own for a new product line that minimized preparation. A former Marine who ate many a meal while hunkered down in a foxhole, Thomas remembered with distaste how all of the food eventually became mixed together in an unappealing glob at the bottom of his mess kit. During a flight to Pittsburgh, Thomas, so the story goes, found himself strangely fixated on the dinnerware Pam Am used to serve meals, a tray with several compartments that prevented the food from mixing together. A mental light bulb flicked on over Thomas's head. Why not use a similar method for packaging a complete, frozen ready-to-cook meal for the harried housewife? In fact, why not make it a meal in which turkey was the main attraction and kill two birds with one stone, as it were?

Immediately upon arriving back to the home office in Omaha, Nebraska, Thomas pitched the idea to Clarke Swanson, a son of the company's founder. It wasn't an easy sell. Meals were more than a source of nutrition; they were ceremonies that helped cement together the most basic building block of American culture: the family. Tampering with traditional methods of preparing and serving meals probably seemed almost sacrilegious at first, but Swanson went ahead and gave the okay for a relatively small production run of 5,000 meals. The woman hired to supervise preparation of the new product, a transplant from Alabama, chose corn-bread dressing and sweet potatoes as side dishes, thereby giving the meal a distinctive southern flair. Most of the dinners were purchased by the manager of a California-based grocery-store chain not because he was convinced frozen meals were the wave of the future but because he figured his female customers would surely be attracted to the unusual meal trays as a place to store loose household items like buttons, sewing needles, and other odds and ends. Whatever the reason, the company ended up selling 10 million of the prepackaged meals in the first year, for which Thomas received a munificent bonus in the amount of 1,000 dollars in return for his efforts.

As it turned out, the TV dinner spawned its own traditions. For example, at our house the Sunday-evening meal became TV-dinner night and commenced at exactly 7:30 PM in order to coincide with another family mainstay, *Walt Disney Presents*. Indeed, that night I was so lulled by the familiar sound of veteran Disney narrator Winston Hibler advising his audience we were about to embark on yet another Disney True Life

Adventure (this one entitled "The Mysteries of Life") that I forgot about my initial line of inquiry until we were well into both our meal and the show.

"This is an authentic story of nature's secret world, of her strange and intricate designs for survival and her many methods for perpetuating life."

"Dad?" I inquired innocently.

"Uh-huh," he replied offhandedly. By now he had set aside his newspaper and like the rest of us was dividing his attention between the steaming tray in front of him and the fuzzy black-and-white picture across the room.

"The compelling urge to continue the species is nature's greatest secret of success, and in all of her creatures from the largest to the smallest she instills a savage determination to re-create their kind."

Picking up my knife and fork, I continued, "Is *fuck* a dirty word?"

The moment the word passed my lips, time literally stood still, and to this day I'm not quite sure why we were not all flung into space or the universe didn't collapse in on itself.

At first I wasn't even aware anything out of the ordinary had occurred, and in my state of blissful ignorance remained focused on the television image in front of me until I realized that other than for the sonorous voice of the narrator, the living room had become suddenly and eerily silent.

Gone were the familiar background noises—bodies shifting in search of a more comfortable position, clinking silverware, even chewing—that usually accompanied these repasts, a white noise one never really notices until it isn't there. A forkful of potatoes dotted with a few stray peas was halfway through its journey from the tray in front of me to my mouth when I happened to look up and catch a glimpse of my older sister staring back at me, eyes wide, her face frozen in disbelief. Momentarily confused, I tried to understand the meaning behind her obvious consternation until it slowly dawned on me that danger was afoot.

Without moving my head, I allowed my eyes to travel across the room where they landed first on my mother, who stared silently, almost blissfully, down at her TV-dinner tray as though it held the answer to all of life's mysteries, and finally to my dad, the true and final litmus test in terms of judging the severity of my predicament.

The look on Dad's face suggested that in this particular instance the battle was pretty one-sided and gave me some inkling of what Custer may have felt like at the Little Big Horn. Apparently, *fuck* was not just any old dirty word. If I'd read the expression on his face correctly, it was the granddaddy of all dirty words. This was important information for a kid to have at his disposal. The only remaining question was whether or not I would live long enough to make use of it.

Experience taught me that in situations like these, playing dumb was often an effective strategy, something, my sister was always quick to point out, came naturally to me. Although Dad's eyes had not strayed from the TV set and he continued chewing his food without interruption, I knew from past history (the way the muscles in his jaw clenched and unclenched) that he was considering his options and that the next few seconds were crucial to my future, if I even had any.

Then I started blathering.

"On my way home from school last week I heard these two older guys in front of me arguing. They kept saying, um, using that, um, you know, *that* word, and I was sort of like, wondered if, you know, it was bad or something," I stammered in what was perhaps one of the lamest performances of my entire life.

Placing his utensils down neatly on the tray, Dad methodically, almost daintily, daubed the corners of his mouth with his napkin and then rose slowly to his feet, his six-foot three-inch frame looming over the room.

"Come with me, young man," he ordered without so much as a glance in my direction before turning and heading for the kitchen. He didn't even bother to see if I was following him. The "young man" part of his command said it all. Whenever a parent used either a child's full given name or the phrase "young man" or "young woman," it was a surefire indicator that serious trouble was brewing.

I glanced over at my sister again, but it was clear I had no allies in that direction; Mom continued to gaze down silently, leaving me to wonder just what could possibly be on that TV-dinner tray that held her so spellbound. Clearly, my only option was to follow Dad into the kitchen, which I quickly did, collecting my thoughts as I went. As soon as I arrived, Dad pointed silently to a chair in the breakfast nook. I took a seat while he leaned against the counter and slowly lit one of the twenty or thirty Lucky Strike cigarettes he smoked each day. With the cigarette now dangling from corner of his mouth he folded his arms across his wide chest and stared off into space, his face expressionless. It was the total absence of any apparent emotion and his studied casual demeanor that disconcerted me the most, that and the fact that he looked so huge as he stood over me. An angry parent is generally easy to manipulate with the proper combination of remorseful body language, a few rueful sniffles, topped off with heartfelt promises of contrition. But an enigmatic parent is a dangerous parent because one is left with no cues to follow. Consequently, I fell back on a time-honored strategy that is best personified in the paintings of doe-eyed children and puppies by artists like Margaret Keane, whose work gave new meaning to the word *kitsch;* and I waited.

"Tell me again where you heard that word?" Dad asked, his tone turning suddenly stern and dangerous as he stared at me with that familiar smoker's squint. I had to hand it to him. He had me on the ropes, and I wasn't really sure why. I repeated my story about overhearing the two imaginary teenagers arguing while Dad looked on dubiously. When I finished I waited quietly for his reaction, unable to control the tears that were beginning to overflow from the corner of each eye. Parents often find themselves engaged in an internal struggle between the overwhelming desire to kill a fledgling member of the brood and the legal consequences of such an action. Although modest in years, I had enough experience under my belt to recognize that this was one such moment.

The only thing certain right then was the fact that if I survived the encounter, I was going to kick Ritchie Dugan's ass all over the school playground the following day. He should've told me, I mean *really* told me, and not left me with the impression that this was merely one more of the many grade-school fun facts we entertained each other with every day. A fun fact was nothing more than a dramatic bit of fictitious trivia, the source of which was sufficiently vague as to allow no opportunity for contradition. Besides, we *wanted* to believe them. Who wouldn't want to be privy to the knowledge that because of its unusually large dimensions, gangster John Dillinger's prodigious pecker was claimed by the Smithsonian Institute for research purposes or that the sewers of New York City were home to hoards of hungry alligators (or was it crocodiles?) discarded at youth by unthinking tourists returning from Florida. Throughout childhood, boy after boy eagerly lay claim to similar richly inventive tidbits and passed them along to one another, thereby adding a veneer of sophistication to our otherwise hopelessly normal lives. In light of this, how was I supposed to know *fuck* really *was* a dirty word?

After explaining yet a third time the fictitious account of how I became familiar with the word (I had to lie because the truth would've constituted a serious breach of the playground code of honor), Dad finally relented and to my great relief seemed prepared to drop the matter with a stern warning of the horrors awaiting me should the word ever again pass my lips.

As he turned to head back into the living room, I silently exhaled in relief and under normal circumstances would've happily dropped the entire matter, grateful to dodge the bullet of parental disapproval. Unfortunately, curiosity got the better of me.

"Dad?" I asked in my best Beaver Cleaver tone of voice. "What *does* it mean? You know, *fuck*." Despite inquiring with what I hoped was just the right mix of innocence and curiosity, I watched as Dad's body stiffened as though my question had struck him in the back like a harpoon. Again I held my breath, aware that I may have pushed the envelope too far this time. The pause that followed seemed to last forever.

Frankly, a small part of me half expected Dad to turn, grin knowingly, and mimic the hand gesture Ritchie had performed a few days earlier. But he didn't, and when he finally did respond, the answer sent my mind, already a hodgepodge of confused thoughts, reeling in a combination of total disbelief, bewilderment, and curiosity.

"It refers to an act of sexual congress," he said, without bothering to turn around. "But the only thing you need to be concerned about is that I never hear the word come out of your mouth again. Do I make myself clear?"

"Yes, sir," I replied automatically, as if there was an alternative response.

With a heavy sigh, Dad returned to the living room, leaving me to grapple with what I had just heard: "an act of sexual congress."

Having recently studied the American system of government in school, I was well aware of the differences between the judicial, executive, and legislative branches of government, not to mention the bicameral nature of the legislative branch itself. But no one had ever mentioned anything about a *sexual* congress. Who were these people? How were they elected, and by whom; what, exactly, did they do? Never in my wildest imaginings had I even considered such a possibility. It was an issue that had been completely ignored by our civics teachers and suggested serious shortcomings in our overall educational curriculum that needed to be addressed, and soon. Clearly, someone had some explaining to do, and when I got to school the following Monday I fully intended to begin demanding answers.

Fortunately, over the next twelve hours, I reconsidered my position and decided not to pursue the matter further, at least not yet. Obviously, this whole *fuck* business was a minefield where even the tiniest misstep could result in disaster, as my own near miss had just proven. It was an issue that was far trickier that I had anticipated, and it required much more prudence than I had evidenced thus far.

Needless to say, it would be years before I could claim to have even minimally mastered the many intricacies and nuances of this intriguing subject despite the best efforts of people like "Uncle Walt." But this in no way deterred me or my friends from incorporating the utterance into our everyday vocabulary, where it quickly proved itself an amazingly agile communication tool, not merely in terms of its most common usage as an everyday vulgarism but as an attention-getting noun, verb, adverb, adjective, or infinitive as well. Occasionally, it even made a dandy gerund, a fact that would've been even more impressive had we known what a gerund was.

Clearly, I had much to learn, but then, my peers and I continued to amuse ourselves by continually adding to the already rich array of synonyms and euphemisms that accompanied the word *fuck*, confident in the knowledge that by doing so we were adding to our ever-growing level of sophistication and worldliness.

CHAPTER 11

The Cowboy and the Cannibals

It took me several moments to realize that the reason I couldn't move was that I was staked to the ground, spreadeagled beneath the merciless tropical sun, my body battered and bleeding from repeated beatings at the hands of my savage captors.

I remained motionless, hoping the pain-induced fog clouding my brain would lift long enough to allow me to plan my escape.

Suddenly, an unexpected but welcome shadow fell across my face, blocking the harsh sunlight that after three days had rendered me almost blind. Squinting through swollen eyelids, I was fully prepared to find myself staring into the cruel, sneering face of one of my captors. But to my amazement, I found myself gazing up at the stunning visage of Dr. Nathan Bennett's beautiful young research assistant, Jillian, as she knelt down beside me. Before I could utter a word, the woman pressed a finger to her full red lips, warning me to remain silent; and after taking one more look around to make sure we were alone, quickly went to work loosening the tightly knotted ropes that held me prisoner.

It was hard work, and soon the shapely young woman, herself a victim of the merciless sun and days of harsh, inhumane treatment, began to perspire from the effort. Despite our dire circumstances, I found myself mesmerized by one shimmering bead of sweat as it made its way leisurely down the gentle slope of her neck on its journey toward the deep, mysterious valley that divided her full breasts. The unremitting assaults of her tormentors had left the young woman's blouse torn in several strategic locations, allowing me a clear view of the white brassiere beneath. I found it distracting, but not nearly as distracting as when, having successfully untied one hand, Jillian leaned over me to free my other hand, thereby placing both bulging, barely concealed breasts within inches of my face. Squirming slightly in response to a familiar stirring in my groin, I cursed my body silently for betraying me at such an inopportune moment. Fortunately, the curvaceous female now kneeling over me was so absorbed in her task that she failed to notice the growing lump in my pants.

Moments later she pulled my other hand free and held aloft the rope in a gesture of triumph. I had to hand it to her. Even if she was a girl, she had nerve, which along with big bazooms was one of the two things I was beginning to admire most in a female.

Slowly, painfully, Jillian helped me to my feet, and after allowing my head to clear for a moment I began considering ways of escaping the village unseen. We both knew time was running out. In spite myself, I glanced over at the severed head impaled on a long pole only a few feet away; and although a black cloud of blowflies concealed most of the face, I could still see Dr. Bennett's sunken, terror-filled eyes gazing back at me. I knew a similar fate awaited my companion and me if we did not get away from the village quickly.

Our predicament had begun as a simple field investigation designed to determine once and for all if there was any truth to the rumors, folklore mostly, that this isolated string of small South Pacific atolls hid the remnants of a primitive tribe untouched by the ravages of modern civilization.

The trouble began within hours of our being dropped off on a lonely beach by a chartered tramp steamer with enough equipment and provisions to last two weeks. Moments after the ship disappeared over the horizon, our small research party of six found itself under siege by a band of bloodthirsty savages dressed in loincloths, their near-naked bodies decorated with strange markings. Three members of our party were killed immediately by poison-tipped arrows fired from the edge of the forest. I was on my way back from the beach with the last load of supplies when the assault began, and I quickly found myself surrounded and held at bay by several natives whose sharp-pointed spears hovered inches from my bare chest. Damning myself for not keeping at least one weapon with me at all times, I could only watch helplessly as the Professor and Jillian were also taken prisoner.

The next several days were a blur of pain as the three of us were taken back to what we assumed was the main village, which consisted of about fifteen primitive huts made of branches and palm fronds. Built in a circle around a central cooking fire, I could've sworn it was the exact same village featured in the old, well-thumbed copy of *National Geographic* magazine I kept hidden under my mattress at home, safe, or so I hoped, from Mom's prying eyes. Even the half-naked women looked unnervingly familiar, the younger ones' sporting tiny pointed breasts no bigger than those I'd seen on my older sister a few weeks earlier after barging into the bathroom unannounced, while the older women appeared to be sporting sacks of wet sand that dangled halfway to their knees.

There was little time to ponder these coincidences, however, as I soon found myself fighting to remain alive in the face of the ceaseless punishment meted out by my tormentors. I watched helplessly at the similar manner in which Dr. Bennett and Jillian, particularly poor Jillian, were treated. Each time I heard the young woman scream, the sound cut through me like a knife, and I refused to let myself think of what the savages might be doing to her full, soft, shapely body.

Now pausing to collect my strength, I was finally able to stand with considerable help from Jillian, and with one of her arms wrapped firmly around my waist, we silently made our way out of the village and into the hot, steaming jungle. Fortunately, most of the adults spent the afternoon out hunting and fishing or collecting wild nuts and berries. What few members of the tribe remained, a small group made up mostly of old people and small children, dozed off during the hottest part of the day, thus allowing us to sneak away undetected.

As my strength slowly returned, my companion and I quickened our pace in an effort to put as much distance as possible between us and the village before our escape was finally discovered. Considering our much weakened state, I was pleased at how long we were able to keep up our pace, and when we finally did stop to rest, I figured the village was now at least a good two miles behind us. Panting from exertion, I ordered a brief rest and we both dropped to the ground in exhaustion. Almost immediately I began to outline a plan for surviving the next two weeks until the freighter's scheduled return.

"If we keep going in this direction, we should reach the coast pretty soon," I explained to Jillian, as the exhausted young woman stretched out on the thick, cool bed of vegetation that made up the jungle floor. I couldn't keep my eyes from traveling up and down the peaks and valleys of her shapely body.

"There's no beach on the other side of the island, just sheer cliffs, which probably means there are caves we can use to hide out during the day. Once the sun goes down, I don't think our hosts are likely to stray very far from the village. They seem like a pretty superstitious bunch to me," I said with a chuckle.

Although she continued to gaze at me intently, Jillian didn't seem to be listening to a word I was saying. It was almost as though she was in a daze, and I feared the trauma of the past two days might finally be taking their toll.

"Jillian, are feeling okay?" I asked the exquisite creature lying next to me.

With languid ease she rolled onto her side and faced me directly. "I don't think I've ever met a braver thirteen-year-old boy in my entire life," she declared almost dreamily.

I felt my neck and face turn crimson. I cleared my throat and was about to dismiss the compliment when, without warning, Jillian reached over and placed her warm, soft hand gently on my thigh. I froze and the reply caught in my throat.

"Let me ask you something." she said in a hushed, inquisitive tone.

Drawn to the sound of her voice, I glanced at her self-consciously and drank in her beauty. Once again there was that undeniable stirring in my Fruit of the Looms.

"Have you ever seen a woman's breasts?" she asked quietly. "Naked breasts."

The stirring became a surge, and I fumbled for words.

"Well, uh yeah, sure, sort of," I muttered in a failed effort to appear worldly beyond my modest years.

As I spoke Jillian reluctantly slid her hand off my leg and rolled onto her back again while beginning to pluck playfully at one of the few remaining buttons on her tight, tattered blouse. "Would you like to see my naked breasts?" she inquired. The hardening hand puppet between my legs lunged forward, forming a tent that even my two quivering hands couldn't hide.

"Sh-sh-sure," I muttered almost prayerfully, "th-th-that would be s-s-swell," and with a flick of her wrist, Jillian released the uppermost button, leaving me to gape as the deep valley between her breasts widened. Now there were two buttons to go, and she moved her hand down a few inches to begin teasing the next one with her fingers.

"But before I show them to you, you have to promise me one thing," said Jillian.

"A-a-anything," I replied instantly. By now it didn't matter if she asked me to pluck out my eyeballs with a soup ladle. "I swear I'll do anything," I stammered, and I meant it.

This said, Jillian released the next and second to last button and her breasts seemed to grow larger, if such a thing was possible. "I want you to promise you will ..."

"... *Get your butt out of that bed this instant!*"

"Huh?" I shook my head in confusion.

"*Because if you make me late for cheerleading practice one more time, I will kill you with my bare hands!*"

What was Jillian talking about? Cheerleading practice in the middle of a deserted island while being chased by a tribe of vicious man-eating cannibals? Then I realized it wasn't Jillian screaming, but a strange albeit familiar new voice. Dazed, I tried to stay focused on Jillian's long, sensuous fingers as they dallied and teased the third and final button on her blouse.

"Oh God," I thought, "please don't stop now."

Suddenly I realized the belligerent voice intruding on this magical moment belonged to none other than the aforementioned older sibling. How the hell did she get on this island and what in God's name was she screaming about? I wondered. I fought to remain focused on that last remaining button.

"C'mon, do you want to see my breasts or not?" urged Jillian.

"Do you hear me, you little twerp?"

"U-u-uh, yeah," I assured one voice while trying to ignore the other, confused about which was which. But it was too late, and slowly Jillian and the jungle with its oppressive heat and the insistent buzzing of insects began to dissolve before my disbelieving eyes; in its place was the figure of my sister as she stood angrily over my bed, fists planted firmly on each hip, her face scowling. Seeing me blink, she took it as a sign I was awake and turned on her heel to leave.

"Wait," I begged, still in a daze. "Please don't go. I really want to see your naked breasts. You promised," I added, pleading as I spoke.

With that, an inhuman shriek pierced the air as my sister launched herself at me with lightning-quick speed. She was on me in a flash.

"*You pervert!*" she screamed as she began to scratch and pummel me mercilessly, "*you vile, disgusting little pervert!*"

I sensed irritation in her voice.

Her bludgeoning continued unabated for what seemed like an eternity, although gradually her blows began to lose some of their original ferocity. The tirade finally ended with my sister suggesting that any future reference to her anatomy was unwelcome and issued a heartfelt promise to oversee my slow and painful demise should I evidence the slightest bit of interest in the topic ever again. In an effort to emphasize her point, after looking hurriedly around the room for a moment, she darted over to a bookcase that housed some of my most prized possessions. Snatching the Magic 8 Ball off the shelf, she hefted it in her hand once or twice, then drew back and hurled it directly at my head. Fortunately, the missile sailed past its intended target only to score a direct hit on a plastic replica of the U.S.S. *Arizona* I had lovingly and painstakingly constructed during my short-lived interest in model building a few years earlier; and for the second time in history, that noble ship exploded in a shower of unsalvageable pieces, just as its real-life predecessor had done at Pearl Harbor two short decades earlier. Then for the second time in as many minutes, my sister turned on her heel and stormed out of the room, slamming the door in an unnecessary effort to emphasize her discontent.

I sighed. I wasn't entirely sure what had just happened, but I knew it wasn't good. Slowly, painfully, I kicked my way free of the tangled sheets and sat up while rubbing the lingering sleep from my eyes. My heart pounded, but whether it was from the dream or the adrenalin-pumping events that followed I couldn't be sure. As I was about to struggle to my feet, I glanced at the floor between my feet where, to my utter amazement, there was Jillian looking back at me—her blouse still torn pleasantly asunder and with that familiar desperate, pleading look in her eyes—from beneath the pile of dirty clothes I'd haphazardly discarded before going to bed the previous night. Leaning down, I reached for her once more, and it all began to come back to me.

My penis and I were at war. What had begun a few months earlier as a few minor skirmishes and a mild suspicion that this appendage had begun to develop a mind of its own had since turned into outright warfare. The former seemed intent on spending most of the day trying to embarrass me in front of my classmates, while I took every opportunity to strangle it at least once, often twice, and occasionally even three times a night. As I increasingly lost confidence in my ability to control *all* of my extremities, the relationship between us grew increasingly rancorous and I often spent the better part of the evening locked in my room poring over an ever growing collection of illicit books and magazines, including the latest addition to my collection, a pulp paperback book, purloined the previous day from the book rack at the back of Spinelli's Drug Store, entitled *The Lost Tribe of Bongo Bongo Island*, featuring a world-renowned scientist named Dr. Bennett, his curvaceous young female assistant, Jillian, and a brave former World War II PT boat captain, who are unexpectedly attacked, captured, and tortured by a tribe of primitive natives during a research expedition. The story goes on to chronicle how through the extraordinary heroics of the captain, both he and the research assistant manage to remain alive until their eventual rescue several weeks later. It was such an inspiring and uplifting story that it inevitably ended the same way every time. I would doze off, whereupon Jillian immediately exposed her extraordinary breasts to me, which in turn I was free to touch and fondle as I saw fit until I awoke, usually with my face pressed firmly against my pillows and a cold wet spot forming beneath me.

Titillation, that's what puberty was all about, and despite whatever guilt I might have felt about acquiring the book through the aid of what we referred to as the five-finger discount, this was war after all. Expanding our knowledge of female physiology often required craft, guile, and, occasionally, even outright larceny because of an unfortunate paucity of readily available sources to aid us in our unquenchable thirst for knowledge. Indeed, when times got tough, one might even be forced to rely on lurid thoughts of such comic mainstays as Betty and Veronica and even Wonder Woman. If conjuring up a lewd image of what exactly was hiding underneath Annette Funicello's gradually protruding Mickey Mouse Club T-shirt would help, then so be it. Jerking off could be serious business if left unattended for too long, and I had no desire to start laundering my own bed linens or, worse, explaining why I wished to do so.

Frankly, it wasn't just my penis but my entire body that seemed on the verge of a full-scale revolt. Hair was beginning to sprout in places that before now had remained smooth and hairless. In mid-sentence my voice sometimes went in search of a pitch different from the one I happened to be using at the moment. If my personal hygiene was ignored even for a day, my body started giving off a rank odor that I quickly gauged—based on the looks I sometimes got—was evident to others besides me.

These affectations of my body's growing discontent, however, paled in comparison to the melee that my face had suddenly become as each day the image in the mirror greeted me with a fresh eruption of those pustules, sores, and furuncles known collectively as zits.

No, being a teenager was turning out to be far less agreeable than my friends and I had lulled ourselves into believing it would be; as if to emphasize this point, as I again attempted to struggle to my feet, I glanced down once more and was greeted by the sight of my Magic 8 Ball, now lying almost forlornly where it had come to rest at my feet after my sister's failed attempt to use it as a murder weapon. Hoping I might tap into its supernatural properties to guide me through the remainder of the day, I reached out to grab it, but froze when I spied a disquieting message in the tiny viewing window. It was the answer to the very question I had not even asked yet: "Is this day going to get any better?"

"Don't count on it," replied the Magic 8 Ball.

"Shit," was all I could say as I returned to the warm safety of my bed-covers and, hopefully, to Jillian's warm embrace as well.

CHAPTER 12

The Devil You Know

The issue of cultural diversity was never a problem where I grew up, for one very good reason. There wasn't any. As in ghettos everywhere, we thrived on the homogeneity and similitude of our environment and swaddled ourselves in the cozy familiarity of those values and mores offered up by our common ancestry. Consequently, because by and large we shared a similar ethnicity, we had to look hard for differences upon which to experiment with our nascent proclivity for intemperance. After all, what was the benefit of being a patio pioneer if one could not feel at least slightly superior to others, and what better way to do this than by taunting those with religious beliefs other than our own?

My earliest memory of anything approximating a religious slight came at age seven. It was the day after Thanksgiving and I had been dragooned by a visiting grandmother, whose roots went back to Northern Ireland's Protestant community, into aiding and abetting in the preparation of that all-American postholiday favorite, turkey soup. As I pulled the last few stringy bits of meat from the carcass of our once proud bird, I came across a rather odd-looking piece and held it up for closer inspection. As I was about to toss it into the soup pot, Grandma's weathered hand stopped me, saying, "Oh no, the Pope's nose goes in the trash, honey, not in the soup."

"Why not?" I asked curiously.

"Because it's dirty, sweetheart. If a turkey could sit down, this is the part that would hit the ground first," she said, swatting my backside for added emphasis. "Besides, that's where the bird poops," she continued, at which point I eschewed any further investigation into turkey anatomy and quickly tossed the offending appendage into the trash as directed.

"Why is it called the Pope's nose?" I continued while washing my hands vigorously. "That's just what it's called," she answered sweetly and without a hint of malice. "That's just what it's called." Her invective meant little to me, and I filed it away with all the other mental debris a typical seven-year-old boy was apt to collect in the course of a day, never knowing when such trivia might prove useful. Thus began my first faltering steps into religious bigotry.

Perhaps bigotry is too strong a word, because as kids we had yet to become very accomplished in the art of blinkered thinking. It was a partiality based not so much on ardent theological beliefs as it was on the kind of fervor and esprit one generally associates with high school pep rallies. It was a rivalry of homecoming-day proportions.

As a kid, I always felt there was a hint of something sinister, almost cult-like about Catholicism, at least in terms of my admittedly imperfect working knowledge of such matters. A few of my friends opined that Catholics were required to venture forth at night in search of souls to steal from sleeping non-Catholic children. Although I didn't put much stock in these theories (they sounded too much like the plot of a bad vampire movie); there were some issues that left me feeling uneasy.

For example, there was the inescapable fact that Catholics organized themselves in a highly structured quasi-military fashion, starting with the Pope, who was obviously the commander in chief of the whole religion, all the way down through the ranks, including cardinals, bishops, and priests; plus a cadre of noncommissioned officers called nuns and brothers whose job it was to keep the parish rank and file, who were actually referred to as Christ's foot soldiers, on their toes.

More intimidating than this well-ordered hierarchy was the presence of what seemed to be like an elite corps of highly trained specialists called saints. In order to achieve sainthood, it was apparently necessary to succumb to some gruesome form of execution preceded, one prayed, by a lengthy period of the most hideous torture imaginable. Like any normal boy, I never tired of the tales my Catholic friends eagerly passed along regarding the suffering and death of various martyrs, particularly those involving immolation, beheading, hanging, drowning, stoning, disemboweling, and a rich assortment of other more colorful forms of mayhem. Fortunately, Catholic educators never seemed to tire of sharing this rich, uplifting religious heritage with the impressionable young minds of the parish.

Exactly how the martyred operated on a temporal plane was unclear, yet obviously they possessed a wide assortment of practical skills and a knack for using them to solve many an everyday problem. For example, everyone knew about St. Christopher, patron saint of bad drivers, and St Anthony, who was particularly adept at finding misplaced objects like keys and wallets. In my estimation his most impressive feat was helping Bobby Craig's older sister, sixteen-year-old Sarah Jane, find a set of padded inserts for her bra that made her chest look bigger than it actually was. Bobby gleefully related how she tore up the house looking for them before a date one night while appealing to St. Anthony for his divine intercession. Meanwhile, Bobby followed her around, wailing in a high falsetto, "Please, St. Anthony, help me find my tits," thus earning himself the disapprobation of his older sister for weeks afterward.

There appeared to be no shortage of individuals willing to strive for sainthood regardless of the difficulties involved. Consequently, there were saints for just about everything, or so it seemed. There were saints for geographical locations, like the European continent, Poland, and, for all I knew Peoria, Illinois. There were saints for every known job and vocation, including beekeepers, arms merchants, spelunkers, and astronauts. There were even saints for things like diarrhea, stupidity, and flatulence—although hopefully not the same saint for all three. Even sainthood had its limits.

Furthermore, sainthood apparently involved a tremendous workload, and notwithstanding the thousands of saints available, the demand for their services was so great and came from so many quarters that most had to juggle an enormous workload. For example, St. Erasmus provided divine intercession to women in labor, babies with colic, ammunition manufacturers, and seasickness sufferers, while poor St. Anthony of Padua had his hands full with shipwreck survivors, amputees, farm animals, the elderly, mail carriers, and airline stewardesses. The overtime must have been enormous!

There were some sticky theological issues dividing Protestants and Catholics as well. For example, we believed that upon death you could expect to wind up in just one of two places, heaven or hell. Catholics, on the other hand, also believed in limbo and purgatory.

Limbo was by all appearances a kind of celestial nursery where unbaptized babies were sent. Popular theory held that you couldn't send these poor unfortunates to Hell because, after all, it wasn't their fault. It wasn't exactly a bad place, like Hell, but it wasn't Heaven either.

Purgatory, on the other hand, was a bad place, and you went there because you deserved to. In some respects, it was not unlike being sent to detention for committing one too many infractions of the school rules. You weren't necessarily a bad person like a murderer or a Communist, but you had crossed the line enough times to warrant punishment. Furthermore, at school, once you completed writing "I will not make rude noises in class" on the blackboard 250 times, you were free to go. Catholics had a similar arrangement involving the repetition of certain prayers, creeds, and invocations as meted out by a priest during confession. Each repetition was counted toward early dismissal from Purgatory.

Catholics also meddled with the concept of sin by splitting it into two subcategories: mortal and venial.

Mortal sins were the *really* bad stuff that got you sent straight to Hell for all of eternity; do not pass go; do not collect $200.

Venial sins were an altogether different story, if they could be classified as sins at all, like eating a hot dog on a Friday. This seemed ridiculous to me, yet my Catholic friends were banned from doing exactly that because it was said to offend God. Even worse, not only was God offended if you ate a hot dog on Friday, but he was also offended if you even *thought* about eating a hot dog on Friday. In my admittedly puerile estimation, this seemed like a terribly inefficient and counterproductive way to run a religion if the goal was to prevent people from actually engaging in certain acts in the first place. For example, Eddie Zellitto became wholly preoccupied with trying to feel up Beth Cranston only because he was already on the hook for innumerable impure thoughts about her, each a venial sin of its own, not to mention a countless number of impure acts. This led him to the inescapable conclusion that as long as he was destined to spend thousands of years in Purgatory because of her breasts anyway he might as well pass the time accompanied by some pleasant firsthand memories.

This is not to suggest that my own religion was not without its own idiosyncrasies. For example, Sunday school had to be one of the most inane conventions of my entire childhood. At the time, it seemed designed solely for the purpose of robbing us of our hard-won emancipation from the humdrum routines of the regular school week. In retrospect, however, it now seems clear that its purpose was to reaffirm many of the secular beliefs already held in common by our community and that the sacred held only a peripheral role in the entire affair.

Our church adhered strictly to the "Dick and Jane Meet Jesus" model of Christian education, one that relied heavily on stories in which two very precocious young children, a boy and a girl both of obvious Anglo-Saxon ancestry, trekked about a surprisingly verdant biblical countryside with an equally bland and colorless Jesus in search of folks to feed, heal, and, in the most extreme cases, even raise from the dead.

The decor of our classroom was probably typical, with walls decorated with illustrations of Jesus in various poses and circumstances. In one he might be gazing into the distance while tending a flock of sheep, in another hobnobbing with a gathering of children garbed in their gaily colored native dress, and in still another, laying his hands on some poor wretch sorely in need of immediate divine intervention.

One artistic style popular with religious illustrators at the time portrayed Jesus in a variety of contemporary settings, often with a distinct bent toward medical themes. In one, called "The Consultation," Jesus silently peers over the shoulder of a modern-day physician, who is obviously on a house call, itself a minor miracle, as he attends to a sickly, bed-ridden child. In another, called "The Divine Counselor," Jesus appears to be enlightening the same practitioner, this time in the good doctor's office, regarding some arcane diagnostic feature of the illness they have both just observed.

One of my favorites has Jesus seated in a lush garden setting surrounded by three adorable and inquisitive children dressed in the quintessential 1950s short pants and pinafores. A little girl seated in his lap peers quizzically into his outstretched palm and inquires innocently, "What Happened to Your Hand?" as the others look on. Clearly, inquiring minds wanted to know.

Not all these compositions were quite so benign or pastoral, however. One in particular, which used to keep me up nights, portrayed a gigantic, hulking Son of God peering in the upper-floor windows of the United Nations building, keeping a watchful eye, one hoped, on the Communists our parents assured us nested within. It was entitled "Prince of Peace," although I thought it looked more like "Attack of the 50-Foot Jesus."

Also standard fare in most classrooms were upbeat religious slogans like "Jesus loves me, this I know, because the Bible tells me so" and "Because I live, ye shall live also." The entire effect of all this was to make a fairly convincing argument that Jesus was not only Protestant but also in all probability a registered Republican as well.

Classroom instructors for Sunday school came from the ranks of the congregants themselves, and as near as I could tell needed no special training or talent, as evidenced by the fact that my own mother was, for a brief period, lassoed into the job by one of our pastors. About the only thing required was a willingness to give up a perfectly good Sunday morning in order to provide a bit of bland and uninspired spiritual direction to a bunch of overindulged grade-school children—who had even less interest in being there than the teachers themselves—through the unimaginative application of some storytelling and arts-and-crafts activities.

My parents subscribed to the theory that for themselves, semiannual appearances at church, usually at Christmas and Easter, were sufficient. However, they did see the importance of having their children receive a proper Christian education because, as things stood then, we were not likely to get it at home. The only real decision was who was going to pry him or herself out of bed early on a Sunday morning to drop us off and pick us up. We usually walked.

Despite these failings, as far as I was concerned, my Catholic counterparts were being hoodwinked. There seemed to be no conceivable way anyone could keep track of all the dos and don'ts of the Catholic Church. Protestants had a much easier time of it. We went to church each Sunday, dropped the quarter our parents had given us into the collection plate, and listened to a service spoken almost entirely in our native tongue. No one bothered us during the week; there were no uniforms to wear, and we were not required to divulge any embarrassing personal matters to earthly intermediaries. In other words, Protestantism had a much more benign and laissez-faire approach to questions of celestial importance, one that did not weigh down quite so heavily on its youngest adherents.

If my friends and I were troubled by some of the religious idiosyncrasies of our Catholic brethren, there were probably an equal number of qualities that so appealed to us, we often debated how they might be incorporated into our own religious belief system. Chief among these was the delightful practice of not only allowing but also encouraging Catholic boys and girls to purchase their very own pagan babies. Second, there were all those really neat Catholics-only holidays, many of which included being excused from school for the day. And, finally, Catholics had a lot of religious ornaments—rosary beads, statues, pins, medals, and other bric-a-brac—to help them with things like driving and sports. Danny Capio told us that Catholics got all their religious tchotchkes from the same place all neat little trinkets came from: Battle Creek, Michigan.

The city of Battle Creek held a very special place in the hearts and minds of children everywhere second only to Disneyland and perhaps Oz. It's where most of our favorite cereals—Sugar Crisp, Corn Pops, Frosted Flakes, Honey Smacks, and Trix—came from, and along with them all of the breakfast-cereal premiums and giveaways we loved so much.

Becoming the breakfast-cereal capital of the world was not something that just happened overnight. As far back as the mid-nineteenth century,

Battle Creek (it was originally named after a dispute between a group of surveyors and the local native population) was considered something of a wilderness outpost for health nuts, including the Seventh-day Adventist Church, which for religious reasons advocated temperance and vegetarianism. The Adventists even ran their own private sanitarium, which they purchased from the Grahamists, yet another cult of health-food wack jobs, this one run by Sylvester Graham, father of the Graham cracker.

Concerned that a diet composed almost entirely of whole-grain food was somewhat monotonous (albeit nutritious), Dr. John Harvey Kellogg, the first sanitarium director appointed by the Adventists, began experimenting with various whole-grain concoctions of his own. Aiding him was his younger brother, William Keith (W.K.) Kellogg, whom he hired to run the business affairs of the sanitarium even though his only business experience prior to that point was as a salesman for his father's broom company.

Like many great discoveries, their first commercially successful cereal actually resulted from a fluke in the manufacturing process. One of their creations for jazzing up the sanitarium's menu was a granola-type product made by taking cooked wheat, forcing it through rollers, and processing it into long sheets of dough. Although a batch of cooked wheat had already gone stale, for the sake of economy the brothers decided to force it through the rollers anyway. Instead of coming out in long sheets, as it always had, it broke up into thin flakes. The rest, as they say, is history. Patients at the hospital loved it, and the brothers were soon flooded with mail-order requests for the new product from former patients, guests, employees, and friends all over the country. Because Dr. John had no intention of leaving his beloved sanitarium for an activity as frivolous as making cereal, it fell to young William to set up a manufacturing facility called the Battle Creek Toasted Corn Flake Company, where the new product, Corn Flakes, could be made and sold in bulk.

Not satisfied to let the product sell itself, the wily William also decided to boost sales by giving each consumer who bought two packages of his Corn Flakes a free toy. Called "The Funny Jungleland Moving Pictures Book," this first-ever cereal premium featured drawings of several different wild animals formatted in such a way as to allow the body parts of one animal to be superimposed onto the body of another animal. It was an instant hit and marked the birth of a love affair between cereal makers, who distributed thousands of different premiums by the tens of billions, and children.

What patio pioneer did not plunge his or her five-year-old arm deep into a box of sugarcoated something or other and rummage around at the bottom for that elusive cellophane-wrapped prize, whether a decoder ring, a miniature plastic airplane, or a frog man that, when placed in water and filled with baking soda, would alternately sink then float to the top again? Who among us did not, in response to some special offer, eat box after noxious box of some cereal product only so we would finally have enough box tops to send away for a "free" prize that took somewhere between four and six years for delivery and usually broke the first time we tried to actually play with it?

In an interesting postscript, in 1891 a former patient of Dr. Kellogg's sanitarium, disgruntled by the fact that his health had not appreciably improved despite his yearlong stay, opened his own health facility in Battle Creek. Seven years later, in 1898, using the same basic recipe as the one used by the Kellogg brothers, he started producing his own commercial cereal product, called Grape-Nuts. His name was Charles W. Post.

In light of my somewhat dyspeptic view of the Catholic faith and despite the alluring claim it had connecting it to the magical city of Battle Creek, it is easy to understand why I rarely entered a Catholic house of worship of my own volition. This changed unexpectedly one year for reasons that can best be described in two words: Diane Halligan.

When the school year began in the autumn of 1963, the air was filled with promise. President Kennedy, whom Grandma referred to as "that Papist in the White House," had stared down the Russian Bear over the issue of nuclear missiles in Cuba and now dared the nation to reach for the moon by the end of the decade. Just a week before the start of school, a Negro preacher by the name of Martin Luther King, Jr., stirred us with his oratory on the steps of the Lincoln Memorial in Washington, DC. Closer to home, although the Beatles were right around the corner, the hit song "Louie Louie" was making all the headlines because it allegedly contained dirty lyrics; at the movies we sat on the edge of our seats as Tippi Hedren was pecked to pieces by a band of barmy birds; and many of the odd changes that had recently begun affecting the bodies of boys and girls alike, things our parents assured us were miraculous and wonderful but that usually left us feeling mortified, continued unabated.

Diane Halligan joined our school's graduating class of 1968 as a transfer student from somewhere in the Midwest. When she appeared at the door of Mrs. Bingham's homeroom class on the first day of school, with her shining emerald green eyes, freckled complexion, and a head topped with long, tumbling red curls, my heart was immediately set aflame. Girls had always been something of an anathema to me, although recently my self-confidence while in their presence had begun to erode in inverse proportion, it seemed, to their physical development—to the point where Miss Halligan's arrival left me positively slack-jawed.

As Mrs. Bingham introduced Diane to the class and directed her to her seat, I remained enthralled and wholly mesmerized. Although the spelling of our last names all but eliminated the possibility of being seated together—our teachers were strict adherents of alphabetical seating charts—I felt fortunate to have her seated only two rows to my left and one row in front of me. Additionally, her seat was right next to a row of windows overlooking the playground, thereby allowing me to stare at her while feigning interest in what was going on outside. Consequently, instead of looking infatuated, I looked merely inattentive.

I knew almost immediately that my aludium p38 solution, the first of its kind ever created in a high school science lab, was becoming unstable by the popping and fizzing sounds it gave off as it started to boil. Normally, school officials would never have allowed such a dangerous experiment, but my reputation as a bright up-and-comer in the field of chemistry afforded me a certain carte blanche rarely given to students. The entire school was abuzz. When Diane heard about the experiment, she stopped me in front of my locker and begged me to let her assist. I told her it was too dangerous, but she kept insisting and finally, against my better judgment, I capitulated. Now I regretted the decision and was about to order her from the room when a brilliant flash of light blinded me. With no time to think, I threw my body between Diane and the rogue experiment. There was a deafening explosion followed by a stabbing pain in my back, then darkness.

I had no idea how long I had been unconscious. When I came to, I was in a dimly lighted room, aware only that someone was holding my wrist. Opening my eyes, I saw the school nurse standing over me, squinting at her watch as a thin stream of smoke rose from the lit cigarette dangling from her lips. "Pulse is good and strong," she seemed to announce to no one in particular. Then I saw Diane outlined in the doorway behind her. As the nurse moved toward the door, I heard her tell Diane it would be okay to stay, but only for a minute. "He really needs to rest," she said.

Diane moved quietly to the side of my bed and sat down. Gently, she took my hand and brought it to her cheek. It was wet with tears. She'd been crying. I cupped her face with my hand and assured her I was all right. "It's just a few minor flash burns. I'll be fine, really," I said. "I'm just relieved you're safe."

She began to cry softly again and I chided her with a gentle "shhh." She squeezed my hand firmly with both of hers. "You know, the whole school is talking about you, and how brave you were," she said. "Someone even overheard a few of the teachers talking about holding a special assembly in your honor." I brushed aside the idea, saying, "I only did what any man would have done," followed by a slight, involuntary cough. Her face darkened in alarm, but before she could say anything more, the nurse stuck her head in and said, "Time to go, dear." Diane turned her head to the door and nodded, then turned back to me. She took my hand from her cheek and placed it carefully on my chest. "Before I go, I have to tell you something very important," she whispered as the tears welled up in her eyes once more. My eyelids were growing leaden with pain and fatigue. "Tell me," I said groggily as my eyes slowly closed. She leaned closer and I felt her warm breath against my ear as she gently whispered ...

"Catching a little shuteye, are we, son?"

I snapped awake and struggled to get my bearings as Mr. Lawless, our science teacher, berated me for dozing off during another one of his scintillating lectures, this one on mold spores. Most of the class found my discomfort amusing and laughed openly. Only a handful, including Diane, made even the slightest effort to conceal their delight. This made me love her all the more.

Unfortunately, this latest disaster was just another in a weeklong series of embarrassing moments that plagued my every effort to get her attention. Fortunately, science was the last class of the day, and when the dismissal bell finally rang, I was out the door and on the way home like a shot. So disconsolate was my mood, I avoided even the company of my friends. Even the fact that it was Friday and I had two whole days of freedom ahead of me did little to improve my frame of mind.

I spent the rest of the day in desultory pursuit of something to get my mind off the fact that I had once again made a fool of myself in front of the very person I wanted to impress most. Even Mom's tuna-noodle casserole at dinner, a family classic and one of my personal favorites, did little to lift my sagging spirits. After moping around the house for the better part of the evening, I finally allowed myself to be drawn into an evening of family TV, including my favorite show of all, *The Twilight Zone*. Regrettably, on this particular night the episode aired was entitled "The Lonely" and had to do with a convicted murderer exiled to a distant asteroid accompanied by a beautiful female robot with which he would spend the rest of his life. Under normal circumstances this scenario would have easily piqued both my curiosity and my imagination with respect to the robot's anatomical exactitude. Given the nature of his crime, I suspected the unfortunate fellow was fated to spend the remainder of his days in the company of an anatomically incorrect Barbie doll. Unfortunately, because of my self-pitying state at the time, the episode succeeded only in reminding me of my own lack of female companionship, human or otherwise.

My parents looked at me curiously when I excused myself before the show even ended and announced I was headed upstairs for the night. When I got to my room, I threw myself on the bed, laced my fingers behind my head, and stared at the ceiling. What happened next is yet more proof that some of history's greatest decisions are often born of desperation.

Subtlety and restraint were obviously not a winning strategy as far as capturing Diane's heart was concerned. What I needed was something so bold, so daring, that it completely overcame any reservations she might have about me. Suddenly, like St. Paul on the road to Damascus, I was struck with an epiphany of such epic proportions that I knew it must be divinely inspired.

Diane was Catholic, a fact confirmed by my friend Danny, also Catholic, who mentioned how nice she had looked at nine o'clock mass the previous week. Furthermore, as far as I could tell, Diane had no knowledge of my true religious affiliation and for all she knew I might well be Catholic myself. What was to prevent me from simply showing up for the same service and masquerading as a congregant? After all, I was not a total stranger to the Catholic order of worship, having attended one or two masses as a guest. If given the chance, I was certain I could impress her with both my piety and my religious *savoir faire*. The more I thought about it, the more convinced I became that my plan was a winner. She would finally get an opportunity to see me as more than just that uncoordinated, narcoleptic nincompoop from school. Instead, she would see me as I really was: the sober, pious young man she had always dreamed of.

I spent all day Saturday preparing for the perpetuation of this heretical fraud. By mid-morning I was out on my bicycle—a jet black Schwinn Panther tracking down Danny and some of my other Catholic schoolmates for advice and further coaching on the intricacies of the mass. I knew there was nothing intrinsically evil about what I was planning, just as long as I was appropriately respectful and refrained from participating in those parts of the services reserved specifically for honest-to-God, bona fide, card-carrying Catholics. I did, however, want to brush up on some of the details in order to appear wholly comfortable and at ease in Diane's environment.

By mid-afternoon the plan began to gel and most of the details were in place. I would spend the night at Danny's with the understanding that I would attend Catholic services with him the following morning instead of coming all the way across town to my own church. I had my best church clothes with me when I arrived at Danny's house that night after dinner, and before bed I meticulously inspected each and every square centimeter of my chin, cheeks, nose, and forehead in the mirror to be sure I would not awaken in the morning to some unexpected and unsightly facial eruption, an exercise commonly known as zit patrol. I was relieved to find no evidence of any impending embarrassment.

We were up at the crack of dawn the following morning. We walked to the church, arriving half an hour early so Danny, one of two altar boys, could do whatever it was altar boys do before a mass. I wandered up and down the sidewalk in front of the church a few times, and pretty soon people began to arrive. When the amount of traffic grew sufficiently large, I swallowed my growing nervousness, took a deep breath and began the long trek up the dozen or so wide stone steps leading to the high, arched outer doorways of the church. As my friends had directed, I kept my head down so as to avoid even the remotest possibility of direct eye contact with any nuns, particularly those as imposing as the one who appeared now to be standing guard at the top of the steps. They assured me from their own unfortunate experiences that nuns could, through eye contact, lock onto your brain waves and suck the thoughts right out of your head. They were also rumored to be trained to smell fear, and even the frailest and most infirm among them could, when provoked, lash out with lightning-quick speed.

As I reached the top step and drew abreast of her, I felt a strange tingling sensation inside my head. Sensing she was about to question me, I stumbled and pretended to lose my footing. Her hand darted out to steady me as she said, "Careful, my son." Eyes still downcast, I mumbled a quick "Yes, sister, thank you, sister" and hurried inside. I'd made it. My ruse had broken her concentration long enough to let me to slip past her mental probing undetected. As my eyes grew accustomed to the dim light inside, I found myself presented with a new dilemma. Before going any farther, each parishioner paused momentarily in front of a silver bowl of holy water set on a wooden pedestal just outside the entrance to the sanctuary. After dipping a finger into the bowl, they dropped to one knee and made what I recognized from what few football games we'd played against Catholic schools as the sign of the cross. Catholic football teams always gathered in a circle to pray and make the sign of the cross before kickoff as though this automatically added God to the roster. I stood frozen as others edged around me. As a non-Catholic I was under no mandate to perform the same rite, but I wanted to do something appropriately respectful before entering the sanctuary myself. I started to bow at the waist but had second thoughts, fearing I looked too much like a Japanese tourist, and opted instead for a smartly executed three-fingered Boy Scout salute, oblivious to the chuckling behind me.

Entering the hushed interior, I felt like a Montague among the Capulets. After allowing my eyes to adapt to the dim interior lighting, I finally spied Diane and the rest of her family seated about ten rows ahead of me on the left side of the center aisle. Not wishing to make myself too conspicuous, I opted for a pew to the right of the center aisle about two rows in front of her, but well within her visual range. Within a matter of minutes, the pew was filled to capacity, including a rather portly, middle-aged lady smelling vaguely of lavender and mothballs to my right who pressed firmly against me pinning me against the side of the pew. As the service commenced, I did my best to appear familiar with the proceedings. At first I was about half a beat off in terms of the constant standing, sitting, and kneeling, but I quickly picked up the signals from the people around me. Indeed, my only flub came during the recitation of the Lord's Prayer, when I stumbled over the part where the congregation asks God to forgive them their trespasses. In my church we asked to be forgiven our debts. How could I know that among Catholics cutting across someone's lawn was considered more egregious than owing someone money?

As the service wore on, I was lulled by the strange smell of incense and the melodic Latin cadences and actually began to feel confident that I could pull off my charade. At one point, I exchanged an accidental glance with Diane and was delighted to see a light of recognition in her eyes. Was it my imagination or did I see the corners of her mouth turn up slightly in a smile?

The smooth flow of events was interrupted when many of the worshipers began to stand and gather in the center aisle before moving slowly toward the front of the sanctuary. Those who arrived first knelt in a row behind a railing that separated them from the priest, and it was then that I realized they were there to receive Holy Communion, a ritual in which I as a non-Catholic was not invited to participate.

I stood graciously and allowed several members of my pew to join those easing their way slowly down the center aisle for their own turn at the rail when suddenly Diane was at my side. She glanced up at me with a look so serene, so seraphic that I stepped away from my post and began following her slowly toward the rail without giving a moment's thought to the impropriety of what I was about to do. As we approached the rail, Diane eased to her knees in a single fluid motion and I immediately dropped down next to her with all the grace of a sack of potatoes. Emulating her pose, I clasped my hands in front of me, bowed my head, and dropped my eyelids to half-mast, unable and unwilling to let go entirely of the angelic vision next to me.

Every man can look back and recall with great precision the moment at which certain elemental shifts changed the course of his life. For me, one such moment came about fifteen to twenty seconds after the priest placed what my friends called a "wonder wafer" on my outstretched tongue before quickly moving to the next kneeling supplicant, which in this case was my own beloved Diane. So engrossed had I become in watching her tongue protrude from between two soft, pink slightly parted lips waiting for that moment of Eucharistic truth that my own mouth continued to hang open. I quickly recovered and resumed my reverent pose, but not before glancing up at Danny, who stood directly in front of me with a barely concealed look of terror on his face. I closed my eyes in an effort to allow what I imagined would be an overwhelming sense of peace wash over me. Instead, for no discernible reason, I remembered a somewhat gory bit of Catholic trivia involving a process called transubstantiation, a miracle of theological alchemy really, whereby the physical properties of one thing are transformed and take on the actual physical properties of something else. According to Catholic doctrine, the soggy object in my mouth was now a piece of actual human flesh.

Suddenly, I broke into a cold, clammy sweat and, to my horror, felt my stomach lurch and begin a one-way express trip straight up my throat. At this, I slapped a hand over my mouth, jumped to my feet, and ran at breakneck speed back up the center aisle toward the front doors of the church. Most of the people still waiting for a turn at the rail quickly moved out of my way, except for one or two elderly people who were caught flat-footed and sent reeling as I brushed past. Reaching the doors at full speed, I straight-armed one door open and dove for the low wall along the steps just in time to send my breakfast spewing into the bushes. Up came the Frosted Flakes, the blueberry pancakes with maple syrup, and a half dozen link sausages. Then, as I stood there sweating, panting, and drooling vomit on my favorite clip-on tie, the dreaded dry heaves commenced. Although there was nothing left, I continued to wretch painfully for a full minute as though my stomach was trying to locate and dispose of the remnants of every meal I'd eaten in the past week.

I was startled by the touch of a hand on my shoulder. I jerked my head up and found myself looking directly into the eyes of none other than the same nun who had nearly stopped me at the door. In my weakened condition I had but one alternative. Run! Escape! Flee!

Letting out a yelp, I tore away and dashed down the steps. I heard her call after me, but I was like the wind speeding down the sidewalk. Fearing this might slow my pace fractionally, I didn't even bother to look over my shoulder for fear that perhaps some of the myths were true and now a nun turned bat was winging its way after me.

I kept up this breakneck speed until I was almost home, and only then did I allow myself a brief glance over my shoulder, relieved to discover I was not being followed either on the ground or in the air. I gradually slowed my pace until, only a few blocks from the sanctuary of home; I paused to catch my breath. As I stood there bent at the waist, hands resting on my knees, huffing and puffing like an overworked locomotive, I could only imagine the chaotic scene at the church now almost half a mile behind me. Certainly by now the congregation had managed to recover from the shock and were at that very moment organizing a posse to track down the heathen imposter who had so boldly infiltrated their midst and desecrated one of the holiest of rites. Would Danny crack under the strain of the moment and blurt out the entire sordid story? Would Diane, shocked at what might well be interpreted as a repulsive attempt to defile this religious sanctuary, reveal my identity in disgust? I could almost hear the pope's bloodhounds baying in the distance as I quickly made my way home.

My attempt to sneak quietly into the house and up to my room was quickly thwarted by my older sister, who glanced up briefly from her usual perch next to the phone long enough to announce my arrival to the entire household: "*Eew, gross, you smell like puke!*" This was enough to bring my mother running from the kitchen and, after only a momentary glance at my disheveled, vomit-stained appearance; she quickly took charge and hurried me up the stairs, clucking sympathetically at my sorry state. In response to her solicitous inquiries, I said only that I had begun feeling ill during the service and left immediately, only to lose my lunch, breakfast actually, on the way home. My flushed, warm skin convinced Mom I had been "bitten by a bug," a fairly universal diagnosis among mothers in those days. There was no way I could explain what had really happened that morning, although I assumed it was only a matter of time before she found out anyway when an angry mob of Catholics formed in the front yard and began pelting the house with brickbats, howling for my blood.

After brushing my teeth vigorously numerous times to remove the taste of bile from my mouth, and a quick shower, I slid gratefully between the sheets of my freshly made bed. Soon the tension of the past two hours began to drain from my body and was replaced with a numbing fatigue that drew me closer and closer to the edge of sleep.

Whatever I'd ingested, it was enough to keep me in bed the following day as well, and it was not until Tuesday that I was finally able to return to school on legs that did not wobble. I was surprised that none of the expected consequences had yet to befall me, but there was still one consequence, facing Diane, I knew could not be avoided. I could only imagine what she must think of me, and it was with a growing sense of dread that I made my way to school that unusually warm, sunny autumn morning. It came as a relief to learn she was also out sick the previous day.

I was standing at my locker the following day when I felt a light touch on my arm followed by a soft, melodic "Hi." It was Diane, but oddly enough she didn't sound at all angry. "I felt bad for you last Sunday. I heard you were pretty sick," she said. I turned to face her, staring into the absolutely bottomless green pools of her eyes, and prayed with all my might that her hand would rest on my arm forever. "Yeah, my mom said it was some kind of bug or something, but I feel pretty okay now," I mumbled. She lowered her gaze slightly. "I know what you mean, I caught it too, but at least it was after church," she continued with a knowing, sympathetic smile.

I spent the remainder of the day floating on air. We now shared a bit of common history, an experience of sorts. This left us free to exchange a quick salutation or a wave as we passed in the busy halls. We could chat before class. We could walk part of the way home without it being any big deal. She never questioned me about my presence in her church that day, or how it was I came to share the communion rail with her, but I think she may have known. I wish I could report that from these humble beginnings a long, romantic relationship emerged, but this was not the case. I continued to carry a flame for several more months, but, as so often happens the vagaries of teenage life took us in different directions.

CHAPTER 13

"Louie Louie"

I first heard the rumor about "Louie Louie" while wrestling with a dis-obliging combination lock before the last bell signaled the start of fifth-period biology class. The bearer of this sordid little news flash was Randy Katz, who had taken it upon himself to mentor me on all matters pertaining to human sexuality ever since we first met earlier the same year. For example, it was Randy who first taught me the significance of an extended middle finger, but because I found it so difficult to believe this harmless gesture might be construed as a nonverbal equivalent of the F-word, I set about disproving his preposterous assertion by shooting my middle finger out the school-bus window at several passing cars on the way home that afternoon. Imagine my surprise (and delight) when the gesture was greeted with a parade of irate glares, disapproving scowls, and a few drivers who chose simply to respond with an extended middle finger of their own! It was an empowering moment, and from that day on whatever pearls of sexually explicit wisdom Randy chose to toss in my direction I was immediately inclined to believe, including the rumor that the biggest hit song on radio in 1964 was actually an anthem to the puerile longings in every teenage boy in America.

Nobody really knows where urban legends come from or how they begin. Yet somehow these modern-day folktales manage to travel just below the radar until they suddenly explode full-blown into the public consciousness and stubbornly resist any and all efforts to eradicate them. Some never die, as evidenced by those who argue with great conviction that at 5:00 AM on the morning of November 9, 1966, Beatle Paul McCartney (the cute one) was killed in a horrible automobile accident after becoming so distracted by the sight of a comely meter maid, he drove through a busy intersection against the light. Or that a crazy man with a deadly hook on his wrist where a prosthetic device would normally go, once escaped from the (insert the name of your favorite lunatic asylum here) and to this day preys upon lovesick teenage couples he finds parked alone up at (insert the name of your favorite local make-out spot here).

Therefore, it should come as a surprise to no one that an obscure Latin dance number found its way into the annals of pop-music history after becoming the focus of a two-and-a-half-year FBI investigation based on allegations, including many from people who had never even bothered to listen to the song, that the lyrics were rife with obscenities.

Later that same afternoon, after an hour of detention for having arrived late to biology, several of us piled into Randy's bedroom to hear the evidence for ourselves. Not that each of us hadn't already heard it on any number of occasions, but now we were prepared to go about the task scientifically by playing the song repeatedly and at various speeds in order to confirm with our ears that which our imaginations had already willingly accepted. We listened and we listened and we listened while Randy insisted with unflagging certainty that he could hear the lyrics clearly. Whenever someone questioned his interpretation, Randy roughly slid the needle across the record back to a particular spot in order to pinpoint a particular word or verse. It didn't take much for us to join the legion of believers.

The original tune had actually been around since 1956, when a little-known West Coast singer-songwriter by the name of Richard Berry (no relation to Chuck) took a Latin dance tune called "El Loco Cha Cha" and transformed it into the lament of a drunken Jamaican sailor for his sweetheart back home. Depending on which version of the myth you chose to believe, Louie was the name of the bartender to whom the lovesick sailor pours out his heart, hence the title "Louie Louie." Berry recorded his composition with a group called The Pharaohs and released it as the B side of another single in 1957, where it immediately sank into obscurity.

A popular Seattle rock band called The Wailers revived Berry's song in 1961 and reworked it into the kind of rough and unruly tune their fans preferred. This latest version did well regionally but never received the kind of attention necessary to get it on the national music charts. Finally, in 1963 a couple of local bands from the Portland area, The Kingsmen and Paul Revere and the Raiders, each recorded and released their own versions of "Louie Louie" within days of each other. However, serendipity chose The Kingsmen for fame, and their version finally made it to the *Billboard* charts on November 30, 1963, where it shared the spotlight with songs like "Dominque," by The Singing Nun; "There! I've Said It Again," by Bobby Vinton; and "I'm Leaving It Up to You," by Dale & Grace. By December it had become one of the Top 10 songs in America, and then the real fun started.

At first the rumor was merely background noise, a modest hum, as the news was passed from teenager to teenager, school to school, and town to town. At some point in the cycle, a nosy teacher or an eavesdropping parent panicked at the possibility that kids might actually have sex on their minds and decided to join the fray, thereby ensuring that the rumor spread like kudzu in a Mississippi swamp. What makes this drama all the more amusing is the fact that, as anyone who has actually listened to the song can tell you, the only definitive thing one can say about the lyrics is that they are for the most part unintelligible. However, this did not stop a young Frankfort, Indiana, teenager from writing to Governor Mathew Welsh on January 21, 1964, to complain bitterly that the song was obscene. The eager youngster even went so far as to include a copy of the lyrics, which he no doubt gleaned from listening to the tune play repeatedly on the 45-rpm record player in his bedroom.

Although to this day former Governor Welsh argues vociferously that at no time did he try to bully radio stations into eliminating "Louie Louie" from their play lists ("My position with respect to the whole matter was never that the song should be banned. At no time did I ever pressure anybody to take the song off the air"), he does acknowledge contacting the president of the Indiana Broadcaster's Association, a trade group that represented most of the radio and TV stations in the state, and suggesting that "it might be simpler all around if it wasn't played."

Soon elected officials at every level of government began to hear the clamor of outraged constituents half crazed at the notion that their spawn were being exposed to such filth. The matter eventually reached the highest levels of government when one parent became so outraged that he took the matter up with Attorney General Robert Kennedy.

"Who do you turn to when your teenage daughter buys and brings home pornographic and obscene materials being sold along with objects directed and aimed at the teenage market in every City, Village, and Record Shop in this Nation?" sputtered the angry dad.

"My daughter brought home a record of "*LOUIE LOUIE*," and I, after reading that the record had been banned from being played on the air because it was obscene, proceeded to try to decipher the jumble of words. The lyrics are so filthy that I cannot enclose them in this letter," he continued.

"This land of ours is headed for an extreme state of moral degradation what with this record, the biggest hit movies and the sex and violence exploited on T.V. How can we stamp out this menace?" he concluded apoplectically.

Soon what had begun as a modest buzz grew into a cacophonous din to which officialdom could no longer turn a deaf ear. Enter no less a personage than J. Edgar Hoover, who unleashed a spirited thirty-one-month investigation into the matter under the auspices of a law that prohibited the interstate transportation of obscene material.

Hoover's minions ranged far and wide in an effort seemingly designed to investigate anyone and everyone who had ever had anything whatsoever to do with the recording, including the song's composer, Richard Berry, record-company executives, producers, technicians, and members of both The Kingsmen and Paul Revere and the Raiders. In fact, the only person *not* interviewed by the FBI during the course of its leave-no-stoned-unturned investigation was the lead singer for The Kingsmen, Jack Ely, and the man who actually sang the lyrics at the recording session (oops!). The results, according to an internal FBI memorandum: "Because the lyrics of the recording "Louie Louie" could not be definitively determined in the laboratory examination, it was not possible to determine whether this recording was obscene." Score: "Louie Louie" 1; FBI—0.

By the time Hoover's FBI released its report, the entire matter was irrelevant really because the song had already served its purpose. Adults were infuriated by something over which they had absolutely no control; nor could they make an example of those responsible because no one could prove what exactly it was they were responsible for! "Louie Louie" had become a nationwide audio Rorschach test in response to which people—teenagers and grown-ups alike—heard whatever it was they were already predisposed to hear regardless of the actual lyrics themselves.

"Louie Louie" remained on the Top 10 charts for a total of thirteen weeks, although it never reached number one, thereby making it the biggest-selling record ever to fall shy of the top spot. Over the years this simple three-chord progression went on to be re-recorded more than 1,200 times, second only to The Beatles's legendary ballad "Yesterday."

The brouhaha surrounding "Louie Louie" evaporated quickly after February 9, 1964, when The Beatles made their first live appearance on American television. From that moment on, not only The Kingsmen but every other popular band found it astonishingly difficult to compete against the Fab Four for attention. Indeed, only the instantly forgettable "Jolly Green Giant" ever got the group anywhere near the *Billboard* charts again, albeit briefly, and then they faded into obscurity altogether.

CHAPTER 14

Chrome on the Range

Second only to the circular imprint of a condom tucked away in his wallet, a set of keys to the family car was perhaps the single most important talisman any teenage boy could hope to possess because it was incontrovertible proof he had finally arrived on the cusp of adulthood. The former spoke of prowess, masculinity, and boundless (albeit misplaced) optimism, while the latter represented independence, maturity, and mobility. Access to the family car allowed us to leapfrog ahead of our peers to a position of prominence, even celebrity, while at the same time offering a portable venue for our busy social lives.

Most grown-ups seemed oddly cool to the notion of placing a teenager, someone who in terms of age was barely into double digits, in control of several tons of glass and steel capable of speeds in excess of 100 miles per hour. It was yet another one of the ubiquitous mixed messages that shadowed us throughout our adolescence. For example, everywhere we turned, cigarette smoking was extolled as a practice that was stylish, wholesome, and agreeable, yet these benefits were denied to us solely by virtue of our tender years. The same held true of our interest in imbibing strong drink. By all accounts alcohol rendered the user both clever and sophisticated, but again we were denied its benefits until we were at least eighteen years of age, at which time we would be far too old and decrepit to enjoy it, or so we were convinced.

To soften the blow, educators, parents, and a variety of civic-minded busybodies conspired in designing a preparatory program with one of two goals in mind. The first relied on a heavy-handed dose of negative rein-forcement regarding the heretofore unknown perils of motor-vehicle oper-ation to the point at which novices were literally frightened out of any further aspirations they might harbor of ever operating any vehicle more powerful than a tricycle. This was achieved through the production of a series of so called educational films, which when considered as a genre, can best be described as the barf-bag school of cinematography.

My Driver's Education instructor was Mr. MacBrady, a sour, gravelly voiced old fart in his late fifties or early sixties, who taught remedial alge-bra and at his own request was assigned permanent duty as detention-hall monitor. Mr. Chips he was not. Moreover, prior to joining the educa-tional establishment, Mr. MacBrady had been employed as a highway patrolman for the state of New Jersey, and his enthusiasm for regaling his young charges with various tales of motorized carnage never flagged. Occa-sionally, the warm embrace of nostalgia became so strong while he recalled for us the details of some particularly gory incident of highway mayhem that one could almost imagine his eyes misting over at the memory.

Mr. MacBrady was nothing if not consistent and began each new semester by screening what was perhaps the best-known Driver's Educa-tion film ever produced, an award-winning classic called *Mechanized Death*. As the film spooled noisily through the sprockets of an antediluvian 16mm projector, the class joined together in a countdown to the film's beginning as the numbers (… 7, 6, 5, 4, 3, 2, 1) flashed across a pull-down screen at the front of the darkened classroom. A card-carrying dweeb from the audio-visual lab, armed only with a shirt pocket full of pens encased in his trusty plastic pocket protector, invariably remained on duty at all times to tenderly nurse the ancient equipment along.

Suddenly the screen exploded with the sights and sounds of screeching tires, crumpled automobiles, and crushed and mangled bodies, and the class collectively held its breath as we began a half-hour roller-coaster ride of automotive butchery. There was no plot or story line to distract the viewer—just scene after gory scene of blood and guts. Production techniques were primitive. The film was little more than a collection of actual accident scenes collected from amateurs who happened to be in the right place—a family crushed by a truck, a mother killed in a head-on collision, a girl hurled through a car windshield as though fired from a cannon after the car she was riding in collided with a speeding train—at the right time. An equally gruesome sound track made up mostly of noises accident victims make while in the final throes of an agonizing death added to the film's stark reality. The only thing holding the entire composition together was the eerily bland voice of a narrator who seemed to pride himself on both his lackluster tone and his attempts to turn a clever phrase ("Speed is a relative matter. How will your relatives feel if you speed and kill?") as the audience absorbed scenes of bodies that had been mangled, burned, and beheaded. I found myself astonished by the possibility certain people actually made a living by mounting a police scanner in their car and rushing to capture firsthand the undiluted sights and sounds of some hideous automobile accident, preferably one rife with opportunities for the careful vivisection of a freshly decapitated human head or any other forms of the macabre.

Within the first minute, we lost most of our female classmates as they charged out the door looking pasty and sick. Although some held on slightly longer, the boys didn't fare much better, and halfway through the thirty-minute gore fest, the viewing audience was down to five hard-core holdouts, including myself, and even I was becoming queasy as scene after bloody scene unfolded before me. By the time the film finally ended and the glare of the projector's bulb lit up the now bare screen like the high beams of an oncoming car, my shirt was wringing wet with sweat and my stomach rose and fell with indecision. So, this was education?

Although popular—*Mechanized Death* won numerous awards from civic groups and police organizations—it was hardly one of a kind, as nonprofit production companies like the Highway Safety Foundation began to crank out a host of similar titles, such as *Highways of Agony, The Last Prom, and Wheels of Tragedy,* all based on the same basic theme: Put behind the wheel of a car, a teenager will be transformed into a maniacal, thrill-seeking sociopath who leaves the nation's highways slippery with the blood and viscera of a thousand hapless victims. Although touted as cautionary tales for teens, these films were little more than a showcase for car wrecks that left the human body mangled, tangled, toasted, roasted, and eviscerated as a result of the homicidal driving habits of the typical American teenager.

Unfortunately, in their zeal to place blame for the skyrocketing number of highway accidents in America on teenagers, do-gooders ignored the fact that the number of cars on the road burgeoned in postwar America as industry began to retool itself in order to meet the unheralded demand for consumer products. Chief among these was the automobile, and the freedom, independence, and financial success it represented.

On February 9, 1942, the last automobile rolled off the assembly line as Detroit turned its full attention to producing the millions of tanks, jeeps, airplanes, and other armament that were the backbone of what Franklin Roosevelt dubbed "the great arsenal of democracy." Back then a car could be had for as little as $800, with gas prices hovering at an eye-popping eighteen to twenty cents per gallon.

Nearly four years later, the War Production Board announced that with the Axis nearing defeat, private industry could resume limited production of consumer automobiles on July 1, 1945, which it did with a vengeance as companies like Buick, Chevrolet, Nash, Oldsmobile, and others began vying for a seemingly insatiable market. Throughout the latter half of the 1940s and well into the '50s, automobile design clearly reflected many of the same design elements that became so familiar during the war years; new models increasingly began to sprout features like tail fins, mini-wings, grilles, protruding taillights, and low-slung, aerodynamic profiles that made cars appear as if they wanted to take flight. It was also a time when Detroit fell in love with the use of chrome, resulting in monstrosities like the 1957 Chrysler Imperial and the 1959 Cadillac, both of which came to represent the useless excesses and ultra kitsch of automobiles from that era.

These were heady days for automobile executives and designers, as appearance all but smothered issues of substance and safety. This led in turn to the breakthrough concept often credited to automobile designer Harley Earl of dynamic obsolescence, which simply allowed the industry to create more and more demand for cars by implementing modest changes in design each year that encouraged buyers to "move up" to a newer model of car. Consequently, automobile makers created cars each year that were considered new because they incorporated some slight change in design. This is turn fueled the desires of consumers who wanted to own a car that was the newest, up to date of its kind. No longer did you merely buy a Plymouth, you purchased the '49 Plymouth. Three years later, while others were tooling about in their new '52 Plymouths, you brazenly announced to the world you were driving a car that, model-wise, was already a dinosaur regardless of how few miles it had been driven or the paucity of engineering changes that may have been incorporated in the newer models. Suddenly, cars were viewed as either new or old and the pressure was on to maintain appropriate appearances, appearances that were consistent with the growing ethos of crabgrass culture.

Increasingly, popular American culture seemed to center around the automobile. Nowhere was this more clearly evidenced than in the entertainment industry, with the rise of the drive-in movie theater. Growing up, we had always gone to the movies. Almost every place I can remember usually had a huge, gaudy theater located right in the middle of town—a throwback to the 1930s, when movies were the favored form of escapist entertainment for the jobless American. Ours still had a huge organ located up near the stage where audiences from an earlier age were entertained during special events like giveaway night or between attractions.

In the 1950s, for less than a dollar a kid could waste an entire Saturday afternoon (on Saturday, movie theaters were always turned over to the hoards of children) watching back-to-back classics starring unforgettable actors like Francis the Talking Mule (*Francis Joins the Navy*), Abbott and Costello (*Abbott and Costello Meet the Mummy*), and even those three lovable lunkheads, Moe, Larry, and Curly (*The Three Stooges Meet Hercules*).

The savviest kids often found strategies that would save them the cost of buying a ticket. This usually involved sending someone in legitimately who then created a diversion that kept the flashlight-wielding theater

Nazis busy long enough to prop open an emergency exit and thus allow dozens of other ticketless patrons to slip in unnoticed. The savings were then used to purchase an additional box of candy (movie-theater candy always came in packages the size of which seemed to indicate an imminent severe food shortage), which could in turn be used to 1) defend ourselves when candy wars inevitably broke out about halfway through the afternoon, 2) start a candy war of our own, or 3) express our editorial discontent for whatever feature happened to be lighting up the screen at the moment.

Although, sadly, drive-in theaters changed all this, they did create a whole new set of cultural phenomena.

Drive-in theaters were hardly new to the 1950s. In fact, the idea of showing films outdoors, where patrons didn't even have to leave their cars, went as far back as 1932, when Richard Hollingshead of Camden, New Jersey, first hung a sheet from his garage, fired up a 16mm projector, and invited a few neighbors to drive over for a movie. This system worked fine as long as no one parked in front of you and blocked your view, which of course happened and which led Hollingshead to invent and patent the idea of utilizing an inclined ramp. He opened what is now considered the first official drive-in theater in 1932 in an open field with room for 400 cars, all pointed slightly downward toward the side of a barn painted white, which served as a screen for the occasion.

To the dismay of neighbors living nearby, the sound system consisted of a single loudspeaker, which could be heard for miles on a quiet summer's eve. This, in turn, led to the development of individual speakers mounted on posts at each parking place, speakers that could be removed from the post and hung from the car window itself, thus relieving local neighbors of the noise. Unfortunately, this did create other problems, since not all moviegoers remembered to remove the speakers before leaving the theater lot and many returned home with the speaker still firmly affixed to the window, its wires dangling limply behind. More than one teenager took it upon himself to begin collecting drive-in speakers as a sign of daring and prowess. This came to an end when many drive-in theaters began broadcasting sound tracks at low frequency so patrons had only to turn on the car radio in order to listen to the movie.

Although first created in the 1930s, the drive in movie theater was clearly a creature of the '50s, and the number of theaters grew from less than a thousand in 1948 to well over 5,000 by 1958.

One of the largest and most notorious—a twenty-eight-acre behemoth with space for 2,500 cars, an air-conditioned (and heated) indoor viewing area for another 1,200 patrons, a full-size restaurant, a cafeteria, a Laundromat, and a playground—was located in the town of Copiague, Long Island, not far from where I lived. It even had a shuttle to transport patrons to different areas of the huge site. The emporium usually opened its gates several hours before sundown (daylight savings time was a problem for the industry as a whole) so that patrons had plenty of time to eat, play, or even do their laundry before the first feature began.

Not surprisingly, many bluenoses saw the drive-in not as just a family-friendly entertainment venue but also as a place where lust-filled teens could gather, thus earning them the name "passion pits" for many. This was not an entirely undeserved appellation. Occasionally, as penance for one sin or another, Felix Lauer's older brother, Eddie, was required by his parents to allow us to tag along on one of his dates to the drive-in with his girlfriend, Sarah Jane Craig. Under pain of death, we were advised by Eddie that once we got into the drive-in (How many ten-year-old boys can you fit in the trunk of a Chevy sedan?), we were expected to make ourselves scarce, even invisible if possible, until it was time to return home. Invariably, our lack of interest in watching the show from the playground or some other far-off location led us to different pursuits. The most popular was to split up into pairs and sneak up silently to those cars containing only teenage couples, which indicated something more interesting than anything we would see in Mrs. Rafferty's Family Life class was likely to take place, something that would further our education into boy-girl relationships.

Along with changing our entertainment and other habits, cars were also responsible for the ever-increasing network of roadways that began to cover more and more of America in concrete. As a nation, we have always had a love affair with the road, from the infamous Route 66 to the first real roadway that ran from coast to coast: the Lincoln Highway, which ran from midtown Manhattan to San Francisco, passing through the states of New Jersey, Pennsylvania, West Virginia, Ohio, Indiana, Illinois, Iowa, Nebraska, Wyoming, Utah, and Nevada as it went.

These paled, however, in comparison to the granddaddy of all road projects, the Interstate Highway System.

The original idea went back as far as the 1930s, when President Roosevelt conceived it as a way of putting millions of Americans back to work at the height of the Depression. Military leaders were also keen on the idea because they knew the importance of quickly moving men and material around the country in wartime. General Eisenhower was particularly impressed with the speed and efficiency of Germany's autobahns in allowing that country to rearm in the years leading up to World War II. He saw this as a federal priority, not something that should be left to individual states to decide. When he became president, he signed the Federal Aid Highway Act of 1956 into law from his hospital bed in Bethesda, Maryland, while recovering from a heart attack. As it was originally intended, the law envisioned a network of 41,000 miles of four-lane highways with no crossings for either other roads or railway lines. Few realize that this law was considered a military expenditure and the road system itself part of a national-defense system in case of war.

Because of its miles of beaches, Long Island had long been considered one of New York City's major playgrounds, along with places like Coney Island in Brooklyn and Orchard Beach in the Bronx. Suburbanites, the new pioneers of Long Island, along with millions of city dwellers, swarmed Long Island's beaches, especially the most endearing and successful of them all: Jones Beach, the creation of megabuilder Robert Moses.

To ensure easy access by automobile to his recreational jewel, Moses also built a series of four-lane concrete ribbons—the Southern State Parkway, Northern State Parkway, Meadowbrook Parkway, and Wantaugh Parkway—to carry automobile traffic to and from what was fast becoming one of the most popular destinations in the region.

But suburbia in general and Long Island in particular had become a haven for private automobiles. Public transportation was almost nonexistent, and for every postwar house built, a carport or garage was also built to house the family car. Almost simultaneously the one-car family was became thing of the past as families quickly found the need for two and even three cars to meet their growing needs. Existing roadways were soon overwhelmed and once again Moses stepped in to save the day by proposing a six-lane ribbon of concrete stretching from the Midtown Tunnel and running eighty-one miles east to the town of Riverhead, Long Island. Known as the Long Island Expressway, its official designation was Interstate 495, which made it part of the nationwide system of highways proposed by Eisenhower.

Moses had hoped to complete the project by 1958, but by 1957 the highway had only reached the Queens, New York town of Bayside. As it made its way ever eastward, the LIE, as it was known locally, finally made it to the village of Roslyn Heights by 1958, and the border between Nassau and Suffolk counties by 1962. It was 1972 before the roadway finally reached Riverhead.

Although it was originally greeted warmly, it soon became clear that the LIE was not the end of Long Island's traffic woes, as the number of cars soon outstripped even the ability of this new, super highway, to carry the load. It wasn't long before the LIE became referred to by many as "the world's biggest parking lot."

The project created other problems as well. More than 10,000 homes were demolished. Towns and villages were literally cut in half as new school, fire, and water districts had to be created. The impact on real estate was enormous as land prices went through the roof, housing tracts seemed to spring up overnight, and industrial parks increasingly dotted the landscape. Gone were the days of falling gently to sleep to the sound of bullfrogs and crickets. Now they were drowned out by the constant drone of traffic interrupted by the occasional honk of a distant diesel horn.

True patio pioneers gave little thought to these now weighty matters. Nor did we evidence much patience for short-lived design fads, although we were outspoken in our efforts to lobby our parents for whatever the latest in planned obsolescence had to offer. I was particularly smitten with the futuristic push-button "power flight" automatic transmission that first appeared in 1957 compliments of Plymouth/Chrysler and openly coveted examples of the many shamelessly gaudy forms of transport as they cruised slowly and self-consciously up and down the main streets of the ever-growing number of towns that dotted the suburban landscape. Alas, we knew in our hearts that the only car our parents would ever buy was that ubiquitous and utilitarian workhorse of the Crabgrass Frontier—the family station wagon.

Station wagons were the cargo ships and barges of the increasing number of concrete rivers—local streets, freeways, expressways, and parkways—that festooned the American suburb.

The earliest iteration of what would eventually become the familiar boxy family station wagon was created in the early 1920s and usually referred to as "depot hacks," or just "hacks," because they were used mainly to haul passengers and the mountains of baggage required for a lengthy train trip. Commercial aviation was still in its infancy, and it would be decades before steel rails were no longer the preferred method of getting from destination to destination and the public began traveling by air.

The fact that these early models were little more than wooden boxes mounted atop a regular automobile chassis, thereby allowing them to carry both passengers as well as large amounts of luggage, earned them the moniker "woodies," a name that stuck even decades after the wood bodies had been replaced with steel.

Plymouth introduced the-all steel "Suburban" in 1949, and the American love affair with the station wagon really began. Automakers began to realize that despite the fancy styling of the more traditional models, American families were growing in size at an alarming rate, and along with it the need for family-friendly transportation. There were dozens of bags of groceries for Mom to bring home each week. Dad had to make his weekly trip to the local hardware store for grass seed, fertilizer, and gardening implements. Someone had to haul the local Little League team from game to game; and Scout troops were constantly in motion.

Obviously, the best seat was in those station wagons that thoughtfully included an extra foldaway seat that faced the rear window, thereby providing endless opportunities for trying to provoke the driver of the car behind you with either funny faces or newly learned obscene hand gestures.

Furthermore, it was an unspoken rule that should your family happen to own one of these ugly behemoths, it had to be given a name like The White Whale, The Green Flash, or The Red Rocket, something that captured what we viewed as the total absence of anything even remotely approaching what we would consider cool.

Regardless of what type of car a family owned, the goal of every teenager was to eventually be allowed the privilege of driving it unsupervised, and that's what Driver's Education courses attempted to either facilitate or discourage, depending on your point of view.

When not engaged in watching the celluloid butchery that made up much of the class curriculum, we spent hour upon mind-numbing hour attempting to memorize the excruciatingly boring details contained in the "New York State Driver's Manual," which included everything from proper hand signals—a meaningless throwback to the days before cars even had turn signals or brake lights—to the differences between the various and sundry lines—solid white, broken white, double solid yellow, broken double yellow—that were used to divide the streets and highways of America. This was made even more burdensome by Mr. MacBrady's reliance on that most despised of all educational strategies: the pop quiz, which was allegedly designed to test our ability to absorb the endless minutiae our state required to regulate our driving habits.

Although these unexpected written inquiries were usually easy—Mr. MacBrady was not exactly known as a mental giant—even the brightest among us were occasionally tripped up by a seemingly simple question like "What's the difference between a flashing yellow light and a flashing red light?" I proffered the most obvious answer, which was "the color." Yet despite the obvious truthfulness of my response, it was marked as incorrect, thus proving that the most obvious answer is not always the correct answer.

However, my *faux pas* paled in comparison to some of those our instructor so gleefully shared with the entire class. In this way I learned many important lessons, such as: When driving in inclement weather, the first thing a driver should do is turn on the headlights and windshield wipers and not, as one classmate suggested, roll up the windows.

Similarly, I learned that if four cars approach an uncontrolled intersection at the same time, the driver with the fastest car is not necessarily the one with the right of way; nor are primping one's hair and waving "hi" necessarily the most important things to do when passing or being passed by another vehicle, particularly if the other driver is a good looking member of the opposite sex.

Eventually, the semester began to draw to a close as we viewed the last gory film, endured the last boring lecture, memorized the last bit of regulatory minutiae, took our last pop quiz, and drove one final circuit around the ersatz streets of Anytown, USA—the name given to the make-believe streets of the practice area set up in the far corner of the teachers' parking lot and easily recognized by the orange cones used to outline the routes we were to follow. When all of the aforementioned was completed, it came time for the magical moment when Mr. MacBrady handed us the keys to one of the three cars in our driver's-education fleet (as Mr. MacBrady called it), each with a large sign on the roof warning others on the road that we were hardly veterans (CAUTION: STUDENT DRIVER AT THE WHEEL) and an advertisement for whatever local dealership had so kindly donated the aging vehicles we used. Now it was time for the big leagues. It was the moment of truth when we got to show our stuff.

Cautiously, we would navigate the local streets of our hometown, the same streets we had been walking and riding our bikes for years, only now we were *driving*.

Sitting behind the wheel for the first time, each of us would take a moment to soak up the ambience of the moment while carefully reviewing each of the initial steps Mr. MacBrady would expect from us.

Hands in the ten o'clock and two o'clock positions?

Check.

All mirrors adjusted to allow for maximum visibility?

Check.

A quick look over each shoulder to ensure no one was standing nearby? Check.

"Well," asked Mr. MacBrady in his most sarcastic tone. "Do you plan on starting the car anytime in the next day or two or are we just going to sit here in the parking lot?"

I'd become so absorbed in making sure Mr. MacBrady saw me covering all the basics that I forgot the most important step of all—starting the car.

Giggles emanated from the backseat but ceased the minute the car roared to life and my fellow students, now much more humble and meek, realized that their fate rested in how well I had mastered all we had been taught the previous eight weeks and whatever eye-hand coordination I might possess. Mr. MacBrady's ability to intervene in an emergency was limited to only two controls—a brake pedal and a button we referred to as the "kill" switch, which when pressed simply killed the engine. Mr. MacBrady occasionally used it to test our mettle in the event the car stalled either at his hand or of its own volition.

He'd used the switch on me only once, and that was to stall the car as I made our way up a steep, twisting hill. It was not his wisest decision. After braking to a stop and putting the car in neutral, I went to restart the car, but the moment I moved my foot from the brake to the accelerator, the car shot backward down the hill. I froze and only Mr. MacBrady's quick use of his own brake pedal prevented us from slamming trunk first into a nearby tree. I had forgotten to put the car in park before restarting the engine.

Notwithstanding the fright it put into all of us, my little memory lapse palled in comparison to the stunt of a fellow student who somehow managed to enter the crowded and dangerous Long Island Expressway *headed in the wrong direction*. Fortunately, New Yorkers tend to consider such shenanigans typical of the local driving public and we were able to recover with a minimum of honking and swerving. The incident did require a stop at one student's house on the way back to school for a change of underwear, however; and the local school board passed a rule that limited all future driving only to local streets.

A few months later, upon reaching seventeen years of age, I finally earned that most coveted of prizes, my own driver's license. Borrowing the keys to the family wagon, I quickly fired up the engine, backed out into the street (without bothering to check the rearview mirror). Pausing a moment to turn on the radio, I placed my left arm along the edge of the open driver's-side window and my right hand on the twelve o'clock position of the steering wheel, and drove off into adulthood.

CHAPTER 15

Boy Meets Girl

Q: What can you do if your date's family clutters up the living room and you haven't enough money to take her out somewhere?

A: Grin and bear it and hope that your date's head works as well as her dimples. Almost any home has a date space, if somebody will find it and fix it. An unused attic or basement room can be transformed with a paint brush, needle and thread, and inexpensive materials. The dining room may not exactly be cozy, but a Victrola or radio can warm up the atmosphere considerably. And what's wrong with the kitchen? Cookie and fudge making aren't exciting, but they're better than spending the evening with the family. It's a girl's responsibility to make her home "datable," and any girl who shrugs off this responsibility is missing a sure road to popularity.

(Dating advice for girls, circa 1955)

Once upon a time, a finely choreographed social ballet existed between adolescent boys and girls, the intent of which was to thrust two very emotionally insecure, physically awkward, and socially inept youngsters together for the alleged purpose of having fun. These attempts at social suicide were called dates, and although dating served many important purposes, it was first and foremost designed to leave the participants feeling generally humiliated, uncomfortable, and socially clumsy. In this respect most of my dates were a huge success.

The only thing worse than dating was not dating. Datelessness placed us squarely outside the social mainstream, the last place any teenager wanted to be, and raised embarrassing questions about our standing within the social hierarchy. Consequently, regardless of how miserable it made us, we dated anyway. Some of my friends called it defensive dating.

For boys, the motivation to date was heightened by the fact that it was the only route available for achieving some degree of physical intimacy with a member of the opposite sex. The concept of voluntary physical contact with girls was relatively new and began right around the time most of us entered junior high school. Previously, our only interest in being around a girl was limited to whatever opportunities it presented for grossing her out with a dead bug or some bodily fluid, although being in close proximity to girls at that age was not without danger given the inherent possibility of catching that most dreaded of all childhood maladies—cooties.

When and where this began to change is difficult to pinpoint. I first noticed the transformation as it affected my sixth-grade daydreams. Although still favoring fantasies in which I brought down widespread carnage on an assortment of evildoers—pirates, Japs, Commies, you name it—at some point a new character appeared quite involuntarily in the form of a mysterious, winsome female. While these idle musings once focused entirely on the adventurous nature of my encounters, a subplot evolved in which the alluring and enigmatic young lady increasingly sought my assistance in rescuing her from the human vermin with whom I was doing battle. Eventually, the story line shifted from one centered on my physical prowess against formidable odds to the favorable impression this prowess made on the young lady herself. Furthermore, not only did the enigmatic young woman continue to physically mature with each new encounter, somehow her clothing mysteriously became increasingly disheveled to the point where it often became necessary to protect her modesty with my own coat or shirt. As time passed and my imagination grew bolder, however, I found the need to cover her nakedness less and less important. Although this involuntary evolution of my recreational musings left me puzzled, the feelings were not entirely unpleasant.

This growing awareness eventually led directly to a burgeoning consciousness of breasts, which overnight began to demand a disproportionate amount of my mental energy. There are experts and even a few feminists who hold that the female breast is little more than a gland, merely deposits of fatty tissue with little inherent value as even a secondary sex characteristic. To the boy who finds himself gazing into the abyss of adolescence, however, nothing could be further from the truth as we increasingly begin to deify this part of the female anatomy.

Our thirst for knowledge about the female body was unquenchable and led us on an endless quest for primary source material in order to study the subject in greater detail, the kind of material that could sometimes be found at the bottom of a father's sock drawer or down at Mr. Spinelli's Drug Store all the way in the back next to the sleazy paperbacks.

Like all boys, I was aware that such resource material existed, but it wasn't until a friend and I discovered a stack of girlie magazines in his dad's closet that I actually saw anything like it with my own eyes. It was a transforming experience.

Shortly afterward, I went on my own expedition, assuming that if other fathers cached away such treasures, my own father must as well, and in doing so unearthed several interesting artifacts. There were matchbooks from various nightclubs and other entertainment venues with images of scantily clad females; a tin ashtray from Mowry's Gulf Service Station, Brooklyn, NY, imprinted with a picture of a leggy lass perched atop a ladder; and a program complete with scantily clad photos of several star performers from the Paradise Cabaret and Restaurant

As interesting as these items were, they paled in comparison to the plastic viewer that when held up to the light revealed a female clothed in nothing but an oversized sombrero or the ballpoint pen handed out as a promotional gift by the thoughtful folks over at Sal's Sewer Service with a shapely, smartly dressed young woman floating inside. It was by accident that I discovered the young lady's clothing disappeared, leaving her clad in nothing but a smile, when the pen was turned upside down. It was like something straight out of an X-rated Johnson Smith catalog.

For the uninitiated, the Johnson Smith Company was a purveyor of some of the finest and most sophisticated novelty items ever invented, including the whoopee cushion, fake vomit, ersatz dog shit, and, for the budding young voyeur in all of us, X-ray–vision glasses. This last item was of particular interest to those of us entering puberty because they allowed us, or so the ad copy promised, "to see right through clothing." The company also promised their product would "amaze everyone." This claim proved to be a hundred percent correct because the moment mine arrived I tore open the package, donned the magical specs, and peered at myself in the mirror. Sure enough, just like the ad promised I was indeed amazed— at how stupid I looked.

Undeterred, I tiptoed down the hall toward my sister's room, where she and several of her high school friends were listening to music and gabbing away. My heart beat wildly at the notion of walking into a room filled with wall-to-wall female pulchritude. I gamely entered under the pretext of asking my sister if she knew when Mom might be home, only to walk face-first into the half-closed door and practically knocking myself unconscious in the process. Quite frankly, with only two tiny pinholes covered with red cellophane to peer through, it was nearly impossible to see anything with my new purchase, let alone through clothing. The girls burst into laughter, not quite the reaction I'd had in mind, as I reeled away in pain, X-ray specs askew and holding my freshly bloodied nose. The only person neither laughing nor bleeding was my sister, who screamed, "*Get out of here this instant, you little pervert!*" a comment I was becoming increasingly accustomed to hearing. Under the circumstances, a strategic retreat seemed in order.

Fortunately, I was not the only one my age lured into the promise of X-ray vision. Boys wearing stupid-looking glasses and bumping into things became a fairly common sight around the neighborhood for a time, until whatever promise the novelty might hold was finally outweighed by the injuries we sustained.

Those with older brothers were lucky because teenage boys seemed to have the greatest access to the research material we desired most. My best friend, Felix Lauer, caused a near riot in the lunchroom one day when he revealed a copy of *Playboy Magazine* purloined from his brother's collection. It contained a pictorial of a remarkably well-developed eighteen-year-old named June Wilkinson, whom Hef had appropriately nicknamed The Bosom. In one photo Ms. Wilkinson stood before a full-length mirror pulling on a tight sweater that barely concealed what by all appearances were two military surplus torpedoes. In another she entertained guests at a Playboy Mansion party clothed in a low-slung black dress while balancing a full martini glass on each breast, an acrobatic feat my friends and I agreed we were not likely to see on *The Ed Sullivan Show* anytime soon. Beat that, Topo Gigio!

Playboy was but one of a whole class of publications known collectively and generically as dirty magazines. A magazine earned this designation by including among its pages photographs of women in various stages of undress, thereby speaking directly to our need for titillation. Although usually tucked away in some unobtrusive corner of the store so as not to unduly ruffle the feathers of any bluenosed customers, we always knew right where to find them and exactly how long each store owner would allow us to browse before suggesting that we redirect our libidinous urges elsewhere.

There were certain patterns in the way dirty magazines were named. For example, many seemed to describe the reader himself, be he a *Bachelor, Dude, Gent, Vagabond, Gentleman, Sir, Casanova, King, Lucky, Knight, Stud, Monsieur, Cad, Dapper, Debonair, Duke, Rascal, Squire, Rogue, Swinger, Mister, Ace,* or *Scamp*. Others tried to describe some type of exploit or activity like an *Escapade, Carnival, Cabaret, Cavalcade, Affair, Fling, Caper, Frolic, Gala, Score, Whirl, Swing, Quickie, After Hours, Rapture, Delight, and Nightcap*; while a handful tried simply to use the title as a way of describing the adventurous nature—*Naughty Ladies, Sassy Ladies, Lively Ladies, Vixens,* or just your basic down-home *Frisky Females*—of the ladies featured inside.

Although generally acknowledged as poorer cousins of *Playboy*, the one true original and Holy Grail of dirty magazines, there was also something more plainspoken and far less pretentious about them as well. The general look and feel of *Playboy* versus all of the other publications available could not have been less similar. Hugh Hefner took the business of publishing pictures of naked women far too seriously when he wrapped them in a glossy package that included editorials, articles on lifestyle, men's fashion, and a wealth of both fiction and nonfiction pieces; it only made the dirty pictures themselves that much more difficult to find.

Being taken seriously was never an issue for others of this genre. There was never any attempt to hide the fact that they were simply printed burlesque shows and existed solely to tantalize and entice. In fact, the magazines usually contained many of the same features of the stage show version, including novelty, humor, fantasy, and, above all, women who wore little or no clothing. Was this not the principal reason for going to a burlesque show or buying such a magazine in the first place?

Most of the written copy was simply filler and a means of separating pictorials. Nonfiction articles, such as they were, usually devoted themselves to such cutting-edge issues as "How to Get Along With Coeds," "Why Nice Girls Abandon Underwear," and "How to Get a Girl to Undress." There were often interviews with well-known strippers and true-life stories of burlesque queens. Fiction leaned heavily toward fairly predictable male-fantasy themes like "The Isle of Lonely Women," "The Girl on the Terrace," "Motel Confessions," and "Passion in Paradise." Not surprisingly, given the nature of the times, there were also many accounts (fictionalized, one assumes) of encounters with large-breasted, love-hungry female aliens, including such classics as "Attack of the Space Maidens" and "Space Vixens from Planet X." Even the Cold War made an occasional guest appearance, with tales of how "Sex Led Me to Communism."

Interspersed throughout were a variety of visual gags, cartoons featuring buxom women and leering men, and ribald jokes that by today's standards would seem hopelessly lame. One feature of many a lowbrow girlie magazine that you never saw in its more urbane and sophisticated *Playboy* counterpart were the classified ads for a variety of hard-to-get products, like the genuine-mink keyhole cover promising "a million laughs," a set of stag-party playing cards ("Difficult to get even in France"), the collection of *Stag Stories for Men* ("The book nobody dared to print"), and yes, even that "laugh of the year and handsome piece of jewelry," the Happy Feet Tie Clip. In fact, much of the advertising was itself an art form more akin to the ads one was likely to find in a copy of "Captain Marvel" or "Archie Comics" than in a so called adult men's magazine, but then again perhaps the audiences for both were not all that dissimilar.

Sadly, somewhere along the road to the sexual revolution, the relative innocence embodied in the classic girlie magazine gave way to a level of graphic gynecological detail that completely objectified the female form. Magazines named *Pert* were replaced by those with names like *Juggs* and *Snatch,* which so corrupted the genre that it lost both its mystery and its appeal. Posing seductively, wearing only what the law requires as a legal minimum, has become so mainstream that the female form seems to have lost much of its numinous and supernatural power over impressionable young boys, leaving them no inkling of the joy inherently associated with a forbidden fruit.

One might reasonably conclude that we spent all of our time thinking about bare-breasted females, and as delightful a prospect as that sounds, such was not the case. Not long after we began noticing some of the more delightful changes girls were undergoing, our own bodies began to rebel against us as well.

Take my penis, for example. I never called it that of course, preferring one of the more colorful appellations of the day like pecker, pud, willie, wiener, weenie, or schlong (I drew the line at Herman the One-Eyed German). All boys had one, and although the appendage had been with us our entire lives, we'd never given them much thought before now. Admittedly, they came in handy on camping trips and allowed us to write our names in the snow, but beyond that most of the guys I knew took them pretty much for granted.

Therefore, imagine my surprise when I woke up one morning only to find mine already wide-awake, standing straight up waving good morning to me. This was a phenomenon I had heard discussed by my peers on many occasions, but nothing had prepared me for the real thing. I had an erection, a hard-on, a woody, a boner, a blue veiner! I was a man!

Although it made waking up more pleasant, I soon discovered my penis had a mind of its own and could become erect pretty much whenever and wherever it pleased. This gave rise, as it were, to any number of embarrassing situations, although fortunately never in the boy's shower room after gym class.

As we began stumbling our way through puberty, another new and generally disconcerting development came to pass regarding this unique appendage. Suddenly, and for no particular reason we could ascertain, our standing in the masculine hierarchy could be measured, quite literally, by the size of our dicks. Without warning, penis size had suddenly become a status symbol, for some anyway, and marked the beginning of a lifetime of insecurity.

Notwithstanding some of the more unpleasant side effects, these changes were not entirely unwelcome and although it might have been easier had this strange new appendage come with an owner's manual, most of us soon understood the causal relationship between our increasingly lascivious musings and the resultant physical consequences. However, because our burgeoning imaginations were no more predictable than our bodies, there was no telling when our minds, already struggling with an overload of hormones, might suddenly and without warning go AWOL, leaving us with the rather awkward task of hiding the evidence. I find it amusing how many grown-ups still think boys who walked around with their shirttails hanging out were trying to make a fashion statement or merely sloppy dressers.

Alone and in the privacy of our own rooms, these erotic musings were not only warmly welcomed, but they became a prerequisite for engaging in what is perhaps the most universal of all pastimes, masturbation; referred to also as jerking off, jacking off, whacking off, burping the baby, tickling the pickle, polishing the happy lamp, choking the chicken, and spanking the monkey. Indeed, as puberty tightened its fearsome grip on us, it seemed as though every waking moment was devoted either to masturbating or to thinking about masturbating.

We were never quite sure what this preoccupation with self-gratification meant. One school of thought held that the practice was both sinful and unhealthy, even referring to it as self-abuse, and warned of potentially dire consequences for those who did not abstain. Football, basketball, and baseball were all suggested as the safe alternatives, which explained why the local Catholic school always seemed to dominate non-Catholic schools in most competitive sports.

When I entered puberty in the early 1960s, a more enlightened school of thought had developed, which suggested masturbation was actually quite normal and a healthy outlet if one did not overindulge to the point of becoming socially withdrawn and isolated. Many parents expressed shock at this heresy, believing their own children had no right to go through puberty with any less guilt than they themselves had experienced.

Another concept taking root suggested that perhaps certain community institutions like schools and churches had some responsibility when it came to educating youngsters about sex. Adults were again shocked and complained bitterly at this further erosion of their God-given parental right to raise ignorant children.

A third school of thought, and the one I adhered to, proposed that boys should jerk off all they wanted and worry about straitjackets, loony bins, and hairy palms at some unspecified later date.

We assumed masturbation was an exercise engaged in only by boys. By all appearances girls were unaffected by sexual urges and were preoccupied instead with things like fashion, makeup, and music. Therefore, imagine my astonishment when I accidentally came across a book entitled *Factors in the Sex Life of Twenty Two Hundred Women*, among a box of old college texts belonging to my mother, a former health and physical-education instructor. Hands trembling, I leafed through what I thought might well prove to be the Rosetta stone that unlocked the secrets of the female gender.

Although I was disappointed that the volume relied so heavily on complicated charts and graphs (I felt the information could have been better presented had the author made greater use of photographic documentation), it nonetheless painted a very different picture of girls than the one we had come to accept. Not only did girls apparently think about sex seemingly every bit as much as boys, they also employed their own unique techniques for self-gratification to relieve the tensions these thoughts were known to produce. I was stunned that girls were seemingly light-years ahead of us when it came to a practice we had always assumed was a predominantly male phenomenon. Girls started earlier, engaged in it with astonishing frequency, and seemed far more creative in how they went about it, as evidenced by the twenty-two-year-old woman who reported that at age ten—at age ten, for Christ's sake—she discovered the joys of hanging her legs over the edge of the bathtub while letting a stream of water pour over her privates. As a ten-year-old, I was still picking my nose in public and playing with toy soldiers made of green molded plastic. No wonder girls were so fucking clean all the time!

It was in the context of these rapid physical changes and emotional dynamics that boys and girls were then thrust together into this ill fitting *pas de deux* that adults insisted was the best time of our lives. It certainly didn't feel like it. Only a few months earlier, I was generally oblivious to girls and almost always happy. Now girls were practically all I thought about and my life was in a constant state of turmoil. From our perspective, girls in general seemed smart, poised, physically self-assured, and graceful. We, on the other hand, usually felt stupid, inarticulate, physically unremarkable if not downright ugly, and maladroit. By all appearances the game was rigged, the deck was stacked, and the cards were marked. We didn't stand a chance.

It is oddly appropriate that baseball, the greatest of all-American sports and perhaps the second greatest of all-American pastimes, was used as a metaphor for measuring the success of our sexual adventures. Sadly, my own sex life, such as it existed at all back then, was filled with more strikeouts, foul balls, and pop-ups than I care to remember. Actual base hits of any kind seemed few and far between.

Part of the problem was simply a dearth of useful information about the mechanics, the how-to of things like kissing or unhooking a bra left-handed with the lights out. Oh, sure, adults had plenty of advice, but it was always the wrong kind and generally focused on what not to do as opposed to how to do it. Everyone from Dear Abby to the makers of those ubiquitous sex-education films approached the subject with an almost missionary zeal designed mainly to prevent any and all physical contact between the sexes. Using scare tactics similar to those employed in most antidrug propaganda, something as seemingly innocent as holding hands was a slippery slope that inevitably led to more intimate forms of physical contact. Adults seemed ignorant of the fact that this is exactly what boys were counting on.

Girls, meanwhile, were barraged with messages designed to scare them away from boys, by suggesting that most of us had developed no further along than had the third fellow from the left on one of those evolutionary charts that hung in our science classrooms, the one who no longer dragged his knuckles on the ground but had yet to walk entirely upright. If subtlety failed, grown-ups were prepared to go straight for the jugular with educational films like "How to Say No," in which an invisible narrator cautions Lucy, "You just can't help getting into situations where petting is likely to start. Just give him half a chance, alone, and there's no stopping him!" This was not quite the ambience we were looking for on a first date.

A date could lead to unspeakable horrors for a boy as well. Chief among these was the possibility that he would be required to dance to some song with a tempo faster than a funeral dirge. By our early teens most boys had, if the music was slow enough, mastered an odd kind of ersatz dancing technique that required little more than swaying back and forth almost imperceptibly while keeping our feet planted firmly in the same spot. Unfortunately, once a discernible beat emerged, any attempt to match the movement of our bodies to the rhythm of the music resulted only in an apparent attack of apoplexy.

Beginning on August 6, 1960, however, boys were actually freed briefly from the fear and loathing that invariably accompanied any trip to the dance floor with the arrival of a young black man by the name of Ernest Evans (aka Chubby Checker) and a song called "The Twist."

It would not be an overstatement to say that the Twist revolutionized dancing forever, for several reasons. Although its roots could be traced directly to the Lindy Hop, the Twist was the first dance that required absolutely no physical contact between partners. Given the generalized fear among adults that moral standards for kids were in free fall, you would think that a dance that required several feet of open space between the two dancers would come as a welcome relief. It didn't, and almost immediately both the song and the dance came under intense fire from the usual cast of civic and religious characters, some of whom decried it as "vulgar jungle dancing," thereby suggesting their concern was perhaps more racial than moral.

Chubby Checker first recorded The Twist in June 1959, but it took more than a year for it to reach number one on the *Billboard* charts and from there into American pop culture history. Pretty soon it seemed that everyone—Zsa Zsa Gabor, Judy Garland, Greta Garbo, Jackie Kennedy; Rob and Laura Petri, Ozzie and Harriet Nelson, and even the Duke and Duchess of Windsor—were doing the Twist.

As Chubby Checker unleashed his new dance craze on the world, and millions of young boys, me included, were in the process of pupating from childhood to adolescence, news that there was a dance that we could actually master spread like wildfire. As one canny observer later put it, "The Twist had not only emancipated dancers from their partners, and from a host of social conventions in the bargain, but put an end to the awful tyranny of ability."

Dozens of us secretly made a trip down to Spinelli's Drug Store, alone, hopefully unseen, in order to purchase a copy of the latest teen magazine containing instructions on how to perform the new dance. I made it home with mine undetected and immediately shut myself in my bedroom to memorize both the song and the instructions.

My debut took place later that evening when, after finishing my shower, I stood in front of the bathroom mirror naked except for a towel wrapped loosely around my waist, the magazine spread open on the sink in front of me. According to an interview with Chubby himself, all I had to do was put my left foot in front of my right foot and pretend to stub out a cigarette while drying my backside with a towel. It sounded easy enough and I certainly had all the necessary equipment, so I decided to give it a try.

Left foot slightly in front of the right, I took the towel from around my middle, held one end in either hand, and softly began singing:

Come on, baby, let's do the twist.
Come on, baby, let's do the twist.

As I warmed to the task, my voice grew louder, and my body began to gyrate wildly. Then I glanced in the mirror where, to my horror, I caught the reflection of my older sister and her best friend, Julie, behind me taking it all in. Eyes wide in amazement, they fought a losing battle to control their mirth, which erupted the moment they realized I was aware of their presence. Every bare-ass inch of me flushed hot with embarrassment, and I quickly tried to cover myself with the towel. By now my audience was practically crying with laughter. Spinning around, I flung the door shut while screaming every epithet I could lay my tongue to. This dismissal would no doubt have been far more impressive had my voice not chosen to crack and slide up into a high falsetto. In the final analysis, Chubby Checker had far more success with the Twist than I did.

Despite all the obstacles and disincentives for doing so, my friends and I ultimately found ways to overcome our own self-doubts and the avalanche of adult propaganda long enough to begin exploring a facet of our lives that up until then had been purely speculative. For boys, leaving our virginity behind allowed us to enter an elite masculine brotherhood where getting laid meant our manhood was proven. It also allowed us to add our own voice to the cacophony of braggadocio that was typical of those first-generation patio pioneers who successfully reached reproductive age. No matter how untidy, fumbling, indelicate, awkward, inept, or loutish our efforts may have been, and generally they were all of these things, we passed through the magic veil, from which there was no turning back.

Q: On a first date with a boy you like, should you let him kiss you good night?

A: It isn't as if you were going out for necking. That isn't your idea of a favorite sport. And you don't want the kind of popularity that's pegged on petting. It's just that you don't want to be pegged as a cold potato. Or maybe his argument is "everybody does it." Or you don't know how to refuse. If you let a boy kiss you good night, you run the risk of having yourself footnoted as an "easy number." Any girl who thinks that lasting romances are built on physical attraction is only kidding herself. The smartest girls think it's better to keep 'em guessing.

Alas, throughout most of high school, I somehow became acknowledged as an accidental expert at finding and dating only the smartest girls in town.

CHAPTER 16

The Crabgrass Frontier Goes to Pot

Adults warned us about drugs, oh yes, they did. Time and time again, we were assured in the most unequivocal terms that drug use would lead inevitably and inexorably to social ostracism, mental mayhem, and an untimely death. As wary as these cautionary tales made me, I was forever mindful of the fact that these same adults were responsible for promulgating what was then perhaps the biggest lie of my entire young life—Santa Claus. If adults had no qualms about lying to a little kid like me about the existence of Santa Claus, I theorized (and don't get me started on the Easter Bunny or the Tooth Fairy), might they not also misrepresent the dangers of drug use as well?

What made the consumption of these illicit substances different from alcohol, in our estimation anyway, was that while drinking was a purely recreational sport, doing drugs (rumor had it) provided an opportunity to expand one's understanding of both the physical and the metaphysical universe. In other words, while drink made us stupid, robbed us of our basic motor skills, and rendered us all but incapable of both coherent thought and speech before we threw up, drugs, it was alleged, would allow us to experience brief moments of expanded consciousness—and then throw up. It was an important distinction, or so it seemed at the time.

Recreational drug use, as it became known, eased its way onto the Crabgrass Frontier and into our lives on cat's paws. One day we were trying to cop a six-pack of Schlitz, the next day to score a nickel bag of Acapulco gold. At first the practice was limited to those kids who prided themselves on living outside the mainstream, who ceremoniously eschewed the social conventions of a typical mid-1960's suburban high school and pursued their identity elsewhere. They enjoyed being viewed as unconventional, in some cases even eccentric, or as my tenth-grade geometry teacher, Mr. Wilcox, put it, "a few degrees off plumb."

Predictably, my first experience with an illicit substance, in this case marijuana, resulted from an overdose of the most common of all naturally occurring chemical substances in teenage boys: testosterone.

In January 1966, having by midyear grown weary of the academic rigors of tenth grade, I decided to pad my class schedule with the most popular of all do-nothing courses—art appreciation. High school art classes were universally acknowledged as a sure way to boost one's overall grade point average with only a modest investment of mental energy. This made them extremely popular among jocks, who were required to maintain a certain minimum average in order to play on any school team, graduating seniors who were for all intents and purposes brain-dead once they took their SATs, and other assorted slackers like me. On rare occasions these classes actually attracted one or two students with an expressed interest in the course itself; however, their numbers were usually so inconsequential, they had very little impact on the overall zeitgeist of the class.

The class was broken up into groups of four, with each assigned to a large high table surrounded by stools instead of chairs, and it was here we began exploring our artistic selves using a variety of different mediums. Three sophomore classmates, including Randy Wiseman, Jenny De Winter, and Penny Marino, joined me at my table. Randy and I had been friends going all the way back to our Boy Scout days. I knew Jenny only casually, enough to say hello as we passed in the halls, although our paths were fated to cross in a big way a year and a half later. I didn't know Penny at all, and even though we had gone through junior high school together, I think the only ten words that ever passed between us were "Take one of these and pass the rest back, please."

It's not that Penny wasn't nice (she seemed pleasant enough) or attractive. She was stunning, almost regal in a way only those who traced their roots back to some small fishing village on the Mediterranean can be, with olive skin; long, shining black hair; and deep pools of brown where her eyes should have been. Unfortunately, her appearance and bearing came at a price, which was a sense that she was not easily approachable. She did nothing to discourage me or anyone else, for that matter, from engaging her in collegial conversation, but neither did she openly invite it. She seemed quite content just being Penny and seemed to assume you were just as content being whoever you were.

Unfortunately, adolescent society being what it is, those who chose to disengage themselves from the pack for whatever reason did so at their own peril. Because teenagers are notoriously cannibalistic and easily prone to sharklike feeding frenzies, they can quickly turn on one of their own. Boys often find themselves physically harassed, while girls become the target of whispered smear campaigns so vicious they could make a career politician blush. Only a few like Penny managed to successfully navigate these tricky social currents and simply remain invisible.

As the semester progressed so too did the frequency of my social intercourse with Penny, to the point where I usually got up enough nerve to bid her a mumbled hello. She always responded in what seemed a genuinely congenial manner.

Our teacher, Mrs. Rudin, to her credit never appeared overly concerned or threatened by the fact that she had to play den mother to a group of ne'er-do-well academics who were there by virtue of the fact that they wanted to be anywhere else even less. That our efforts were usually boisterous and lacked any serious intent did not appear to bother her in the slightest. This was uncharacteristic inasmuch as most teachers were generally considered humorless, self-important martinets with an overly inflated opinion of the importance of their own subject areas. In this regard, Mrs. Rudin was a breath of fresh air in an otherwise stale environment.

By late March, we began to experience the first signs of approaching spring. With the sweet smell of graduation growing stronger, the seniors in our class became all but catatonic, while those disposed to athletic endeavors gave themselves over completely to the promise of taking to the softball and touch-football fields once again after months of sweaty confinement in the gym. For the rest of us, those who belonged in neither camp, we tried to find diversion in the class itself, and increasingly I found myself concentrating with uncharacteristic intensity on one class assignment or another. In most of these, Mrs. Rudin valiantly attempted to draw from us a level of artistic self-expression that few had known since the paste-pot and Crayola days of grade school. Although our efforts were for the most part stilted and amateurish, she encouraged and cajoled us with such relentless good cheer that it was difficult for me not to drop my guard on occasion and become genuinely enthusiastic about what I was doing. Notwithstanding these lapses, I was nonetheless surprised one day when Mrs. Rudin asked me to remain after class for a minute with Penny. I looked quizzically over at my tablemate for some indication that perhaps she might know the reason for this unusual request, but during that brief moment when our eyes made contact, she just shrugged her shoulders and gave no hint that she might be privy to any more information than I was.

When the last of our classmates had retreated, Mrs. Rudin came over and sat down at the worktable with us. After a few pleasantries she got down to business.

"As both of you know, each year I choose two students from this class to work on a project together that is submitted to *The Inkwell*," she began, "and from what I've seen so far this semester, I think the two of you could come up with some very interesting ideas."

The Inkwell was a student literary magazine that the school put out at the end of each academic year. It contained a collection of student essays, short stories, poems, and artwork chosen by a special panel of teachers. Among the modest cadre of literary and artsy types, getting something published in *The Inkwell* was considered quite a coup, but for the rest of us it was generally considered a pretty ho-hum affair.

Actually, one year it did receive rave reviews from the great unwashed masses after a wily and obviously disgruntled young artist successfully published a pen-and-ink drawing so elaborately detailed that the judges failed to spot the Hirschfeldian incorporation of numerous earthy four-letter references. Only after the magazine reached our hands did word of this perfidy become public, spreading joy throughout the student body and panic among the faculty and administration. From that day on, the vetting process used to screen student submissions became so byzantine that the number dropped significantly; score: grown-ups—1, artistic expression—0.

"Sure," Penny responded immediately. "I think it might be fun."

Meanwhile, I sat there with my mouth open looking dumb while my mind tried to get a grip on the idea. Why on earth had she picked me? Penny I could understand; she was the artsy type anyway and even expressed an interest in making it a career, but me?

Before I could express any of this, I heard myself add my own mumbled assent. "Good," said Mrs. Rudin, looking quite pleased with herself. "Why don't the two of you take a few minutes to come up with a few ideas and we can talk about them next week."

"Can't," said Penny as she stood and gathered her things. "I've got an English Comp essay due next period." Turning to me, her eyes locked onto mine like radar. "But if you meet me by the door to the student parking lot after last class, we can walk over to my house and start. It's only a couple of blocks away, okay? Later," she said and she was out the door before I could respond. Things were moving much too fast.

Sensing my befuddled state, Mrs. Rudin reassured me, "Don't worry, you'll do fine. You have a good eye and some very original ideas. I've watched you. You and Penny will make a great team. Now get going so you're not late for your next class."

Frankly, my biggest concern was not so much the project as it was the partner. Unlike most of my classmates, Penny was not easy to pigeonhole. Some of my classmates thought she was stuck-up, the worst label a teenager could receive, but I didn't share that opinion. Penny just seemed to prefer to keep her own counsel on most matters and was oblivious to what those around her thought. Unfortunately, Mrs. Rudin had given little or no consideration to the social ramifications of the pairing, only to the fact that our abilities, such as they were, complemented each other, at least in her estimation. That there might be no interpersonal chemistry, no shared interests or common ground to work from, seemed irrelevant. For all she knew, she might have paired a Montague with a Capulet, a Jet with a Shark, or even a Yankee fan with a Boston Red Sox fan. Only time would tell.

As the 3:05 bell rang, sounding our release, I allowed myself to be carried along by the loud, bustling flow of students as they made their way toward the school exits. Although outwardly I remained unperturbed and kept up the usual steady patter of salutations and cheerful one-liners with friends and acquaintances as we passed in the hall, inside I was still unsure exactly what I had gotten myself into. Perhaps there was still time to back out, I thought; just tell Mrs. Rudin that the combined burden of my current academic load, family obligations, and whirlwind social life simply did not permit me to take on another major responsibility.

"Hi!"

My reverie was broken by the sound of Penny's voice as she suddenly emerged from the crowd and took up station next to me as we approached the two large wooden doors to the student parking lot. Once outside we were greeted by a warm, sunny afternoon that held great promise for the days and weeks ahead. Groups of students, arms piled high with textbooks and three-ring binders, made their way off in different directions or gathered around the cars of friends; a few stood chatting, while one or two footballs arced in flight high over our heads. It was exactly the kind of boisterous scene you would expect from several hundred high school students freed after six hours of academic sedation.

During the five minutes or so it took to walk to her house, Penny seemed relaxed and easygoing, far more so than in school, and surprisingly easy to talk to. Because of its proximity to the center of town, her neighborhood was far more modest than I expected. The homes were smaller and packed more tightly together on smaller lots, many showing the signs of wear that suggested the owners were not nearly as prosperous as others in the community.

Soon we were making our way around to the side of Penny's house, where we entered a small but warm and brightly lit kitchen. After dumping her own books unceremoniously on the kitchen table and inviting me to do the same, Penny, like all good teenagers, made a beeline for the refrigerator.

"Coke?" she asked, holding up two of the familiar green eight-ounce bottles. "Or I think we might have some 7-Up or orange juice, I'm not sure, I usually do the grocery shopping on Saturday."

"Coke is fine," I replied. "Thanks," I added. "Is your mom home?" I wondered aloud.

"No, she doesn't get home usually until six or seven o'clock, sometimes even later," answered Penny. "She works as a bookkeeper for a doctor's office in Queens," she explained.

I didn't know anybody whose mother worked even part-time. For both me and my friends, mothers were people who took care of the house and were always home when we got there, if they weren't out shopping or running some other domestic errand, like picking up Dad's shirts at the Chinese laundry. This got me wondering about Penny's dad.

"My dad was killed in the Korean War," said Penny as though she had just read my mind.

I mumbled a hurried condolence of sorts, but Penny interrupted, saying, "Hey, I never even met the guy, so it's always been just me and Mom."

Penny opened the Cokes, and then started rummaging about for snacks in a small pantry next to the refrigerator. "We have Twinkies, HoHo's, and there may still be a package of Ding Dongs in here someplace," came her muffled voice from inside the pantry.

"Nothing for me, thanks," I replied. "I'm fine with just a Coke." I could not help noticing that Penny was just as attractive from this angle as she was from the front.

"Suit yourself. You know where to find them if you change your mind," she said, handing me a cold bottle of soda. "Let's go up to my room and get started," she suggested, and with this Penny headed for the stairs at the front of the house. After a moment of puzzled hesitation, I followed.

Except for my sister's, the last time I had been in a girl's bedroom for social reasons was in third or fourth grade. The accepted protocol for girls and boys assigned to the same class project was to meet at the library either after school or during the weekend. Meeting at someone's home was acceptable, but the project was then done at the kitchen or dining room table, not in the bedroom.

Furthermore, there was no parental supervision. Although by no means a prude, this violated a number of unwritten rules of teenage culture. Had we been going steady and Penny had been wearing an ID bracelet engraved with my initials, that would be one thing, but we hardly knew each other. Clearly, I was on unfamiliar ground, blazing a new trail where many of the old rules did not seem to apply. All I could do, I figured, was to remain alert and follow Penny's lead lest I commit some blunder that revealed my ignorance in such situations.

As I entered her room, Penny slipped past me, her arms full of clothes, heading for the bathroom. "I'm just going to change my clothes. I'll only be a minute," she announced over her shoulder. "Make yourself comfortable."

Comfortable, indeed, I thought to myself as I looked warily around the room.

In retrospect, what surprised me the most was the fact that Penny's bedroom did not look anything like I'd expected. Although I could not claim to have an inordinate amount of knowledge in such matters, I did expect a room decorated in pink with lots of frills, shelves filled with cuddly stuffed animals, and perhaps a poster of two of her favorite heartthrobs. There were posters all right; one of Bob Dylan, another of Joan Baez, and two or three jazz musicians I'd never even heard of.

The next thing that caught my eye was the odd-looking light on her dresser, called a lava lamp. Along with the black light and the psychedelic poster, lava lamps would become almost essential to the well-appointed teenager's room within a few years, but at the time they were still something of a novelty. And were it not for the fact that the inventor of the lava lamp was disposed to cavorting about in his birthday suit with those of a similar disposition, these peculiar-looking decorative accoutrements might never have come into being in the first place.

Legend has it that World War II veteran, travel agent, and inventor Edward Walker stopped by The Queen's Head Pub in New Forest, England, for a pint one evening in the early 1950s when he spied what he later described as a "contraption made out of a cocktail shaker and old tins." The contrivance was actually a homemade egg timer created by one Mr. Dunnett. Filled with a mixture of oil and water that was then heated by a bulb in its base, the light it cast created eerie, ever-changing shadows that so fascinated Walker he set about to track down Dunnett, only to find the eccentric inventor had already gone to his great reward. Undeterred, Walker purchased the rights from Dunnett's widow and spent the next fifteen years exploring what he was certain were the enormous commercial possibilities of this most unusual object.

Inventing weird lamps was not Walker's only interest, which also included getting married (he did on four separate occasions) and getting naked, which he apparently did quite regularly.

Walker first embraced the philosophy and practice of what in polite society was referred to as "naturism" in the early 1950s while visiting the coast of southern France. So enamored did he become with the *au natural* lifestyle that he, using the profits from his design business, the Crestwood Design Company, made several films featuring (no surprise here) naked babes. One film in particular, entitled *Traveling Light,* was so successful it allowed Walker to purchase a beach resort in the south of England, which he named the District Naturist Center of England, and which became the country's best-known nudist colony. Walker fell out of favor in some nudist circles when he later tried to ban fat people from the resort, claiming that obesity was antithetical to the naturist ideal of physical health.

In 1963, using Dunnett's concept, Walker, using a fifty-two-ounce container filled with oil, wax, and thirteen other, "secret" ingredients, finally came up with a device he called the "Astro Lamp." Local merchants at first looked upon the globulating lamp with jaundiced eyes, fearing the design was too ugly. However, as the Age of Aquarius dawned and began to dominate almost every facet of popular design, the unusual light, with its decorative and meditative qualities, began finding a home in the rooms of millions of teenagers around the world.

In 1965 two American entrepreneurs spotted Walker's lamp at a German trade show and bought the rights to manufacture the product in the United States. With the help of the growing psychedelic movement, sales of what was renamed the Lava Lite skyrocketed both here and abroad, reaching nearly 7 million a year in the late 1960s and early '70s.

By the late '70s and early '80s, however, with the Love Generation now defunct and the once mighty herds of hippies almost extinct, sales plummeted to a mere 200 a month before Walker threw in the, uh, towel, sold his company, and used the profits to continue his pursuit of naturism until his death on August 15, 2000. One can only speculate how much of the profits were used to purchase calamine lotion and sunscreen for his guests at the Naturist Center.

Obviously, I didn't know any of this as I stood in the middle of Penny's bedroom and watched in fascination as weirdly shaped bubbles of the glutinous liquid oozed their way endlessly up and down the body of the lamp.

It was clear from the many shelves crammed with books that Penny read a lot too; and it didn't seem to be the usual stuff you might expect a high school girl to read. Some claimed to be poetry, but the one I flipped through, called *Howl* and written by a guy named Allen Ginsberg, seemed to be nothing more than a jumble of incoherent, disconnected thoughts; wasn't good poetry supposed to rhyme? On a table by her bedside sat *On the Road,* by Jack Kerouac. It seemed well thumbed, as though it had been read several times, and even had handwritten notes in some of the margins. I could tell by the tiny, neat lettering it was Penny's handwriting, and I wondered what kind of book required the reader to take notes, outside of school, that is.

"Do you like Kerouac? He's one of my favorites," Penny said as she reentered the room. I quickly placed the book back on her table, afraid she might think I was snooping in her absence.

"Uh, no, I haven't read any of his stuff, but I hear he's pretty good," I answered lamely.

Penny was dressed in blue jeans and what looked like an old white dress shirt with smudges and smears of paint here and there. Even dressed down she looked pretty fantastic.

"What do you read?" she asked, dropping cross-legged on the bed and gazing at me with those big, unblinking brown eyes of hers.

Always a quick study, I sensed right away that Penny was not referring to comic books and scoured my memory for something that sounded vaguely serious.

"I liked that one about the man in the rowboat, you know, the one where he catches a real big fish and …"

"You mean *The Old Man and the Sea,*" Penny interjected, much to my relief. "Ah, yes, Hemingway's classic allegory about man's eternal struggle with the forces of nature," she continued. "Yeah, it's pretty good, but I think Hemingway spends too much time extolling the virtues of courage and tenacity in his characters, particularly men, and not enough time exploring their vulnerabilities, don't you think?"

"Yeah sure, uh, their vulnerbles, right …" What the hell was she talking about? Before she had a chance to continue, I quickly changed the subject and asked if she would put on some music: "Hey, do you have *Rubber Soul?*"

"It's over in that stack somewhere," she said, nodding toward a pile of vinyl LP's and a record player near the closet door. "I'll put it on. Some of their stuff is too commercial, but this one's pretty good," she added.

I once had a girl, or should I say she once had me.

"So, what do you want to do?" Penny asked while motioning for me to sit. Gingerly, I sat on the edge of the bed as she reached into the drawer of her nightstand, pulled out a small wooden box, and placed it in her lap.

She showed me her room, isn't it good, Norwegian wood.

"Uh, about what?" I asked, watching her open the box and sort through the contents.

"Our art project, silly, what else would I mean?" she chirped airily, glancing up briefly from her efforts. What was she doing? I wondered.

She asked me to stay and she told me to sit anywhere.

Setting the Kerouac book in front of her, she pulled out a tiny square of white paper and placed in on the book. Then, opening a small packet of aluminum foil, she began to carefully sprinkle small bits of dried green leaves onto the paper. It looked like something my mother would use for cooking and gave off a sweet pungent smell. I sat there mesmerized as Penny closed the foil packet and returned it to the box. She then carefully rolled the paper into the shape of a cigarette, ran her tongue along the edge, and sealed it.

So I looked around and I noticed there wasn't a chair.

"A little something to help the creative juices flow," she said with a knowing smile as she reached back in the box for a wooden match. "Care to join me?" and with this Penny slid the match across the top of the box and a small flame sizzled to life. As she carefully brought the twisted home-made cigarette to her lips and touched the tip with the flame it suddenly struck me: *Penny was smoking marijuana!*

Fear surged through me and I broke into a cold sweat. Penny was a drug addict!

Puffing once or twice to make sure it was properly lit, Penny then drew hard on what I now realized was, oh God, *a reefer*. Inhaling deeply, she drew the deadly smoke deep into her lungs and held it there for what seemed like hours, then slowly let it out in a cloud of pungent smoke. I sat hypnotized as my mind grappled with what to do next.

My friends and I had been warned over and over about the dangers of drug use in general and marijuana in particular, because as harmless as it appeared, marijuana was considered a gateway drug, meaning it always led to other, more self-destructive forms of drug use.

The previous year when we were freshman, school officials had lectured us relentlessly about the inherent dangers of using drugs in any form, whether pot smoking, popping pills, or tripping on acid. Companies specializing in educational films again jumped in and helped hammer home the dangers of drug use with classics like *Drug Addicition* in which the protagonist carelessly drinks from a broken Pepsi bottle while under the influence of some unspecified drug, then laughs hysterically as blood pours from his torn lips. In another, called *The Terrible Truth,* we learn that the

Russians are really the ones responsible for promoting drug use among American youth in order to "undermine national morale," something most parents suspected all along. In *Marijuana,* Sonny Bono, of all people, becomes a spokesman for drug abstinence by warning that we risk becoming bummed-out "weed heads" and then watched with us as a kid stares at his reflection in a mirror and his face is transformed—into an image of a cheap rubber Halloween monster mask. Bummer.

I watched with fascination as Penny inhaled a second time, held in the smoke, and let her head fall back in deep repose. Was she … stoned? I wondered? I thought about leaving.

Under the influence of drugs like marijuana, some girls became quite, uh, sexually aggressive. I knew this for a fact because only recently while sneaking a few furtive glances at some of the dirty magazines down at Spinelli's Dug Store, I came across several paperback books on the subject, books like *Marijuana Girl, Reefer Girl,* and *Love Addict.* Although I didn't have time to examine the contents of each book closely, the covers seemed to tell it all. Amply proportioned women, their clothes disheveled, their eyes glazed with yearning; this is what became of girls who played Russian roulette with drugs.

I decided it would be best if I stayed.

Exhaling slowly once more until the room filled with the heady aroma of pot, Penny tilted her head forward again, slowly opened her eyes as if waking from a deep sleep, only to burst suddenly into a fit of giggling. "You should see the look on your face," she said pointing at me gleefully. "You look like you've seen a ghost."

This observation so amused her that even after clasping both hands over her mouth, she continued to snort with laughter. I wondered if this signaled the onset of some bizarre "trip." Perhaps it was even the prelude to her ripping off her clothes as waves of drug lust washed over her. I waited expectantly, but alas, after a moment or two, Penny seemed to regain some of her composure.

"I'm sorry," she said. I could tell she was sincere, but that didn't stop her from smiling anyway.

"It's just that you looked so surprised, I couldn't help it," she said.

Now I felt stupid, like a kid who had just tripped over his own shoe-laces. I felt my face grow warm with a blush. Sensing my embarrassment, Penny tried to reassure me. "Really, I'm sorry, it's just that, I mean, you looked so startled it was cute!"

Cute? I thought. Cute is better than stupid, cute is definitely better than stupid.

"Nah, don't worry, it's just that I don't know too many people who, you know, take drugs," I replied.

She smiled again and said, "I'm not sure I would call smoking a joint taking drugs, exactly, but hey, I know what you mean. I guess you and your friends are mostly into beer and stuff, huh?"

"Yeah, when we can find someone to buy it for us. I guess finding some-one who sells drugs, um, marijuana, in this town is pretty hard too," I replied.

Penny shrugged, trying not to let any of the tainted consciousness-rais-ing fumes from a second pull escape her lungs. I waited for her to exhale.

"It's not like you think," she said as she carefully extinguished what remained of the joint, tucked it into the box, and placed the whole thing back in the nightstand drawer.

"Don't believe everything you've been told about drugs," she said firmly, "at least everything they've told you about marijuana anyway. Most of it's a crock. I mean, I smoke, and do I look drug-crazed to you?" Admit-tedly, she did not.

"Getting high now and then just helps shift things around in my head, it slows life down a little so I can enjoy it more," Penny continued. "It sharpens my senses so everything seems more intense, like this song, for instance." We listened to the haunting words of The Beatles singing "In My Life."

"Isn't it amazing," she said softly and with a hint of awe. Clearly, Penny was enjoying the Fab Four at a level a mere mortal like myself could only imagine, which piqued my curiosity all the more.

We continued talking—about music, school, grades friends, peer pres-sure, love, whatever came to mind, and the hours slipped by until dinner-time was upon us and it was time for me to get home. Penny had already made three separate trips back downstairs to the kitchen for more HoHo's and Twinkies and had even managed to find the missing package of Ding Dongs.

"It's called the munchies," she explained between ravenous bites. "Marijuana makes you really, really hungry, and everything you eat tastes delicious."

The following day was a Saturday, so Penny and I agreed to meet at the public library in an effort to make up for the time we'd lost in quiet, albeit intense, conversation.

Walking home, I marveled at how different Penny was from most other girls my age, how self-assured and easygoing she seemed. With most girls, I was always alert for the ever-present verbal and nonverbal cues that guided, stage-managed actually, my every word, and particularly if it was someone I was attracted to. It was hard work pretending to be genuine, but with Penny it all seemed to come naturally. Being genuine, I mean.

The following day we met at the library in the late afternoon to work on our project as planned. It was fun being with Penny, and we laughed enough to earn several stern looks from the librarian. After an hour or two, however, the confinement began to chafe on both of us, so we packed up and left. When we got outside, the last warm rays of sun greeted us.

"Want to walk me home?" asked Penny.

Was she kidding? "Sure."

As we walked, we continued talking about the project and volleyed ideas back and forth like two tennis pros in a heated match. I was surprised at how enthusiastic I had become over a lousy art project for school. It had been a long time since anything related to school had been this much fun. At one point she became so passionate about the point she was making that she began tugging on the sleeve of my coat as we walked. I looked at her and wondered if the enthusiasm was natural or if she had received some herbal assistance. She glanced over, caught me staring, and stopped short.

"What?" she demanded?

"What, what?" I replied innocently.

"Why are you staring at me like that? Do I have something stuck in my teeth or something?"

We had just entered a small park, which actually had once been the water hazard on the sixteenth hole of a private golf course before the area had been developed. The pond remained and was now surrounded by a stand of maples and oaks. A brick path wound its way around the whole thing. Following the path, we started down the gentle slope toward the pond.

"I was just wondering if you were, you know … I mean you seem so intense and everything, I just thought maybe you were, uh …" Could I have sounded any dumber? I thought to myself.

"You mean am I stoned?" she asked as a smile washed over her face.

I nodded.

"No, I'm not, but that's something we can correct in a jiffy," and with that she grabbed my arm and pulled me toward a solitary bench near the edge of the pond.

Dropping to the bench, she began rummaging around in her purse and pulled out what looked like a small black change purse. I sat beside her as she opened it and took out what I now recognized as a joint.

"Want to join me this time?" she asked.

I hesitated, still unsure how seriously to take all the warnings. Was this the first step on that slippery slope to drug addiction?

"Listen, it's okay either way as far as I'm concerned. If you're going to try it, do it because you want to, not because you think I want you to," she said, patting her pockets for matches. As a regular cigarette smoker now, I politely handed her mine. "Well, what am I supposed to do?" I asked.

She placed the joint between her lips after first making certain the coast was clear and any unwanted company would not interrupt us. "You smoke it just like a regular cigarette, except you have to inhale the smoke as deep as you can and hold it in as long as you can," she explained, and for the second time in as many days I watched as she demonstrated the proper method for smoking marijuana. Inhaling deeply, she handed it to me. "Here," she said tightly between pursed lips, "try it."

I hesitated momentarily, then gingerly brought the joint to my lips, paused, drew the smoke into my mouth and inhaled quickly. Then just as quickly I broke into paroxysms of hacking and coughing in response to the sudden fire that had erupted in my esophagus.

"Slowly," she cautioned. "It's much harsher than regular cigarette smoke, so you have to inhale slowly."

"Thanks for telling me," I said between coughs as I wiped the tears from my eyes. Passing it back to me, I paused, cleared my throat, and tried again. This time I was ready for the harsh burning sensation and managed to stifle the cough reflex long enough to keep the smoke in for several seconds. I passed the joint back to Penny.

Passing it back and forth for another minute or two, the joint was finally down to a tiny nub. Penny brushed away the burning tip on the bench then licked her thumb and forefinger and pinched it to make sure it was out. Carefully placing the tiny bit that was left (I later learned that this was called a roach) back in her change purse, she put the whole thing away in her bag and turned to me.

"Feel anything?" she asked."

"I don't think so," I replied. "I've never been stoned before, so I don't know what I'm supposed to feel. Is it like being drunk?"

"No, not at all," Penny replied. "But if you're stoned you'll know it, believe me. There's no feeling like it."

"Well, if being stoned means you have a pounding headache and a sore throat, then yes, I am definitely stoned. Otherwise, I just have a headache and a sore throat," I said.

She smiled at this. "Don't worry about it," she said. "Some people just aren't affected the first time, but we can try it again sometime if you want."

"Sure," I said. "How about you, did it affect you?"

"Oh, yeah," Penny assured me with a grin. "It most definitely did."

We sat quietly side by side for a minute or two, each of us wrapped comfortably in our own thoughts. Suddenly I was struck by something.

"Have you ever noticed," I began, "that if you look very carefully at this bench, you can almost see the imprint of each and every single individual hair on the brush used to paint this bench. Look at this," I said while star-ing intently at a wooden bench.

It was strange how my mind had suddenly pulled this realization out of thin air, as though my powers of observation had experienced a sudden growth spurt and I was able to see things—small, inconsequential things—in a way I had never seen them before.

Penny didn't respond. Tearing my eyes away from the bench, I glanced up only to see her looking directly at me with an incandescent smile.

"What?" I asked.

"Hello, stranger," she said. "Welcome to the other side."

Her voice sounded like it had come from inside a long tunnel. "What do you mean?" I asked again.

"Don't look now, my friend, but you are ripped," she answered.

Ripped? I thought. I'd never realized what an odd word it was. It was one of those few words that is spelled the way it sounds. I mean, when you rip something, it makes a sounds like *rrrriip*. Pop is the same way. *Pop! Splat! Plop*! The English language is really very interesting when you stop and think about it, I thought to myself.

"Hey, Spaceman, are you in there?" Penny pulled me from my reverie and suddenly I realized what was going on. Slowly I turned to Penny.

"Guess what?" I said as a huge grin spread across my face.

"Um, you're stoned?" Penny answered. I just grinned and nodded.

"Pretty wild, isn't it?" she asked. I kept nodding and grinning.

"Not anything like you expected, is it?" she continued.

"No," I replied as my head kept nodding up and down. She laughed and said, "You want to feel something else really wild?"

"Sure, but it would have to be something to beat this," I said, and with that Penny leaned toward me and pressed the warmest, softest lips I'd ever felt in my life against my own. Sliding closer, she slid her hands behind my neck and drew me to her. I felt her tongue begin to gently explore and opened my mouth slightly to greet it. I felt like I was falling gently down a deep hole, drowning in pure warmth as all awareness of the outside world ceased to exist except where our hands, lips, legs, and bodies touched. If I could have stopped time and lived the rest of my life in that moment I would have done just that. I needed nothing else to survive, neither food nor water, air nor sleep. After only sixteen short years on the planet, I had found the true meaning of life.

After several moments—it could have been seconds or it could have been days—Penny pulled back hesitantly and looked at me with eyes that seemed capable of seeing right into my soul. "Wow," I said reverently after several seconds. "That was ... amazing."

"Think you can handle another one?" she asked teasingly, and this time I reached out and drew her to me.

After a bit, the evening chill burrowed its way inside our light spring coats and we noticed for the first time that night was almost upon us. We sat in silence with our arms entwined for a few minutes more before reluctantly continuing on our way. Finally, we arrived at the now familiar back door and kissed one last time—deeply, longingly, achingly, as only teenagers can.

And so the door to altered consciousness was opened to me. Over the next several years, I would learn that marijuana was actually just one of many doors available to those of an inquisitive nature. "Inside the Mind of a Teenager," our joint art project, was published in *The Inkwell,* and for several weeks I fancied myself a budding young Picasso. Even after we finished the project, Penny and I continued our liaisons, often in the same little park. We talked ... mostly. But every now and then we would kiss, not make out really, like boyfriend and girlfriend, but just kiss, and each time it was the same: incredible.

What surprised us both was the fact that we never really fell head over heels for each other. Penny was one of the prettiest girls I had ever known and, hands down, the best kisser, but for some reason it never seemed important to push it to the next level. It seemed far more important, to both of us, I think, that our friendship remain intact, and the only realistic way of doing that was by not burdening it with the angst that seems to accompany every teenage romance.

As for drugs, I continued to dance with the devil for some time thereafter in the form of one illicit substance or another. Despite the dire warnings, my actions did not lead to the abyss of addiction, despair, and a ruined life. By the same token, I can also safely report that neither was my consciousness raised nor were my mental abilities significantly expanded, at least not so you would notice. Indeed, when all is said and done, about the only lasting effect drug use did have on my life, good or bad, was that it left me with a profound appreciation for Hostess Ding Dongs.

CHAPTER 17

The Final Frontier

Because of the male predilection for revisionist history and the funny tricks time plays on the memory, what today we recall with a measure of hubris, particularly if it pertains to some early sexual conquest, was in all likelihood not quite as pretty as we remember it. Take Jenny and me for example.

Jenny and I dated through most of 1967, up through the end of our junior year in high school. As the academic year drew to a close, we became almost inseparable, and although our extracurricular activities had not yet tested the ultimate boundaries of probity, the countdown to "going all the way" had definitely begun and we were rapidly approaching the point of no return. Already we had experienced evenings in which we both went home with damp underwear, not the most delicate way to describe our amorous encounters, but there it was.

Like all good high school students, with the end of the school year only a few days away, that round thing sitting atop our necks was pretty useless except as a place to store our eyeballs. In my own mind, I was already a senior, the highest rank achievable until it came time for college, where we would once again start at the bottom of the food chain. For now, however, I was going to enjoy every single moment of being a BMOC.

It was a Monday afternoon, and my last scholastic assignment for the year was a three-hour Regent's exam in algebra the following day beginning at 8:00 AM. I studied X's and Y's until it felt as though my eyes were about to bleed, and by three o'clock that afternoon I decided to end the madness and close my books for good. I rationalized that whatever I hadn't learned by then, I probably wasn't going to learn in the next few hours. I called Jenny and we arranged to meet in a few hours at a local watering hole where bartenders turned a blind eye to underage drinking. We decided to down a couple of beers in order to slow the feverish pace of the previous two weeks and go straight home for a good night's sleep in preparation for our last respective academic battles of the school year. Unfortunately, because moderation is not something that comes naturally to teenagers, we were still winding down when last call was announced at 12:45 AM and a good night's sleep was no longer an option, nestled as I was in the collegial bosom of my friends and classmates; while bosoms of another sort sang their siren song to me.

Leaving the bar rather than accept a ride, Jenny and I chose instead to enjoy the warm night air of late spring and walk the half mile or so to her house, where I would say good night before hoofing it on to my own house a mile or so beyond. It was, therefore, with the heady scent of freedom in the air and a goodly amount of alcohol in our bloodstreams that we set out hand in hand to answer the call of Kismet. Accompanying us was the transistor radio I'd swiped from my sister's room right after she left for college the previous fall. I carried it wherever I went, giving my life what amounted to its own sound track. Like every other couple on the planet that spring, "our song" was a mawkish, sappy release by The Happenings called "See You in September." Jenny would soon be leaving for New Hampshire where she'd been hired as a junior counselor for the summer. I would remain at home, working as a bag boy at the local A&P. The song was our way of swearing our everlasting love to one another for at least three months

The quickest way to Jenny's house included a well-traveled shortcut through the golf course of a local country club. We paused now and again to exchange ardent physical expressions of our shared affection before surrendering completely to our passion on the grass near the edge of the green on the eighteenth hole, a par four.

To the best of my knowledge, the first time any of my friends had gone all the way, it had rarely been preceded by a conscious decision to do so. Desire, yes. Decision, no. It wasn't something you chose, it just sort of happened. Conscious choice implied intent, premeditation, and if we intended doing it that meant we might have to take responsibility for our actions, a step so radical, no teenager in his or her right mind would knowingly do such a thing. Generally speaking, both participants shrouded the entire affair in a conspiracy of silence, preferring instead to believe forces outside their own control had swept them along, thereby setting the stage for the classic youthful lack-of-discretion defense in the event anything went awry.

Oblivious to our surroundings, we sank to the grass and began loosening buckles, buttons, snaps, hooks, and zippers until most of our clothing was either bunched up around our necks or down around our ankles. We had reached this stage before, even to the point of positioning ourselves in the classic missionary position and vigorously grinding our pelvises together in a mock coupling, but somehow I knew this time would be different.

Rolling off Jenny, I reached for the wallet in the back pocket of my jeans, now tangled around my ankles. After some effort, I succeeded in extricating it and fumbled for the condom I had stored there like a talisman for so long it had left a familiar circular imprint in the side of the wallet. It ultimately required both hands and a sharp set of teeth to open the familiar Trojan-brand foil packet. Slipping it on was not a problem. I had practiced this part on more than one occasion in the privacy of my bedroom in order to familiarize myself with the process, sort of a dry run, if you will.

Jenny spread her thighs as wide as her hobbled legs would allow, and I rolled back on top of her, not quite sure what to do next other than to poke and stab in the general vicinity of her vagina with my eager but untrained penis. But without the aid of any sort of navigational or internal guidance devices, these efforts remained ineffectual. To my enormous relief, Jenny reached down between us and guided me along until the maneuver was successfully completed. A few years later, the memory of this moment came rushing back when I heard Neil Armstrong utter the immortal words "The *Eagle* has landed," when Apollo 11 arrived on the moon. Although for slightly different reasons, I recognized in his tone the same sense of relief, pride, and excitement I now felt although instead of landing on the moon I was lying half naked on a damp golf course after having successfully achieved the one goal, getting laid, I had been chasing since the appearance of my first pubic hair. Both of our goals had been about seven long years in the making.

Although the *Eagle* had indeed landed, the next big question was, Now what? I had a rudimentary grasp of the basics, but a dearth of practical experience to guide me through the process. Should I move or remain still? What if I ejaculated too soon? What if I don't ejaculate at all? Is Jenny enjoying it? Shouldn't she be moaning or something? I thought.

I lifted my head to look at Jenny. With her eyes squeezed shut, her face suggested a mixture of pleasure, pain, and uncertainty, but there was little to indicate she had been swept away by my effort thus far. Once again she saved the day as she began to slowly rotate her hips in a delightful easy motion. Obviously, this sort of thing came more naturally to girls.

As these gyrations continued, our breathing became more ragged and labored, and I felt a familiar tingling sensation deep down in the center of my groin. I was thinking about how to slow the pace a little while Jenny seemed to move with more insistence. She dug her fingers into my back, urging me on, but I needed no encouragement. The feeling in my groin began to grow until it reached a rousing crescendo, every nerve ending quivered, and for a few brief moments I was transported to a place I'd never been before.

Almost immediately after breaking over me, the wave receded and left me feeling physically deflated, like someone had let all the air out of me, and with it went the passion, tension, and energy I'd felt only moments before. My whole body relaxed, and another wave came along, only this time it was fatigue. While my brain processed all of this new information, I couldn't help but notice that Jenny continued to grind her hips as though she wasn't aware we were done. Already my once mighty love sword (Hey, that's how those sleazy paperbacks referred to it!) had begun to retreat, and my entire body felt like lead. Eventually, Jenny abandoned her efforts and squirmed at the discomfort of being pinned under 135 pounds of dead weight. I got the hint and moved to her side, trying to read the expression on her face in the pale moonlight as our breathing slowly returned to normal. Again to her credit, before I could ask what I would come to learn was the single most inane question a male can ask—"Was it good for you?"—Jenny turned her head toward me and gave me a sweet but enigmatic smile before lifting her head and kissing me softly on the lips. I decided to take that as her answer and not inquire further.

As we both struggled to tug our clothes back in place, I grappled with the additional problem of how to politely remove and discard the sperm-filled condom that hung from my now deflated penis. Unfortunately, I couldn't seem to get it off without tearing out most of my pubic hair with it. Rather than appear unschooled in such matters, I decided to just pull my underwear and pants on over it and leave the whole mess until later.

We cuddled and kissed there on the dewy grass of the eighteenth hole, each thinking our own private thoughts. I wasn't quite sure how I felt about the experience, and other than a sense of relief that, from a technical standpoint anyway, I had apparently performed the act correctly in most aspects, I wasn't quite sure how I should feel. In some weird sense, it was almost anticlimactic because I had anticipated this moment for so long and now it had actually happened. It was almost as though the anticipation of doing it was nearly as much fun as the real thing and now a big part of what made the whole exercise so thrilling all these years was gone. How strange, I thought. You look forward to something for so long and when the moment finally arrives, you discover wanting it was half the fun. Not that the experience itself wasn't extraordinary and beat the hell out of jerking off by a mile. And, besides, now I was a member of the brotherhood and no longer had to lie through my teeth when queried by my peers about matters of experience.

I awoke with a start. It had started to rain. No, not rain, pour! Jenny and I jumped up screaming and cursing simultaneously at the rude awakening. It took us both several moments to realize that our quiet reverie had turned to sleep, which in turn had been rudely interrupted when the sprinkler system on the golf course started up automatically. Dodging jets of water from every direction, we ran for it and didn't stop until we squeezed through a hole in the fence and were back on dry pavement. We stood there a moment, both of us completely soaked, and assessed the situation. Jenny grabbed a handful of her long, curly brown hair and began wringing the water out of it. At least I'd had the presence of mind to grab the radio, but a steady stream of water continued leaking from its innards. I reached down and pulled off a sneaker and dumped out the water before repeating the process with the other sneaker. It was well past dawn, which meant it was already after 5:30 AM, and which meant I had only two and a half hours before my math final. We turned and began to half walk and half trot toward Jenny's house.

"My parents' alarm clock goes off at six-thirty. If they find out I was out all night they'll kill me!" she exclaimed. "I'll be grounded for life, if not longer."

"And if I don't make it to this final, I'll fail algebra," I said, adding my own woes. Getting caught staying out all night was less of a concern for me because my parents thought I had spent the night at a friend's house diligently studying. In terms of the relative severity of possible outcomes, Jenny clearly had the edge, which only added guilt to my ever-growing burden of misery. As we passed what few people were already up this early either walking a dog or grabbing the morning paper, we just tucked our heads down and kept moving along at a steady clip, hoping to avoid recognition.

As we drew near Jenny's house, she breathed a sigh of relief that the upstairs bedroom curtains in her parents' room were still closed. "The first thing Mom does when she gets up is open the curtains," she reported in a loud whisper, as though her parents might hear us even from a block away.

Up the driveway, we practically tiptoed around the two-car garage to the back of the house and scrunched down. Jenny raised her head slowly and peeked in the kitchen window. "All clear," she whispered hoarsely as she reached under a flower planter by the back door and grabbed the key. While she fumbled with the lock, I risked my own peek inside the kitchen window, where my eyes spotted a wall clock that announced it was six-twenty-seven.

"Shit, hurry," I urged her. "It's almost six-thirty," and with that we simultaneously heard the distant buzz of an alarm clock, her parents' alarm clock.

Just then the door opened and Jenny pecked me on the lips and quickly closed the door behind her. I wished her luck, but now I had my own problems to worry about. First, I had to get away without being spotted. I couldn't risk being seen on the street in front of her house, so I made my way through several backyards and crossed over to the next block, my feet automatically taking me toward home.

Shit, I thought to myself. Shit, shit, shit, shit, and double shit! I can't go home like this. My parents think I'm at Jimmy's house. They'll both be up by now, and if they see me in this condition, I'm dead! I immediately did a 180-degree turn and headed in the other direction toward school. Besides, I thought, even if I could get home and clean up, I could never make it all the way back to school by eight o'clock. And once the test began, the classroom door was locked for the duration. Even going to the bathroom required an escort.

I tried to pull my thoughts together, which was difficult under the circumstances. My hair and clothes were still wet, my shoes squished with every step, and a sudden wet sensation in my pants told me the condom had slipped off and dumped a load of cold sperm in my still damp underwear. I stuck my hand down my pants and became so possessed with the task of grabbing the offending object that I never noticed the elderly woman as she approach me with her dog. "Got it," I said aloud while simultaneously pulling a stringy wet latex object from my pants. Looking up, my victory turned to ashes as I hurried past the startled senior. I couldn't imagine what she was thinking right now and glanced over my shoulder only to catch her doing the same. We hurried our separate ways.

It was time for Plan B, which consisted of rushing to school, cleaning myself up in the locker room and changing into my gym clothes before the test began. Fortunately, although the high school was nearly two miles away, I made it with fifteen minutes to spare.

Heads turned as I entered the classroom wearing dirty gym clothes, including torn, sweaty, grass-stained shorts and a T-shirt, a jock strap in lieu of underwear, and a pair of untied sneaker,s one of which was held together with masking tape. Because I had not taken the gym clothes home to be washed all semester (we were supposed to have them laundered at least every two weeks), the other students in all likelihood smelled me coming before I actually arrived. The fact that my hair had apparently been combed with an eggbeater and my eyes were red and sagging with fatigue added to the general sense of curiosity. Cadging a few No. 2 pencils from my classmates, I sat in the back of the room in an effort to draw as little attention to myself as possible, no mean feat given my condition.

At eight o'clock on the nose, our test monitor arrived and began rattling off a series of instructions while placing a copy of the test facedown on each desk. As she did so, I began to notice an odd itching sensation on my nether regions. Demurely, I tried to relieve the itch without drawing still further attention myself. Arriving at my desk, she was sufficiently taken aback at my general demeanor to pause as though to comment. However, she merely wrinkled her nose in distaste, placed the test booklet on my desk, and moved on.

As the test proceeded, I found myself struggling to keep my attention focused on the numbers as they swam on the page in front of me. Fortunately, it was a multiple-choice exam, which at least gave me a fighting chance, but the itch refused to dissipate and began driving me nuts. I squirmed in my seat with increasing animation, which in turn began drawing glances from my fellow students, a few of whom snickered at my obvious discomfort.

"Is there a problem, young man?" I nearly jumped from my seat, startled by the sudden appearance of the test monitor at my elbow.

"Uh, no, m'am," I stuttered, then corrected myself and said, "Actually, I would really appreciate it if I could use the restroom." Once she called the office for reinforcements, I was accompanied to the lavatory at the end of the hall by none other than our very own Vice Principal and Chief Executioner, Mr. Biddleman, who urged me to go about my business as swiftly as possible so he could return to his. He did not comment on my attire.

Fortunately, the stalls all had doors, and upon closing mine I immediately dropped my shorts and began scratching my buttocks with a vengeance. Letting out a huge sigh of relief, Biddleman apparently ascribed to other sources, he called out, "I'll be waiting right outside the door. Let's not procrastinate."

When a swoosh of air from the closing door told me he was gone, I opened the stall and waddled over to the mirror in order to inspect the damage at close range. The second my fingers stopped scratching the itch returned, seemingly worse than before. Positioning my bare buttocks toward the mirror and looking awkwardly over my shoulder, I saw what appeared to be an explosion of red dots that looked suspiciously like mosquito bites, and the more I scratched, the worse they itched. Biddleman rapped on the door urging me to "speed things up in there," and I quickly pulled up my shorts lest he discover me in this somewhat unflattering position. After splashing water on my face and slapping myself a few times, I gave my butt one last frenzied scratching before being escorted back to the classroom.

I cannot understate the horror of the next two hours. It seemed like two years, and no amount of squirming and surreptitious scratching could relieve the agony. By the time I reached the last section of the test, I simply started filling in answer boxes next to each question with my No. 2 pencil at random. I'd reached the point where if my only two choices were to take the class over again or to continue to endure the itch now plaguing by buttocks, I would gladly have chosen the former. After filling in the last answer box, I leaped from my chair, raced to the front of the room, and deposited my test on the monitor's desk. She started to say something, but the words had barely formed in her mouth when I was out the door like a shot, scratching my ass vigorously with both hands as I went.

From the moment the first Crabgrass Cowboy and Cowgirl began play-ing "I'll Show You Mine If You Show Me Yours," grown-ups have cau-tioned their progeny about the dangers of premarital sex. We were told it was wrong, bad, iniquitous, sinful, a big-time no-no; and anyone who did engage in such activity would be punished—severely. This was simply the way God in His infinite love for the human race set up the universe to operate. Rob a bank and you went to jail. Jerk off and you went crazy. Vote Democrat and the country would be taken over by Communists. It was just that simple.

The list of potential consequences for those kids foolish enough to engage in such folly seemed almost endless. For example, your girlfriend could end up pregnant, which meant you had to quit school and spend the rest of your life toiling away at some meaningless and degrading dead-end job involving the worst kind of backbreaking physical labor. At some point you would turn to hard drink in an effort to numb the pain of your lost youth and now meaningless existence. Your wife would leave you, your boss would fire you, your friends would shun you, and eventually you would die a lonely, bitter old man. Yes, that was one possible scenario—if you were lucky.

Another outcome, one the makers of classroom sex-education films seemed to favor most, was the gleeful possibility the two errant teens would contract some horrific strain of venereal disease, one that rendered their genitals useless. In an effort to allay any doubt that such diseases did exist, the purveyors of this barf-bag cinema attacked our senses with images featuring a rich assortment of oozing skin ulcerations, blisters, warts, sores, lesions, abscesses, boils, and every other pleasant form of der-mal eruption imaginable.

If the images themselves were not enough, the narrator's cheerful voice-over was always there to assure us that venereal disease "could cripple you, kill you, and destroy your brain." Wow, and all this just because two kids got a little frisky.

Unfortunately, I was now learning about those consequences firsthand and although it was not an entirely unpleasant experience, an ass full of mosquito bites and a failing test grade seemed like a relatively fair exchange for being allowed to enter the Sacred Brotherhood of which I was now officially a member.

POSTSCRIPT

Generations

Christa Speck is now eligible for Social Security and has come to grips, one presumes, with the effects of Newtonian physics on the human body; the man who published the magazine in which she was so prominently featured more than four decades ago has become a dotty old fart shuffling about his mansion in a bathrobe and bedroom slippers. Clearly, the eschaton is upon us.

The eschaton, or end time, as it is known in theological circles, comes not with a great apocalyptic bang, but quietly, stealthily, and incrementally so as to avoid notice until it is already a foregone conclusion. Rotary telephones are gone, as are doctors who make house calls, typewriters, gas-station attendants, and the inimitable smell of burning leaves on a crisp, clear autumn afternoon. Vinyl records, telegrams, drive-in movies, human directory-assistance operators, and girdles are also gone, all gone. Ask a kid today to explain the significance of Battle Creek, Michigan, and all you get in return is a blank stare.

My third-grade teacher, Mrs. Levinger, told us that Daniel Boone woke up one morning to the sight of a thin plume of smoke rising from a mountaintop many miles away. After learning it came from the chimney of a new settler, Boone packed his belongings and headed further west, where the population was less congested. Along with inferring that perhaps the legendary woodsman was perhaps wound a bit too tight, this anecdote frames an interesting question: When does a frontier cease to be a frontier?

When we first settled in that no-man's-land between urban and rural America it was considered the very fringe of the civilized world and a new ethos had to be created where none had previously existed. This we accomplished quite handily by ignoring any hint of our own preexisting cultural identity and replacing it with a new one that faithfully mirrored the values and mores of the emerging crabgrass society around us. Mayonnaise, Wonder Bread, Velveeta, Jell-O, and Tang became our ethnic foods. Our living accomodations were so similar in every exquisite detail, it was not unheard-of to completely misplace your own house. The images on our TV screens linked us together in ways that rendered moot any differences in custom, outlook, and taste. There were uniforms for everyone, including a gray flannel suit for Dad; capri pants and an open-necked blouse for the *hausfrau*; dungarees, T-shirts, and a pair of high-top Keds for the boys; and a colorful little frock for Missy.

Young patio pioneers like me didn't spend a lot of time pondering the meaning of our social, cultural, or economic differences because, quite frankly, there weren't any. I had every reason to believe that the rest of the world was exactly like the one I lived in and populated by people like those who lived in our neighborhood; amazing at it now seems, I somehow managed to journey many times around the sun without once giving serious consideration to the prospect I might be sharing the planet with people who were very different from me. When it arrived, the realization that this was not so created more than a little consternation and seemed to needlessly complicate my life at a time when additional vexations were not entirely welcome. To suggest we were culturally myopic is like suggesting The Beatles were a pretty good rock-and-roll band.

In many respects the safe and welcome predictability of life on the Crabgrass Frontier was illusory. Each generation evolves not by happenstance but in response to the social, economic, and technological circumstances from which it emerges. As these circumstances change, so do the customs, tastes, values, and habits—in other words, all the things that make life familiar and comfortable—they produce. Inevitably, every generation reaches a point at which life begins to feel slightly alien and marginally uncomfortable, like a piece of clothing that doesn't fit quite right. It's as though life is supposed to be governed by a new set of rules, but nobody bothered to tell us what they were. This is when our atavistic impulses kick in and we begin longing for the good old days.

This divergence doesn't happen just once, it happens repeatedly throughout our lives, starting with childhood. We tend to notice it first when some comforting behavioral routine suddenly seems out of place or unacceptable to those around us. The first time it happened to me was shortly after I began junior high school. While engaged in a bit of boyish hijinks with some of my friends in the hallway between classes, I darted into a hidden alcove behind one of the stairwells and in doing so almost collided with two of my new classmates who were intertwined in an extraordinarily amorous embrace. Their tongues were locked in what by all appearances was mortal combat while his hands roamed freely underneath the back of her tight skirt. She had one leg thrown around his hip and gripped his hair fiercely with both hands. "Geez," I thought to myself, "that's gotta hurt," and as if on cue they both began to moan softly.

Just then the boy opened his eyes and spotted me as I stood there gaping in wonder. As he drew his mouth away from hers, I was relieved to recognize him from my homeroom.

"Hey, Eddie," I chirped in a cheerful albeit awkward greeting. "What's up?"

"Beat it, punk, can't you see we're busy?" he growled menacingly.

The girl glanced over her shoulder imperiously but didn't say a word. She seemed unconcerned that her clothing was in a state of utter disarray or that I was gawking impenitently.

"Uh, sure Eddie, sorry, I was just playing a quick game of tag with the guys before the bell," I responded lamely.

"Tag with the guys," he snorted derisively as I turned to leave. "Didja hear that?" he asked his partner in a mocking tone. "Wadda little homo." She giggled in reply, then she and Eddie resumed their tongue-wrestling competition and there wasn't much for me to do but slink away, embarrassed and confused.

On the one hand, I found myself fantasizing about activities like those I had just witnessed with ever-increasing, one might say even say alarming, frequency. On the other hand, games like tag had been a recreational mainstay for as long as I could remember. Here in a nutshell was something I had determined to be a basic flaw in life: Everything kept changing. Nothing in my life seemed certain except perhaps uncertainty; and just when I thought I had reached the acme of my existence, things shifted and I was forced to adopt a whole new set of strategies in order to maintain some semblance of order in my existence.

The almost mythological figure of the humble neighborhood milkman is another example. Most baby boomers have a clear memory of the early-morning deliveries, the sound of clinking bottles as the empties were removed from the ubiquitous wood or metal box that sat beside the back stoop of almost every house in suburbia. They recall the tower of fresh cream that erupted from atop the new bottles of milk if not brought inside quickly on cold winter mornings. They remember with awe and fascination the milkman's ability to decipher the notes our parents hurriedly scribbled on any old scrap of paper they could find with instructions for the next day's delivery. They remember the envelope containing a few crumpled dollar bills and some change in payment for last week's deliveries—all done on the basis of trust. They remember the milkman as such an integral part of neighborhood life that he was often called upon to assist in any number of very unmilkman-like activities—filling a saucer for the family cat, helping an elderly customer move a piece of furniture—involving none of the sexual prowess that suburban legend and suspicious husbands often bestowed upon him.

Yet as these memories unspool, we are quick to forget that it was the rise of the baby-boom generation itself that helped speed the demise of this familiar icon. In the 1930s, more than 50,000 milkmen plied their trade, most working for large dairy companies that went to great lengths to train their employees. Many sent their fledgling deliverymen off to spend a week in the country in order for them to learn firsthand where the products they sold came from and how they were processed. Milkmen were not unlike earlier seers of human behavior and were encouraged to read their customers and divine the category into which they fell. Was the customer impulsive? If so, the milkman was encouraged to make use of that knowledge in pitching the dairy products. The same held true if the customer seemed suspicious, impulsive, or uncertain. A good milkman learned how to read these signals and use them to sell more of his company's products

The war itself began to erode the industry as gas, rubber, and other consumables became less and less available. The big dairy companies had to cut back and start looking for other ways of making their products available to the American consumer. As special chilled display cases became available, dairy companies began relying more and more on local markets. Soon dairies found the cost of sending a single man out in a truck to sell its products was far more expensive than it was to sell them through the burgeoning supermarket industry, since even the small neighborhood mom-and-pop markets began to disappear. After a time, milk became a mass-produced generic product as brand loyalty became yet another victim of the changes taking place in almost every American custom following the end of World War II and the rise of the Crabgrass Culture.

From the outside each generation appears as a solid, enduring, monolithic whole. Only when we view it from the inside do we begin to fully understand the fallacy of this perception. Then we recognize that each generation is in actuality a phenomenon that is at best fleeting, inconsequential, always evolving, and that each has its own built-in shelf life, thus ensuring that no matter how hard we may wish otherwise, it begins to change almost from the moment of its birth and gives way to the next generation, and then the next, and then the next....

978-0-595-45169-
0-595-45169-1

Lightning Source UK Ltd.
Milton Keynes UK
UKHW011840270519
343405UK00001B/99/P

9 780595 451692